So Why Have You Never Been Married?

10 Insights Into Why
He Hasn't Wed

So Why Have You Never Been Married?
10 Insights Into Why He Hasn't Wed

By
Carl Weisman, M.S.

New Horizon Press
Far Hills, New Jersey

New Horizon Press
P.O. Box 669
Far Hills, NJ 07931

Carl Weisman, M.S.
So Why Have You Never Been Married?
10 Insights Into Why He Hasn't Wed

Cover design: Wendy Bass
Interior design: Susan Sanderson

Library of Congress Control Number: 2007939909
ISBN 13: 978-0-88282-326-3
ISBN 10: 0-88282-326-4
New Horizon Press

Manufactured in the U.S.A.

2012 2011 2010 2009 2008 / 5 4 3 2 1

DEDICATION

This book is dedicated to
never-married people everywhere.
May you find your own brand of happiness,
no matter what it looks like.

TABLE OF CONVERSATIONS

FOREWORD

Thank you, Carl Weisman, for this long overdue sociological study of the unmarried; for putting this stigma under the microscope and examining it from all angles. It is no secret that our society affords benefits to the married and even the divorced. Rarely are married persons asked "So, why are you married?"

This study is an illuminating venture into the psyche of persons who are deemed nonconformists, at best, to standards that our society deems normal. Peeling back the assumptions and labels of never marrieds, this study gives voice to the myriad reasons for these choices. What affects some of us, affects all of us: marrieds, never-marrieds, divorcees, men, women, over and under forty years of age. This book delves into men's psyche, not just the never-marrieds. Ultimately this book is for people: men, women, married, divorced, single, everyone. I believe it is a must-read, a primer if you will, for those in the launching years (late adolescence and early twenties) so that they can listen to their own inner voice over the "They say...." statements and the sound of the sociological clock ticking.

Perhaps readers will be more sensitive to asking never-marrieds that dreaded question, or with a different intention behind that question. Perhaps never-marrieds will feel freer to answer that question more honestly, rather than politically correctly. Much like someone who is inordinately tall might grow tired of the question "How tall are you?," never-marrieds experience discomfort when questioned about their marital status. In my mid-thirties, I dated a divorced man in his mid-thirties who was completely flummoxed that I had never married. His perpetual probing became so interrogational and his stare so discomfiting, that I terminated the relationship with him because I was tired of feeling like a circus freak.

I am reminded of the *Sex and the City* "missing shoes" episode where Carrie (played by Sarah Jessica Parker) is outraged by the discrimination of singles. "I'm not taking anything away from weddings and marriage, but where's the Hallmark card for those who choose to be single? There's no 'Good for you, you didn't marry the wrong person' card." Perhaps those brave enough to defy society's rules are more thoughtful and respectful to the institution of marriage.

What I expected to see in this book was "the men's view" as opposed to "the women's view." I didn't get that. I got something much better: evidence that our fears and hopes and dreams are genderless. What the author probably was looking for was a simple and absolute answer or two. You won't get that. What you will get is something much deeper: most of these men are really happy as they are. Most of them really like and respect women and the institution of marriage, so much, in fact, that they want to wait to do it right. This should be very flattering and comforting to women, and to unhappily married men and women who may be fearful of re-entering the single world. I expected that I would see anger, fear of intimacy, misogyny, hedonism, axe grinding and "Peter Panism" as primary themes. While there are some of all of those issues, what I saw was what is reflected in my own patients: men and women who have similar fears and hopes and dreams. We basically want the exact same things. Our social masks may reflect mores and conditioning, yet deep down, we all want respect, affection, acceptance and love, perhaps even more than children and security.

While there are some playboys and some wounded men, most of the responses are quite refreshing. These men want something different than they've seen in their parents' and friends' marriages. Some but aspire to that and feel inadequate to do so; many simply want more, but have no role model to follow and they feel lost. Granted, the respondents to his survey are seekers themselves. The angry misogynist and the sex addict would probably not care to respond to such a survey. What is blindingly apparent here in this pioneering study is that we are ready for a new menu of styles of relationships.

While I know of no empirical evidence to substantiate a genetic predisposition to independence/singleness vs. mating for life/ bonding, I'm convinced it exists. Perhaps "chronic singledom" is simply a feature of innate personality, but many of us are simply happier with less social bonding and more privacy. If we could go through the genealogies of this study's respondents, we may see a strong "single gene." This is certainly the case in my own family tree.

As a forty-plus, never-married female, I saw a piece of myself in most of these men's fears and hopes. This collection depolarizes the genders; the author could easily change the respondents' names and pronouns and instantly have a companion book from the female camp. I can also see a *So Why Have You Never Been Divorced?* for men (and women) who "followed the rules" of society's expectations, but not their own hearts. While I am only one therapist, I can tell you that I have personally seen and professionally treated many, many more distressed married couples than bitter, lonely-heart never-marrieds.

Social psychology tracks tendencies among groups. Nevertheless, in matters of the heart, one must focus on the individual's perspective. I am reminded of the ancient Indian parable of the three blind men and the elephant:

Upon touching the elephant's tail, the first blind man exclaimed "I declare, an elephant is exactly like a rope." The second blind man, bumping into the elephant's side, said "No sir, you are wrong. an elephant is exactly like a wall." Then the third, having grasped the elephant's trunk, declared "You are both mistaken. The elephant is exactly like a snake!"

Just as the nature-nurture debate is nondiscursive, we must take into account each person is a unique mélange of culture, race, religion, socioeconomic status, birth order, life experiences, generational influences, innate personality, social learning, parental influences, community, population density, geographic location and family dynamics to name a few factors. As a doctor of clinical psychology with a cognitive-behavioral bent, I am trained to use a phenomenological approach: that is a patient-based, individualistic approach. Mr. Weisman makes it possible in this book for these men to be heard in this way, valued for their own uniqueness, rather than cookie-cuttered by stereotypes. The same freedom from judgment that they got in these blind interviews is what patients get in the clinic from a therapist. It's as if this book has opened a psychologist's patient files and exposed the truth for all to see. Now, those who choose to ask the title question can stop looking for what is wrong with the never-married, and see what they've done right in their own model of the world.

What I hope this work will do is bridge the gender gap, benefiting women by seeing their own issues reflected, freeing other men to question their choices and authentically express their own individuality, and to encourage us all to abandon looking at people's marital choices through a right-wrong, normal-abnormal lens. Never-marrieds are not freaks; they are not abnormal. Perhaps in the field of social psychology that group is considered abnormal, but in the field of clinical psychology, they are perfectly normal. "Abnormal" connotes "wrong." Never-marrieds are atypical, exceptional, a minority, individual, introspective, creative, sensitive, out-of-the-box thinkers. One could say the same about the extremely successful.

Marrieds may be surprised to find that this book presents data that these never-marrieds are overwhelmingly pleased with their choice. Approximately 50 percent of marriages in our culture end in divorce ("...the rest end in death!" quipped the late, great comedian Richard Jeni). While this is only one sample, comprised no doubt by the more aware and curious respondents, I wonder that if a similar questionnaire were put to marrieds, if 66 percent would say they had no regrets about their marriage. (Do I hear the sound of the presses rolling on *So Why Have You Never Been Divorced?*)

Interestingly, most of the men in this sample came from homes that were stable and "normal." Again, these are thinkers and individuals. If and when they choose to marry, they will do so as a proactive choice vs. a reactionary one. The power and beauty of this book is in the simple truth that men and women are not from different planets. We have many more similarities than we have differences. It is my hope that this book will be a landmark study for de-stigmatizing and normalizing the never married status. We are developing new models for relationships, just as new choices of sexual behavior have become more normalized. This book may do for never-marrieds what Ellen DeGeneres's sitcom and *Will and Grace* did for gays.

As a psychotherapist, I am encouraged by this work, for it sets a stage (as the therapeutic setting does) to stop looking for the simple and the obvious. People are complex, and you must dig deeper to understand intimacy. Unfortunately, the success rate for couples therapy is very low. Generally, couples enter therapy after it's too late, when they are deeply distressed and in search of a magic wand to repair them. Like sex education, marriage/relationship education before the fact is the new model for successful relationships. Couples will fare much better if they set aside the traditional roles and customs they are used to and design their own marriage/relationship. Communication and relationship skills are not taught in school, yet should be, as they are as important as learning to drive. This breakthrough study may very well be a pivotal step in the right direction of creating conscious relationships.

Dr. Nancy B. Irwin
Los Angeles, CA

ACKNOWLEDGEMENTS

I could not have done this alone. I would like to acknowledge the positive influence on this book by Frank Simonelli. It was his admonishment to not write the book without first doing the survey that made it all possible. A special thank you goes out to Alexi Holford, my proofreader extraordinaire. I appreciate her tolerating my impatience. Her meticulous editing and creative input made this a better book. And I would like to thank my very efficient web master Neil St Clair who effortlessly (and magically) transferred the survey onto the Web without a hitch.

I also received tremendous encouragement and support during the researching and writing of this book. I am grateful to Kimberlee MacMullan. She was there when I first dreamed up this harebrained idea and not once did she ever think I couldn't do it. I am indebted to Rebecca Forster, an accomplished author in her own right, for her mentoring me throughout this process. My heartfelt appreciation goes out to my friends, Don Coleman, Dave Guelff, Larry Herman and Tim Mayfield, for tolerating what had to be my endless stories about the "men I spoke to." And I offer my deepest affection to Cassandra Matek for her encouragement, and because she waited patiently with open arms for me cross the finish line.

Thanks also goes out to the over 1,500 men who took a chance and participated in the online survey. It was their initial response to the survey that convinced me to continue with the project. And finally, my most sincere gratitude goes out to the thirty-three men who took time out of their lives to share their thoughts, philosophies, hopes, dreams and fears about being over forty and not married. Without them, there is no book. In a perfect world, I would have already met them face-to-face, and maybe that will still happen. Until then, I consider them all friends, and I am eternally grateful to them.

CHAPTER 1

Introduction

But if my life is for rent
And I don't learn to buy
Well I deserve nothing more than I get
Cos nothing I have is truly mine
— Dido

I will never forget the moment the idea for this book hit me. It was New Year's Day 2006, and I was at one of those house parties that are only attended by the survivors of the previous night's festivities: in other words, people with young children and those of us who did not have a date the night before. I was at the house of my friend Kevin's new girlfriend, a single mother with three young children. Kevin is one of me: over forty and never married. Because I had not seen him in a while, I arrived early so we could catch up on life. He sat on the arm of the sofa while I sat on the arm of a La-Z-Boy chair across from him. As we were talking, his new girlfriend's children came running in between us screaming, temporarily capturing our attention and halting our conversation. After what seemed like several minutes, but was probably only a few seconds, I looked back over to Kevin and asked him sarcastically, "How the hell did we get here?" He had laughed boisterously because he knew exactly what I meant.

How does an over-forty, never-married man find himself, on New Year's Day, at the home of someone else's children? Why isn't he at home with his own children? Why wasn't I at home with a family of my own? What is wrong with me?

Why I Wrote This Book

This book is as much about self discovery as it is about researching the subject of never-married men over the age of forty. For me, the book could have been titled, *So, Why Have I Never Been Married?* That is one of the two questions I sought to answer when I began this project. And since I am over forty and have never been married, there was another question I wanted to answer: What is wrong with me? This book is about my search for the answers to those two questions.

You might think that at the enlightened age of forty-eight, I would know the answer to the first question already, or at least have sufficient insight to avoid the lengthy process of writing a book. Not really. In the past, if someone—most likely a woman—asked me why I have never been married, I would have answered, more sarcastically than honestly, that it had never occurred to me. Strangely enough, at least one of the men I spoke with in researching this book answered that question almost the same exact way. Thankfully, the same cannot be said for the rest of the men. They knew exactly why they have yet to marry. For some, it may have been a deliberate choice; for others, they were victims of circumstance.

Admittedly, my second question (*What is wrong with me?*) comes with a built-in negative bias: it assumes there *is* something wrong with me. Any objective researcher would never ask such a leading question for fear of biasing the answer, but I did not care. That is the question I felt most compelled to answer, as it is what many people think. Now, the easy answer to that question is *nothing at all*. But even if that is the answer, I wanted to know why. If there really is nothing wrong with being over forty and never married, then why does society look at us the way it does? Why are we seen as the ones with the commitment problem? Why are we looked at suspiciously? And what is that suspicion: *What is wrong with him?*

A great deal of the book has to do with how we handle the consequences of our life decisions. In this circumstance, it is the life decision of men over forty not to marry. We all make important decisions we have to live with—not just us never-married types—and on some level we want to know that we did not blow it. That given all of the options available to us, we chose wisely, if not perfectly. That is what I wanted to confirm for myself in writing the book. Given all the options that were available to me—and I am certain there are at least a few women who would have said yes had I asked for their hand in marriage—that I chose wisely in remaining single up to this point. I wanted to know that I made the right decision for me, regardless of what anybody else thinks or how many times I have to answer that awful and uncomfortable question in the title of this book.

Since I truly did not know the answer to that question before I began writing this book, I thought if I could just ask it to enough other never-married heterosexual men over forty, I would hear the answer—my answer—from at least one of them. It would be an answer that would resonate with me the instant I heard it, and then I would know. As a result, I was prepared—no, I expected—to hear my answer from at least *one* of the men to whom I spoke. What I did not expect was to hear my answer, or at least part of it, from each of them. Every one of them said something I aligned with; it fit me like it fit them. Maybe that means there is no single answer to that question, at least not for me, and certainly not for the men in the book, but that was never its purpose: one simple solution that ties everything up in a neat little package. The lives and relationships of human beings are much too complicated. But simply because there is no one single answer to that question does not mean the many, varied answers are not valuable. I have always believed no matter what challenging situation you are going through in life, whether it is a traumatic event or a question that haunts you, it makes you feel good to know you are not going through it alone. You can take comfort in knowing there are others with the same challenge, and I believe there is strength in that. So, if you are a never-married man over forty, or a never-married woman over forty for that matter, maybe this book can be a source of strength for you as you read it. Know you are not alone.

My Approach to Writing this Book

So, what can be learned from this book? A lot. You can see the limits: the highs and lows of being over forty and never married. You can see the whole gamut of cause and effect. You can see the adopted beliefs and the consequential behavior. And you can hear the stories. That is what the book is really about: the stories. I spoke with thirty-three men in researching this book and heard completely different stories from each of them. I am convinced that had I spoken with 133 men, I would have gotten 133 different stories. But that is a good thing, because somewhere in there, amongst all those varied stories, is my story, my answer. It cannot be found in one single story though. It is more of a mosaic I had to put together from all the stories, but it is there, and it has changed me. If you are looking for the answer to this book's question, perhaps you will find it somewhere in here too. I hope so.

I am not a doctor. (Dr. Carl? *Oy vey!*) Nor do I attempt to play one in writing this book. I was careful to avoid psychoanalyzing the men because I am not qualified, nor was that the purpose of the book. I was not trying to "fix" these men. (Many of them are pretty damn good the way they are.) I was just an investigative reporter. I like to think of myself as the Mike Wallace (from *60 Minutes*) of the over-forty, never-married crowd. During my conversations with the men, I did my best to remain objective, inquisitive and non-judgmental. In writing the book, I felt qualified to do only two things: I felt I could ask the questions I provided, and I felt I could share my responses to the men's answers. More often than not, my response was more questions. At times, I felt like Hercules fighting the Hydra: each answer I evoked only served to generate more questions. I suppose that's how the discovery process works. With increasing levels of understanding comes an expanding sense of curiosity. We become smarter so we can ask better questions, but be forewarned: most of the questions go unanswered. It's almost as if my job were merely to pose the questions.

The plethora of questions made the book draining to write at times. I felt as though I no longer had my own uncertainty to deal with, but rather all of the men's uncertainties weighed upon me. And instead of converging the information into a manageable number of answers, it tended to diverge into an ever-expanding jumble of questions that only seemed to amass as I continued to write. Therefore, as I wrote, I did not think summarizing these men was valid, useful or even possible. These men are as diverse and varied as any other population of men you are likely to come across. Perhaps the only thing these never-married men have in common *is* that they have never been married. Nevertheless, I was convinced I could produce a work that shared the flavor and understanding of these men without trying to come to some sort of grand conclusion: All never-married men over forty are...and that is exactly what I have attempted to do.

As you read, it may appear that I am speaking from authority. In reality, I am simply thinking out loud while going through the discovery process. Many of my observations occurred *while* I was writing. To the extent that I wrote it, it was what I was thinking at the time. And the most arduous thing I had to do was to keep myself from defending these men and their (and my) decision regarding marriage. I did my best, but I was not perfect.

I began this process by posting an online survey advertised for never-married heterosexual men over forty, the complete results of which are in Appendix A in the back of the book. To my pleasant surprise, 1,533 men (and one woman) responded by taking the survey. The survey afforded me two important pillars as starting points for this project. First, the results of the survey provided a foundation from which to understand never-married men over forty. I have woven the results of the survey throughout the book to supplement the conversations. Second, the survey provided me a pool of more than 1,000 men from which I could randomly select a small group to have a conversation. I hesitate to use the word *interview,* because I really did not want these conversations to be interviews. I wanted to avoid any possibility of a student-teacher dichotomy, or any other structure that would have had the men believe I was superior to them in any way. I wanted it to be a dialogue of equals and a conversation among new friends. Consequently, when time permitted,

I would share my stories with them as well. I owed it to them.

Of the more than 1,000 men in the survey, I randomly selected about sixty, thirty-three of which ended up speaking with me. When I chose these sixty men, even though they were randomly selected, I was careful to make sure all constituents were represented. As a result, there are men from all regions of the United States and Canada; there are men as young as forty and as old as sixty-four; there are men with limited education and men with multiple college degrees; and there are men who are financially challenged and others who do not have a worry in the world when it comes to money.

All the conversations took place by phone, and all the men were total strangers to me prior to our call. At first this arrangement might seem like a limitation on my ability to really connect with and get to know these men. In fact, just the opposite was true. I probably know a dozen men over forty who have never been married. (One of the consequences of being never-married and over forty is you tend to surround yourself with people in similar situations.) I asked just one of them if he would have a conversation with me, and he turned me down without hesitation. After pondering his response for awhile, it hit me: he declined to participate because we know each other too well. It would have made discussing the intimate topics of the book awkward and uncomfortable. There was a certain vulnerability and honesty I was counting on and that just was not going to be possible with somebody I already knew. My not knowing these men allowed them to open up during our exchanges.

A similar benefit was derived by using the telephone, as opposed to having the dialogues face-to-face. The telephone acted as a barrier, a safety shield that protected the men and their anonymity. It enabled us to avoid the uncomfortable stares and awkward fidgeting that were bound to have occurred during the more personal questions. Consequently, the men were free to be open and honest and that is exactly what happened. In retrospect, I was shocked at how forthcoming the men were in telling their life stories to a total stranger. Speaking with the men was the best part of writing this book. As you experience their conversations, you will hear them say funny things, sad things, politically incorrect things, and even some things that make you mad. But it is honest, and that is what I wanted from them and for the book.

I had several important creative decisions to make in writing the book, not the least of which had to do with the structure of the chapters. I had to choose between telling each man's story as a stand-alone chapter or organizing the chapters by topic. I chose the latter. I have read a handful of books (on different subjects) that are organized in such a way, where each chapter tells the story of one individual. I found frequently I was not interested enough in a particular person and would skip the chapter. I did not want that to happen here. Every man that I spoke with had something unique and interesting to say, and I did not want the reader to miss the message because they could not identify with the messenger. Besides, my feeling was, and still is, that the particular individuals I spoke with are not nearly as important as their stories. Thus, you will not get to know the men as well as had I chosen otherwise, but you will get to hear their stories in a more organized fashion, by topic. (If you are interested in any of the men I spoke with in particular, you will be able to find a brief description of each individual in Appendix B.) And in keeping with my belief that the stories are more important than the men, no real names are used in the book: neither the men's names nor any of the people they mentioned during our conversations.

Another creative decision I had to make had to do with editing: what to keep in, what to get rid of and in what order to write it. People rarely speak in a way that you would want to read in a book. They add unnecessary interjections, they repeat themselves, and sometimes they even transpose the words they mean to say. I did the necessary edits to make the conversations readable, and in places where I had to add words for clarity, I did so within square [brackets]. I believe I maintained the integrity of the conversations in doing so.

Survey Results

All surveys are challenging to create, and even more so with online surveys. Crafting an online survey is a study in tradeoffs and limitations. For one thing, the survey must be quick and simple, or you will never get 1,533 people to take it. Nevertheless, you want it to be as comprehensive as possible, so there is a tendency to ask a lot of questions. The questions must be unambiguous, or there can be little confidence in the results. And, of course, there are the limitations on the questions themselves: multiple choice, true-false or open-ended? I made the creative decision to utilize only multiple choice questions because I did not want those taking the survey to have to use a keyboard—just the mouse was required (except at the beginning to enter their first name and zip code). The questions solicited information on the men's demographics, family situations, past relationships, current situations and outlooks for the future.

Since it was an online survey, there was the unavoidable bias toward those never-married men over forty *with* Internet access. That meant a bias toward the younger end of over forty and better educated with higher annual incomes. The survey results confirmed the biases. In particular, according the 2000 U.S. Census, 32 percent of all never-married men over forty are between the ages of forty and forty-five. Contrast that to my survey results, in which 62 percent (almost double) of the respondents are between those ages. Clearly, there is a bias toward younger men, which is what would be expected considering older men's relative lack of Internet acumen. Over 21 percent of respondents claimed an advanced college degree, which is much higher than current national averages indicate. The same bias held true for annual income. According to the Census, 61 percent of never-married men over forty earn less than $25,000 per year and only about 3 percent earn over $100,000. But from the survey, only 11 percent of respondents earn less than $25,000 per year, while over 21 percent earn greater than $100,000. Again, this is a bias toward more affluent men, which was also not unexpected. Finally, there is a bias toward Caucasian survey takers. Over 84 percent of the respondents were Caucasian, while the expected percentage from the Census would have it at closer to 65 percent. This bias is most likely a reflection of the method used to attract the online survey takers.

Even with all the inherent biases from the online survey, there were still some intriguing, and perhaps even unexpected, results that are worth highlighting. One of the more interesting areas of the survey had to do with the influences of sex as it relates to never being married. For instance, almost one in five men have had over 100 sexual partners, but almost one in four have had less than ten. To my way of thinking, ten sexual partners in over twenty years of sexual activity is not very many. I interpret that to mean never-married men over forty are more likely to be serial monogamists than philanderers. A statistic from the survey that confirms this is almost six in ten men said they could be satisfied with just one sexual partner for the rest of their lives.

As expected, a majority of the men (68 percent) have lived with at least one woman, and 15 percent have lived with more than three. Building on that serial monogamist theme, slightly over half the men have had at least three serious love relationships; however, over two-thirds have never been engaged, so perhaps there is a commitment issue. Over two-thirds believe in soul mates, and about half of those are still waiting to meet theirs, which could still further explain the delay in marrying. Finally, less than one in four are in a relationship right now, and 15 percent of the men in the survey consider themselves lonely. What does that say about their future?

The Conversations

I attempted to limit the telephone calls to thirty minutes out of respect for the men's time. Almost all of the conversations were at least thirty minutes, with the longest one lasting for over an hour. I used a list of questions to help guide the discussions. In developing the list of questions, I wanted to be as comprehensive as possible, while still remaining neutral. I was careful to ask questions without a bias, especially a negative one. As an example, I avoided asking questions such as, "How have your feelings about marriage impacted your decision to not get married?" That question assumes that their feelings about marriage *have* impacted their decision to not marry—a negative bias. Instead, I asked more neutral questions like, "What do you think about the institution of marriage?" One consequence of sticking with these neutral questions is that all but one of the chapters in the book could apply to married (or divorced) men as well. In some respects, this book is about all men over forty.

In crafting the questions, I especially wanted to make sure I investigated every possible factor that may have had a significant enough influence on the men to get them to avoid or postpone marriage. To that end, I asked them about their family, infidelity, divorce, children and sex. I asked them what they thought about marriage, what they thought about women, and if they had ever been in love. I also wanted the men to reflect on their past, to see what lessons they learned and how it had changed them, if at all. I asked them if they had any guilt or regret over any of their relationships, or if they saw any patterns in their behavior. I asked them one of the most difficult questions you can ask anybody on any subject: If you had to do it over again, what would you do differently? The question is difficult because it calls into question our life choices and it is easy to deny the truth, but examining a life choice is exactly what I wanted the men to do with regard to marriage. I also wanted the men to peek into their futures. I wanted to know where they saw themselves in five years, and if they hoped to be married. And of course, I asked each of the men why he had never been married. In the end, I crammed all of the questions into just a handful of categories that ended up becoming the chapters in this book.

I began with the list of questions written in a specific order, but rarely did the dialogue stay on track. I had to let the conversations go where the men wanted them to go. Regardless of where the conversations went, I always began and ended each call with the same two questions. I began each call by asking the men what they thought about the *institution* of marriage. It was a benign question that got the conversation started and set a foundation for the rest of the call. I ended every call by asking the men what advice they would give to twenty-something young men about relationships. Theirs is a unique perspective, to say the least.

Quite a few of the men were caught off guard by my questions. They had not given as much thought to this subject as I had, and frequently the initial response to a question was, "I don't know." I was constantly surprised at how many did not really know the answer to some of life's most important questions. Were they afraid to be truthful, or did they just not know? Later, what I came to realize was, saying "I don't know" was just a delaying tactic the men used unconsciously to give themselves time to address the question and gather their thoughts. Eventually the answers came out, and sometimes the answer really was that they did not know. There were instances where I could almost hear the men trying to convince themselves the answer they were giving was what they truly believed. It was not that they were lying or did not want to be open; they just had not given much thought to my questions prior to my call. In essence, they were answering these questions for *themselves* for the first time.

Most fascinating of all, though, was the small number of men who had taken time to address these questions long before my telephone call. I sensed it immediately. They answered the questions with a clarity and certainty that was impossible not to detect. They became philosophers and preachers, preaching the gospel of the never-married. They knew exactly why they had never gotten married, even if it was not their choice. These were the easiest men to speak with because a single question might have lead to a five-minute monologue. You will probably recognize them as you read.

In speaking with thirty-three never-married men, there were bound to be themes that came up repeatedly. Opinions of marriage, lost loves and the influence of family are just a few, but the most fascinating by far—and the one that permeates the book—is the notion of "the right one." Everybody, it seems, is looking for the right one, especially the men in this book. What does that mean—"the right one"? It is the question that intrigued me the most, and one I explore in great detail during the conversations.

The Men

They are all in here. Think of any male stereotype, and they are in this book. The first one that probably comes to mind for most people is the playboy bachelor who does not want to settle down, cannot commit and will never grow up: the philanderer. Certainly he is in here, but less frequently than you might imagine. So, too, is the forty-year-old virgin, the momma's boy and the male chauvinist. There is even one man who has been in a committed relationship with the same woman for thirty-eight years, never married. Each of the men I spoke with is an entire story in and of themselves. They are all forty-plus years of hopes and fears and triumphs and mistakes and uncertainties, just like married men, divorced men and everyone else. The men I spoke with are so diverse and varied, as I suspected they would be before I began, it did no good to try and organize or categorize them in any meaningful way. No matter how I tried, there would be almost as many categories as there are men.

So what is it that these men have in common? For one thing, their honesty. They are honest about their strengths, their shortcomings and the mistakes they have made along the way. They know what they got right and what they got wrong. Not one of the men I spoke with has consciously lied to himself about why he is not married. Perhaps that is a consequence of the maturity that comes with being over forty. It is my belief that their ability to be honest with themselves *is* the pre-dominant reason why most of them have not married. They know themselves too well and they also understand too well the realities of making a marriage work. And for a small group of them, society be damned, they know marriage is not for them. I applaud their honesty.

The other thing these men have in common is acceptance. Satisfied or not, they have accepted their never-married situation for what it is: the life they chose. None are panicked over the thought of never getting married. They are either comfortable not being married (and potentially never getting married), or they feel confident they will be some day. Perhaps acceptance, like honesty, is another consequence of getting older. We stop running from ourselves. We accept ourselves and come to terms with our decisions, and that is precisely what these men have done.

The fear of being alone as old age approaches is a far bigger concern to them than never having taken a wife. Almost without exception, every man said he would like to find somebody he cared about with whom to share the latter part of his life. In that respect, these men are no different from any other man (or woman) over forty: nobody wants to be alone as they grow old. Most of the men were not in a relationship when I spoke to them, but they wanted to be, whether in a marriage or something else. And even though they wanted to find somebody, I was a little surprised at how many of them—even those still in their early forties—were resigned to their current situation (without somebody). It was not that they had given up on finding a partner, it was more fatalistic: if it happens, it happens. For those who were not in a relationship, they knew why and, more importantly, they knew what they had to do to change it. But whether they thought it was too late for them or that they could not change, it did not occur to them that they still have the power to affect the rest of their lives, and that includes finding someone with whom to share it. I don't know the answer. Perhaps some of them are just tired. Tired of a life spent looking and not finding. Speaking from experience, it wears you out.

Misconceptions are easy to have about never-married men over forty, such as they disdain marriage, hate women, have no interest in children and are generally selfish people. These descriptions are the exception rather than the norm for the men with whom I spoke. All of the men hold marriage in the highest of esteem, even if it is not for them. In fact, it could be argued that one reason these men have never married *is* the seriousness and permanence with which they view marriage. Even the ones who know marriage is not for them still greatly respect the institution. Their love for and appreciation of women is universal. And do not confuse their lack of a marriage certificate for their lack of desire to be in a relationship with a woman they love. Every one of them wants that. Most love kids, some still want them and a few actually have them. Even the ones who do not want children respect and admire those who have undertaken the awesome responsibility of parenthood. And yes, some of these men are selfish, but most know it and have proceeded through life accordingly by *not* getting married. For the most part, when it comes to marriage, it is far less about bachelor stereotypes and a lot closer to "it just hasn't happened" with these men.

The Existing Research

I suppose another reason I wrote this book is because I wanted to read a book on this very subject and found the selection lacking. A search on Amazon.com for the subject of never-married men over forty (I figure if you cannot find it on Amazon, it probably does not exist) produced only a handful of meaningful books, the most recent of which was published over a decade ago—before the dramatic impact of the Internet. Most of the pertinent information on this subject is found in tombs with intimidating names like *The Journal of Clinical Psychology* and *The Sociological Review*. I would not read these articles even if I knew where to find them, and it is not because I think they are without merit. If anything, I think they have too much merit. The books and articles written on this subject are primarily scholarly works produced by MDs or Ph.Ds. They have a certain structure to them, which almost invariably includes some sort of organizing and categorizing of the men in an effort to understand them and make sense of their behavior. Most of the research done on this subject tries to fit never-married men over forty into some small number of classifications to help other professionals understand them better. One such book, *The Psychology of Men Who Haven't Married* (1996 Praeger Publishers), attempts to fit all of its subjects into one of three categories: conflicted bachelors, flexible bachelors and entrenched bachelors. As I read the book, I certainly saw traits of myself in each of the bachelor archetypes. It's true: sometimes I am conflicted, sometimes I am flexible and sometimes I am entrenched, but who isn't? It was apparent to me that I did not fit neatly into any of the categories.

I felt only the slightest need to augment the research I had done for the book with research that was already out there on this subject. There are several reasons for this. For one, the research is already out there—I would not be adding anything new. Also, it would be easy for me to selectively use the research to my advantage, to either prove or refute something I discovered in my own research, and I wanted to avoid any possibility of selection bias. But most importantly, I found myself wanting to defend the men in this book—and all never-married men over forty—against what I perceived to be research results that contradicted what I had found. Nevertheless, I have included some recent research, either directly or indirectly related to this subject, as a way of adding some perspective to the conversations.

Probably the most interesting research out there has to do with the hormone oxytocin, known as the commitment chemical. According to Wikipedia, the source for all things obscure, oxytocin is "a mammalian hormone that acts as a neurotransmitter in the brain. Oxytocin is released during orgasm in both sexes. In the brain, oxytocin is involved in social recognition and bonding, and might be involved in the formation of trust between people."

Without going into too much of the biochemistry, basically what the research seems to indicate is that other hormones, such as testosterone, may inhibit the effects of oxytocin. And mammals in which the oxytocin is inhibited are less interested in bonding with one mate. Several studies of North American men showed that guys involved in committed relationships such as marriage or fatherhood tended to have lower testosterone levels than their single counterparts[1]. Of course, nobody knows whether this is because mated men have lower testosterone levels *because* they are in a relationship, or that men with lower testosterone levels are just more likely to be in a relationship. Could it be that the men in this book have too much testosterone? It certainly would be interesting for someone to do a study on that. I can see it now: a woman seriously in search of a committed relationship meets a man for the first time and inquires as to his testosterone level. Until someone shows me otherwise, I refuse to believe testosterone levels are the culprit. When you listen to the stories of these thirty-three men, it just cannot be that simple. The stories are too varied and diverse. There are too many factors at work, too many causes and too many effects. Research has shown that only 3 percent of mammals mate for life, and needless to say *Homo sapiens* are not among them. Still, we are the only ones with a marriage contract. Viewed in that way, never-married men are no different than divorced men: neither has mated for life.

When you delve further into the research, you find that never-married men are more likely to suffer from mental illness, earn a below average income, suffer from alcoholism or kill themselves. But is their never marrying a cause or effect? Other than the one drawback of weighing more, married men live longer and are healthier than their never-married cousins. The one exception is those men in unhappy, long-term marriages. Theoretically, if you could foresee an unhappy marriage in your future, you would do better to remain as a single man. I wonder how many of the men in this book benefited from that intuition?

According to the Census Bureau, in 1980 only 6 percent of men in their early forties were never married, and as of 2004 that number is up to 16.5 percent, which is a statistically significant increase. Certainly the trend is toward delaying marriage or never marrying. I don't think anyone finds that surprising, given the societal changes that have taken place over the last quarter century. What is compelling is there are 61 million men over forty in the United States today, and 6.2 million, or slightly over 10 percent, have never married. At the same time, there are 68 million women over forty, of which only 5.2 million, or less than 8 percent, have never married. There are two conclusions you can draw from this. First, there are also a whole bunch of women over forty who have never married, so whether it is a problem with commitment or a problem with oxytocin, we both have it. Second, more men than women, be it by numbers or percentage, never marry. Whatever the cause, it affects more men than women.

[1] *American Way*, November 1, 2005 page 37

CHAPTER 2

Marriage

So, what is it that never-married men over forty think about the institution of marriage? If there is one overriding theme to their beliefs, it is this: marriage is good for some people and not so good for others. They especially see the utilitarian purposes for marriage, such as child-rearing and certain financial reasons. Of the 1,533 men responding to the survey, most believe that marriage definitely serves a purpose, at least for some people. In fact, a majority (62 percent) would like to be married someday, while only 8 percent of the respondents have no desire to ever get married, with the remainder still undecided. I also found that to be true of the thirty-three men with whom I had conversations. A significant proportion, if not the majority, would like to get married someday. Of those who would like to get married, the thing they mentioned most often that would actually cause that to happen is finding the right person.

With regard to their overall feelings toward marriage, the men surveyed differed quite a bit from those to whom I spoke. For those responding to the survey, roughly equal numbers view marriage positively (40 percent) as opposed to negatively (42 percent), with the remainder being neutral. But of the men I spoke to, very few have negative feelings about it. Ironically, most have positive feelings toward the institution. At first, it might seem like a contradiction: never-married men thinking highly of marriage. As I thought about it though, it made perfect sense. They have never had a reason to feel badly about marriage *because* they have never directly experienced it first-hand. The idyllic perceptions can linger within them unabated. Quite frequently during the course of the conversations, I found myself wondering how the answers to my questions would have differed had I been speaking with married men or divorced men. How does being married—or having been married—change a man's perception about marriage? Had I interviewed thirty-three divorced men, I may have gotten far worse feedback regarding their feelings toward marriage. What was clear was that the men had separated, in their minds, what they thought about marriage in general from what they thought about marriage for themselves. In other words, the institution of marriage is fine, even if it is not for them.

One of the intriguing things I found during my conversations is how these never-married men could have such understanding of, and convictions about, the demands and rewards of marriage, having never been married themselves. One thing is abundantly clear: these men understand what it means to be married, or at least they think they do. They have learned from their parents, their siblings and their friends. They have internalized and synthesized their observations and have drawn their own conclusions. These men are not bachelors out of ignorance or for lack of options. If anything, they know too much.

While most of the men think marriage is good for some and bad for others, the area in which they differ are the reasons *why* it is bad for some people—usually them. Of those who think marriage is not for them, they question its purpose, its restrictions and the requirement for monogamy. They view marriage from a historical perspective and have rightfully noted that the "rules" of marriage have not exactly kept up with the changes in modern life.

To put things in context, I wanted to see what historical research had to say about marriage and monogamy. In particular, how far back does the concept of monogamous marriage go? Did ancient peoples get married? And if so, did they somehow figure out a way to conquer the urge to have sex outside of marriage? Were they somehow able to keep marriages together, forever? If yes, what was their secret? What I found was a little shocking, as I truly expected behaviors like infidelity and divorce to be a result of our modern culture. I learned that monogamy has been the primary form of human relationship for as far back as anyone can investigate, but that is not all I discovered. According to George Howard in his book, *History of Matrimonial Institutions* (1964):

"The researches of several recent writers... confirming in part and further developing the earlier conclusions of Darwin and Spencer, have established a probability that marriage, or pairing between one man and one woman, though the union be often transitory and the rule frequently violated, is the typical form of sexual union from the infancy of the human race."

Building on that theme, Edward Westermark, in his book, *History of Human Marriage* (2000), points out that concubinage (the practice of forming a union with a woman other than a wife) has prevailed to some extent among most peoples, even among some that attained a high degree of civilization, such as the Greeks and the Romans. Westermark found that adultery has been sufficiently common at all stages of world history. Marriage goes back a long way, but true everlasting monogamy does not. When never-married men question the validity of marriage and the achievement of monogamy, they are not unjustified in doing so. These are questions that have existed for a long time and have not gotten sufficiently answered. Consequently, some have decided not to participate in a ritual that comes with expectations they believe are impossible to live up to.

I was also impressed with how cognizant the men are about more recent historical influences on marriage such as the Victorian Age, European culture and arranged marriages. I respect how progressive they are in their thinking about more liberal ideas like renewable marriages, open marriages and the fleeting nature of *romantic* love. In general, these men are insightful, introspective and very aware of why they are where they are, which is unmarried. However, that does not mean they do not have strong opinions about the institution of marriage.

Separating Marriage from the People in it

Martin, a fifty-four-year-old writer and actor from Missouri, offers an honest assessment of his life, his relationships and himself. Often speaking with hesitation, as if he is collecting his thoughts, his recent role as a senior caregiver has greatly impacted his way of thinking, even to the point where he now considers himself a little selfish and emotionally closed off. Having been raised with traditional values, he is a Christian and claims he relates better to women than to men. In line with many of the men I spoke with, Martin's responses indicated to me that he had not given much prior thought to the questions I asked him. I began by asking him his views on marriage.

"I think the institution of marriage is great," he responded. "It's one of the bedrocks of society. I don't know that society could function without the institution of marriage."

"Why do you say that?"

"Because I think it's the basic relationship; it's the basic institution in society. What other institutions do you have? You have the government, you have churches, you have whatever, but it seems like the family and marriage is something that almost every society in history has had, at least, certainly every advanced society. So, it seems hard to have a society without that."

"What would you change about marriage if you could?"

"I think the way people have related to each other in the family situation often holds much to be desired."

"Can you elaborate on that?"

"As much as I've said about how important marriage is as an institution, it's like any other —one that's made up of people who have a lot of flaws and who bring a lot of baggage and a lot of problems. I think most families are probably, to some degree, dysfunctional. I guess if I had a magic wand, I would change that and make everybody that's in a family healthy and unencumbered by a lot of the psychological problems."

"It sounds like marriage is okay, it's the people in them that are flawed."

"Right."

It is an interesting distinction Martin makes. Marriage, in and of itself, is not the problem; it is the people in the marriage who are the problem. But how can you separate marriage from the people in it? Is he saying some of the people who get married should not, or perhaps they should, but to different people? That somehow the marriage would be okay if only the people in it were altered in some way? I thought this concept of separating the marriage from the people in it would be unique to Martin, but it wasn't. Another man who thinks similarly is Chuck, a forty-one-year-old soft-spoken engineer from Colorado with an easy laugh, who had just recently broken up with a woman when we spoke. Like Martin, I sensed that Chuck had not given a lot of thought to my questions, because many of his responses seemed tentative or qualified. It would have been easy for me to think of him as indecisive, but as the interview progressed, it was clear that Chuck was simply more comfortable operating on instinct—both during our dialogue and in his relationships. At forty-one and feeling as though he was going through some version of a mid-life crisis, he was ready for another relationship, although it did not have to be marriage. His qualified answer intrigued me. I thought, how can someone be over forty and still unsure whether or not they want to be married? The reason it intrigued me so much is because I, too, am still unsure. Maybe he could give me some insight into my own uncertainty. I really wanted to get his take on marriage. He said, "I think it is a good institution, but I'm not totally dedicated to it, obviously."

"Why not?"

"I go back and forth on it. Sometimes I think it's a great thing, and then I see people trapped, friends, and whatever. I am forty-one and I've had friends that were married two or three times. Then I've seen people that have been happily married with their high school sweethearts and are totally dedicated. I see it is a good thing in some cases and a bad thing in other cases. It is almost like a crap shoot."

"Do you have any fears about being married?"

"The biggest fear about being married is I've been in a couple of relationships, and it's good for a year or two and then real soon, it goes sour."

"What typically goes sour (for you) after one or two years?"

"The girl starts finding other things she wants to do or moves in another direction. Eventually, you just have differences of opinion and you end up with two hard-headed people that don't compromise."

"Would it be fair to say that marriage has not been a priority up to this point?"

"I would say, yeah. Like all my relationships, all I've done is entertain the thought. I might get caught up in it for a while, and then I start to pull the reins back and say, 'Whoa, wait a minute.'"

Things change, relationships change, people change. Perhaps the fear of change is what kept Chuck unmarried to this point, but change happens to everyone, not just us never-married folks. So, how do married people do it? How do they stiffen themselves against the inevitability of change long enough to make a lifetime commitment? Do they not know things are going to change when they get married? Do they know and not care? Or is the allure of marriage, and all it has to offer great, so that it is just a price they are willing to pay? Could the fear of change keep Chuck (or myself) from ever getting married? Of the men who responded to the survey, almost three quarters (72 percent) are not afraid of marriage, but almost half (45 percent) are afraid of divorce. There is a cost to being paralyzed by the fear of change. I asked Chuck how he would feel if he got to the end of his life and had never gotten married. In a not unexpected reply, he said, "I think it would be nice to be in a committed relationship, whether it's being married or not. I think as long as I feel good about what I did, and I made sure I helped people, and always was a good person, I don't think I would have any regrets. It's something I want to do, but I wouldn't want to force it."

He wants to get married, but wouldn't want to force it. What does that mean — to force a marriage? I suppose it means either marrying the wrong person or marrying for the wrong reason(s). I am sure some people have done that, but not the men in this book— and certainly not Chuck. Chuck has a vision of marriage for himself and a strong belief: I will have the marriage of my dreams or I will not have one. Chuck does not have a commitment problem; he is totally committed to achieving his standard of marriage and won't settle for less. Perhaps a better word to describe him would be *uncompromising*. That word describes most of the men I spoke with, and just might be the reason why they never married. After all, isn't that what marriage is about: compromise?

The Only Reason to Get Married

There is a group of men whose opinion of marriage made me uncomfortable, because what if what they believe is true? What if the only reason to get married is for children? (And if that is so, does that mean marriage ceases to serve a function, once the children are grown and out of the house?) It is true that in most modern societies there is little real social or economic reason to get married. Unmarried couples co-habitating no longer experience much social stigma, especially among young people. With regard to taxes, property ownership and even inheritance, many countries treat long-term cohabiters the same as married people. Other than for religious conformity or to create a more traditional child-rearing environment, does marriage serve a purpose any longer? One man who digresses is Paul, a fifty-three-year-old CPA from Texas who is amiable, soft-spoken and has a good, quick laugh. Financially cautious, as you would expect an accountant to be, Paul is also "into" numerology. A generally conservative person, he bores quickly and seeks variety, including in his relationships. He believes he was put here to help people and sees himself as a rescuer and an enabler, by his own admission. He cherishes independent women, which makes the rescuer in him somewhat of a contradiction, and when I asked about marriage he stated, "I feel it's an important institution."

"What makes it important?"

"I just think that bringing up a family, especially in today's age, is a very difficult thing to do, and I think a stable marriage would ensure that you could teach your children morals and things like that, which is very hard to do in today's age."

"What if there are no kids involved?"

"Then I'd say, why get married?"

"Do you mean that?"

"If you really care for someone, if you really have a relationship with someone, then why do you need a piece of paper just to say you're married. As a CPA, because of the tax consequences, marriage would be a benefit. Insuring a spouse would be an issue. There's just some issues like that that may be advantageous to be married, but other than that, if things don't work out, it's much easier to say 'bye' (big laugh)."

"How would you change the institution of marriage if you could?"

"Maybe, somehow, ease into dissolving it if it doesn't work."

If all you have is a hammer, everything looks like a nail. To an accountant, the choice for marriage is merely a series of decisions to be made about taxes and insurance, but he is not the only one who thinks that way. Another man with an almost identical belief about marriage is James, a forty-year-old software technician from the South. A stereotypical male in his younger years with his share of casual sexual encounters, James bores easily and is self-centered by his own admission, which greatly impacted his earlier relationships. Even though he has extremely liberal views on marriage and does not really believe in it, in my estimation, he is the man in this book most likely to be married a year from now. He said about marriage, "I could take it or leave it. My general thought on it is that historically people got married for much different reasons than are really applicable today. Today it's more of a tradition than anything else. I do think there are financial reasons to marry, especially if there are kids involved. Outside of the kids thing though, I don't really see that it's necessary. It's really just a label, if you ask me."

"Have you always felt that way?"

"For most of my adult life, I've felt that way."

Aiden, a fifty-year-old mortgage and real estate broker from Southern California, also believes the only real purpose for marriage is to raise children. Aiden has a strong, confident voice and an energetic laugh, even if it is at his own expense. Originally a lawyer from Texas, he is happy, upbeat and, I imagine, he has an almost permanent smile on his face. He is financially well-off and wary of women who are not. He explained why he thinks the only real purpose for marriage is to have children. "It's good for some people and bad for others. I think that the institution of marriage is probably for people that want to have kids, or people who have kids, or people who are about to have kids. The only reason to get married is to have kids."

"Where does that line of reasoning come from?"

"I'm originally from Texas, and in Texas when you get married, you have kids and you stay together for the rest of your life."

"Have you always felt that marriage is only for kids?"

"Well, after my study of the laws in California and Texas, it seemed to me that was probably the only reason to get married."

"What did you find in the law that made you think that is the only reason to get married?"

"The laws are severely skewed toward women."

"How so?"

"If you go back to common law, Texas and California are community property states [and in] community property states, the wife is entitled to half, whereas in separate property states, she's only entitled to her share. As a single guy, it's really not to my advantage to get married. It's more to the woman's advantage."

"Why?"

"Because she gets half of my income, and usually she doesn't make as much money as I do."

"What happens in the situation where the woman makes more money than the man?"

"Then it's to my advantage."

"So, you tend to look at it solely from a financial standpoint?"

"Yes, the cost versus benefit, because that's how women look at it."

"Really?"

"Being in the mortgage and real estate industry, I have a lot of experience dealing with divorce. In a household where the guy is usually the breadwinner, the woman tries to get everything she can."

Maybe everything they said is true and the only real reason to get married today is to raise children, but I could not help but notice that there wasn't a single mention of the word love. The accountant (Paul) sees taxes and insurance, the software technician (James) sees financial reasons and the ex-lawyer (Aiden) sees community property as reasons to get married, but no mention of love. These men have severed the connection between the feelings they might have for a woman and the utility of marriage. In their minds, they have made a clean break: marriage serves one purpose and that is to raise children. And if they choose not to have children, then their decision regarding marriage has also been made. It works for them and I respect them for adhering to their beliefs.

An Institution Whose Time has Passed

A more extreme view of marriage was offered by men who believe that it serves no useful purpose any more. One such man is Trent, a fifty-two-year-old retiree from Vancouver, who speaks with a hint of a Scottish accent and so softly that I have to strain to hear him. Moving frequently as a child caused Trent to become introverted and distrusting of many things, including himself. Describing himself as "not very macho," I could tell by his voice that he was a gentle person. The overriding theme during our conversation was fear: fear of making mistakes, fear of disappointing people and fear of hurting people. I wanted to know what somebody so driven by fear thought about marriage. He stated, "I don't really understand the purpose of it. I've never been attracted to it."

"Why not?"

"Two people can live together and don't need to have a marriage."

"Have you always felt that way?"

"I guess so. My friend had a real good marriage, but things [began] breaking apart and I thought, well, this isn't something that naturally works."

Conceivably, he is right; marriage is not something that works naturally. I know even in the best and happiest marriages, it does not happen without a lot of work. But maybe that is what makes it so precious, the fact that it does not come easily or naturally—you have to work at it. Maybe the struggle is what makes the marriage. I know that humans rarely value things we attain too easily. I once heard an analogy that surmised that the purpose of marriage is for *mutual irritation.* In the same way a grain of sand irritates the oyster and produces a pearl, the struggle results in something beautiful. Is that what Trent is really saying, that he does not want such a struggle? That the cost is not worth the benefit? I think it is honest of him to admit that, but I am not sure if that is what he is doing. Since he did not see any purpose to marriage, at least how it exists today, I asked him how he would change the institution of marriage, if he could. He said, "I think there is a problem between the responsibilities and the liabilities, and the formality of it all seems to cause a lot of people a lot of grief. I guess it hasn't been updated to the way things are now."

I know he is right on this one. Marriage, at least in the United States, is in need of an update. The same vows, restrictions and expectations exist today that existed a hundred years ago, in spite of the changes in life expectancy, science (i.e., birth control) and even the divorce rate. Almost everything changes over time: laws, science, people's behavior, but not the rules of marriage. Is that a failing on the part of marriage? Does the institution of marriage share some responsibility for changing in response to the realities of the day, or would this cause its value to diminish? It is an interesting question and one that is starting to attract a great deal of debate today.

Dwayne, a sixty-three-year-old retiree from Oregon who grew up in a conservative home with a religious influence, is another man who thinks marriage has not kept up with the times. Colored by his parents' divorce at an early age, Dwayne never really bought into the concept of marriage. And while he has an unquestioned confidence in his beliefs, he is filled with the resignation you might expect from a man in his sixties who never married. He wanted children earlier in life, but put career and school before relationships and never achieved that lesser goal. He had a unique response when I asked him what he thought about the institution of marriage: "As defined by our culture, bewildering."

"Why do you say that?"

"Because it represents an era to which I no longer belong. Perhaps I never subscribed to the notion of marriage. Although the establishment of a significant relationship with another is something desirable, but not in the context of marriage."

"Tell me about that era you no longer belong to."

"I grew up in a conservative home, conservative community and conservative religious environment, and I feel it's alien to me. Perhaps it always was. I never really bought into it."

I failed to see the relationship between finding marriage to be an alien concept and growing up in a religious home. I would have thought just the opposite, but Dwayne's conservative upbringing affected him sufficiently for him to remain unmarried for sixty-three years.

Kyle, a forty-eight-year-old massage therapist from Texas, also does not believe in marriage as it exists today, but unlike Trent and Dwayne who dismiss it outright, he actually expands the definition of marriage. An adopted child from parents who are still together, Kyle has a progressive view of marriage and relationships, and it is clear he has given some thought to these topics prior to our conversation. Articulate and self-aware, he lacks a strong desire to marry. He said with regard to the institution of marriage, "It seems the need for marriage has shifted a great deal. I don't know if it came out of the women's movement or the social movements in this country, but certainly for those people who still find the need to get married, it's a wonderful thing. For some people, marriage is probably the worst thing that could happen to them."

I agree: marriage is good for some and bad for others. I just wish that was the prevailing sentiment in our culture today, rather than what it is: that there is something wrong with you if you are not married or have never been married. Perhaps, as time goes by, and we continue to evolve, it will become the accepted notion: some people get married and that is good, and other people do not get married and that is just as good. Kyle believes it, I believe it, and so do most of the men in this book.

Kyle elaborated, "It seems that over time, this other thing has emerged. Whereas marriage is a way to placate the state and more of a legal thing, there's this other kind of marriage that is a merging of hearts, in a spiritual sense. The idea of marriage has expanded. It's a complex word that has a lot of levels now."

"Which level do you identify with?"

"I identify more with the marriage of the heart, more than the financial, law-oriented type of thing. I feel that if I were to meet somebody that I truly wanted to marry, I guess one of the things that we would have to have in common is this idea of, let's not involve the state in this in any way, shape or form. This is between myself and that person. At the same time, if, after a period of time, my partner wanted to be married, I don't think I'd put up a fight. I think I would just go along with it, because of her sentiment. But my own personal orientation would be that the institution of marriage is basically something that's not really applicable to me or my partner."

"So, you would not resist it, but you would not choose it."

"Yeah."

Kyle is right. There are two aspects to marriage: the legal contract and the spiritual contract. So, which part is more important? Somewhere out there are marriages that are only "legal" without a "merging of the hearts." These marriages are more utilitarian, in that both parties just wanted to be married badly enough that the other form of connection was not important (or not considered). Yet, the other way also exists. Is the relationship between Kurt Russell and Goldie Hawn or what Tim Robbins has with Susan Sarandon any less meaningful, important or real since they are not officially married? Perhaps a more enlightened title for this book would be *So Why Have You Never Been Legally Married?* Could it be that this marriage of the heart that these men are waiting for and the legal marriage without this other connection is something that does not appeal to them? Certainly that is true with Kyle. Admittedly, this brings into question the whole notion of the changing nature of relationships and is way beyond my intentions for this book. Nevertheless, this topic is covered comprehensively and with an open mind by Daphne Rose Kingma in her book, *The Future of Love*. In essence, she writes that love will take many forms in the future, not just the traditional structures we think of. I agree with the book's assertion. Are the men in my book pioneers? Are they actually helping to create the future of relationships by *not* getting married? Perhaps.

The Marriage Flaw

Some men feel marriage, as it is structured today, has a flaw—it is too restrictive. Is it reasonable to think you will get everything you need from your partner when you get married? Is it okay to have relationships outside of marriage, and if so, what kinds are acceptable? And would relationships outside of marriage make it more palatable for the men in this book (and the millions who have gotten divorced)? Are we asking too much of marriage, with all its rules, about how to relate to people *outside* of the marriage? One man who thinks so is Nathan, a fifty-two-year-old high school student counselor from New Hampshire. Affected at an early age by repressive parents, Nathan was also impacted by a young lover who abandoned him and left him feeling as though he would never meet anyone as good ever again. He is liberal in his thinking, loves children—works with them for a living—and enjoys his solitude. And while he has many female friends, he claims he has not had a sexual relationship in many years. He said, referring to marriage, "It's okay for some. Whatever floats your boat. If that's what people want, to spend the rest of their life with one person, that's fine. If they don't, that's fine too."

"Have you always felt that way?"

"Yeah, always."

"So, from the time you were a young child, you were thinking those thoughts?"
"Yeah."

"How would you change (the institution of) marriage if you could?"

"Who made the rule that somebody should be married? Why can't people be with different people if they really want to be? Why do you have to be married to just one person? It's funny because when I mentioned it at school to the secretary and nurse they couldn't get their thoughts around it. Who made that rule?"

"So, if you could change it, would you make it ok to marry more than one person?"

"Yeah."

There are other ways in which marriage is restricting that have nothing to do with sex. Samuel, a forty-seven-year-old teacher from Colorado, shared his views on this. Samuel is soft-spoken, with a voice that borders on soothing. I think it would be fair to say that he is a little jaded in his views about women and dating, as a result of many brief, unfulfilling relationships. Very pragmatic in his views on marriage today, he often quotes relationship research as justification for his beliefs. Because of his background coaching and teaching kids, he relates well to younger people, including younger women. Samuel claims he has never been in love and is still trying to find his place in the world. Naturally, I wanted to know what he thought about the institution of marriage. He said, "I don't have a problem with it. I see good and bad in it. I think there [are] some very fundamental purposes that it serves for society as a whole. Unfortunately, once people get married, they think everything is going to be perfect, and that's not the way it works. So, it becomes restrictive, based on the assumptions and presumptions that the parties bring to it, and I don't think it should be."

"How should it be less restrictive?"

"You look at the number of people that go outside the marriage for various activities. By various activities, I mean they feel like they're not getting something in their married life. I think the marriages that are successful are those couples that realize that there are actually three parties involved: the married couple and then each of the individuals. I think the couples that get trapped forget this. I'll give you an example. With some couples, it's like, we have to be together every weekend and every night. Now, I have a friend who got engaged and he went camping with his buddies and she had something else to go and do, and I thought that was really refreshing. It doesn't mean that they're doing their own thing all the time, but it means that they understand that their interests are not a hundred percent [aligned]. I have another friend who is recently married and never spends time away from his wife, which I just think is crazy. He needs to spend time with men. Some of the research I've read says that men need to spend time with men away from their wives, and that doesn't mean they are out chasing skirts; it just means they're out doing stuff with other men together. The same goes for women."

Is Nathan's idea inherent in all marriages, or is it self imposed? The couples I know, who have stayed married for any length of time, seem to not have this restriction. They do not do everything together. They have friends and interests and hobbies outside of their marriage. I suppose there really are three parts to every marriage and the really successful ones are those that nurture all three parts: the couple and each individual.

Monogamy is Not in Our Nature

As far as monogamy goes, amongst primates, humans lie somewhere between the gibbon (true romantics) and the chimpanzee (incorrigible lechers). So, when men say monogamy is not in our nature, they are actually being truthful. There are two fascinating aspects to monogamy though. First, monogamy may not even be in our own best interest. In his seminal book on evolutionary biology titled *The Moral Animal: Why We Are The Way We Are*, Robert Wright explains that as far as survival of the species is concerned, polygamy would actually serve the human race better than monogamy. In essence, what he postulates is, some women would do better sharing a man who has more to offer (money, health, intelligence, better genes, etc.), than being in a monogamous relationship with a man who has less to offer. If that is true, not only are we non-monogamous by nature, it does not even serve us well.

The other intriguing thing about monogamy is there are two ways to be non-monogamous: philandering—cheating on your spouse— and serial monogamy—being in a series of monogamous relationships. The philanderer obviously cannot, or will not, be monogamous, but what about the serial monogamist? Is serial monogamy (and serial divorce) merely a natural consequence of the changes that have taken place in our society, including the fact that we are living longer? Is the validity of marriage-for-life only now coming into question because we are living long enough to ask these questions?

Hundreds of years ago, our ancestors lived in an agrarian society. Most people worked on a farm eighteen hours a day, never traveled more than fifty miles from home and, if they were lucky, died in their forties. Today, we live into our eighties and beyond and can be on the other side of the planet in twelve hours. I once heard someone say that the single biggest predictor of infidelity is opportunity. A long time ago, the opportunities to be non-monogamous were severely limited. Today, the possibilities are boundless, but the structure and restrictions of marriage were created back then, when monogamy was more achievable. Is it possible we have combined two things that were never meant to be together: everlasting monogamy and modern life? In the future, as we live even longer, will the "forever" marriage be the exception rather than the norm? The men in this section think so. Unlike the men in the previous section, who think it is too restrictive and want to know if are we asking too much of marriage, these men are asking the opposite question: is marriage asking too much of us? A man who falls into this group is Evan, a forty-one-year-old mathematician from Virginia. Evan is insightful, well-read and articulate. He speaks with a sturdy voice, which makes him sound more mature than his forty-one years, and is one of those rare men who had already given some thought to my questions. A self-described introvert, his beliefs run the gamut from liberal to conservative, but he is level-headed and almost always considers both sides of the story. He said, "Marriage means different things to different people. I think a long time ago, as far as I can tell, you didn't marry for love. It was kind of a childrearing thing. Now we have the notion of romantic love, especially here in the United States, and it serves a very different purpose. So, I think people tailor their marriages to what they want. I have friends in open marriages, so certainly fidelity is not an issue in a marriage like that. So that doesn't define a marriage."

"Would it define a marriage for you?"

"Not necessarily. I'm not set on the idea of a closed marriage. I think it certainly is a simpler thing, where one can have a deeper relationship. I wouldn't be against an open marriage, but I would have my suspicions."

"Where do you think that kind of open-mindedness comes from?"

"I think it might just be a matter of practicality. I don't know if we're biologically geared to have a single partner for our entire life. I don't know if everyone's geared toward monogamy or if humans in general are."

It doesn't matter whether or not we are geared toward monogamy, because Evan believes we aren't, and so do I. If we believe it, is it any wonder we are over forty and never married? It does not mean Evan and I will never get married, but it does mean, if we do, we will do so with our eyes wide open regarding its expectations and limitations. Since he does not believe we are monogamous, and *that* has impacted his decision not to marry, I wanted to know how he would feel if he got to the end of his life and he had never gotten married. He said, "That's fine. Ultimately, I don't think it's going to make me any happier or sadder. I'm a fairly content person now, and I don't think getting married would change that. I think you come back to your own level of happiness. People usually gravitate toward their own plateau of happiness. So, if you're a happy individual to start with, you will remain a happy individual afterwards."

Winston, a forty-five-year-old corrections officer from Boston with a strong Bostonian accent you'd expect to hear at a Red Sox game, agrees with Evan when it comes to monogamy. Winston is well-off financially as a result of savvy real estate investments he made as a young man. An admitted chauvinist and a little cynical about relationships in general, he leans more toward the European culture when it comes to his ideas of marriage. And while he has many insightful and objective observations about the way marriages are today, he often couples these with antiquated views or extreme liberal positions. More than any other man I spoke with, Winston replied to my questions with multiple answers, making it difficult at times to get his true bent on things. When asked about marriage, he said, "I don't believe human beings in general are meant to be monogamous by nature. I think that marriage served a purpose, and if you really look into the history of marriage, it was more of a necessity back in the day. Marriages have always been arranged throughout history and throughout cultures up until the 1800s in the United States. They started being for love, which I believe is the first time in world history that that's ever come to be. I'm sure it was considered before, but pretty much, marriages were arranged. I think marriage in that sense is sensible, but I don't believe marriage in today's society, based on love, is a wise decision because people fall out of love, they move on. That's why 50 percent of the marriages in the United States fail. That's why there are so many extramarital affairs and all that other crap that goes along with it. I don't think marriage should exist in the form that it is today, an institution based on love."

"How would you change it if you could?"

"I would return to arranged marriages, much like the European marriages as I understand them. They're there for the purpose of having kids, raising kids and creating an economic base for you and your mate and your children. I don't want to say open marriage, but a respectfully open marriage. Marriage in the old days you were faithful and monogamous because there were venereal diseases and stuff like that, and there were no cures. That's no longer an issue per se in this day and age. We do have HIV, but even that is held in control."

"Tell me more about this respectfully open marriage."

"That would be the way I understand it's been for thousands of years in Europe. In Europe, it seems to be more civilized. Women take on a lover, a man takes on a lover, and it's understood and there's no jealousy about it. The guy comes back, the woman comes back, there's no rubbing it in each other's faces. There's no threat of breaking up the family circle."

I inquired further. *"It seems as though here in the U.S. we have those issues, and in Europe, and maybe even in Asia, they are a little more open to it. Where do you think that difference comes from?"*

"The difference comes from the Victorian pressures that we've inherited from the Victorian age. They're standards that just can't be lived up to. Human beings are not monogamous by nature. Some are and that's fine, but most of us are not."

"And that's in direct conflict with this sort of Victorian pressure?"

"Exactly."

I know it is not what most people want to hear, especially women, but Winston is right. People do fall out of love, 50 percent of marriages end in divorce, and maybe basing marriage on love is futile. Maybe we are carrying the weight of the Victorian ethos on our collective shoulders and it is starting to break our backs. What if the Victorian standards are too high? What if the Europeans have it right?

During the whole Bill Clinton-Monica Lewinsky episode, I read somewhere how things are different here in the United States compared to Europe when it comes to extramarital affairs of the heads of state. Supposedly, the Europeans looked at all the fuss the Americans were making and pointed out the only time they would make that much fuss in France was if the Prime Minister did *not* have a mistress. I don't know if that is true, but it raises an intriguing, if not uncomfortable question: could accepting a more open "European" style of marriage actually serve to strengthen and preserve the ideal of marriage? Would bringing marital infidelity out into the open reduce the divorce rate and increase the likelihood of fulfilling the commitment *till death do us part*? Can open marriages save marriage?

I respect Winston because he has the courage to say exactly the way he sees the world, regardless of how politically incorrect it might be. I agree with him and have always thought we are a little naïve in this country. We are a culture that tolerates adultery and accepts divorce, but at the same time holds fast to our idyllic notions of what marriage is supposed to be. Maybe open marriages are the next logical step in the evolutionary process. Only time will tell.

Modern Marriage is Not Realistic

Dale, a forty-five-year-old mortgage analyst from Seattle with a Ph.D. in finance, thinks that the requirements of marriage, as it stands today, are unrealistic. Originally from Texas, Dale answered many of my questions with long pauses and nervous laughter. Describing himself as intense when he is in a relationship, he prefers strong, independent women. When I asked Dale what he thinks about marriage, he stated, "I guess I have mixed feelings about it." He then echoed sentiments similar to Evan and Winston.

"What are those mixed feelings?" I asked.

"Well, it's a long-term contract. It's for life, and I don't know if that's realistic. I guess if you approach marriage without worrying about it being forever, then you're better off."

I have to admit the "forever" aspect of marriage intimidates me. I used to joke that the Grand Canyon started out as a leaky faucet. The point being that time is a powerful force, and given enough, it can create a crevice large enough to be called grand. And if time can erode a hole in the Earth a mile wide and four thousand feet deep, it can erode the best, most loving relationship. One reason I have never married is fear. I have seen people smarter than I am and better equipped for marriage stand up in front of God and everyone they know and declare they would love their spouse forever and ever no matter what…and they didn't. They missed something. And if they—who are smarter than I am—missed something, what makes me think I won't miss it too? I want to avoid the mistakes many others seem to make. And I am afraid to make those mistakes because of my deeply-held belief that marriage *is* forever, and until I can better understand the reasons why marriages fail, I am going to abstain, and so is Dale.

I continued by asking him, *"How would you change it (marriage) if you could?"*

"I've heard the term 'option to renew' before."

I have heard it too, and I like it. From what I understand, marriage is the only open-ended (meaning without an end date) contract into which we can enter. No other legally-bound endeavor asks for a commitment of such duration. Pragmatism, it seems, has crept into every facet of human life except marriage. According to Dr. Lynn Brown in her forthcoming book *A New Marriage for the 21st Century* (excerpts of which can be found at NewMarriage.net), the four-year renewable marriage contract may just be the answer to some of our marriage woes today. She asserts that the permanence of marriage, rather than being its strength, is actually a shortcoming. Working with many couples in her practice she says:

> I notice a high rate of mutual disrespect, rudeness, intolerance and lack of intimacy. It appears most couples change how they treat each other once they have acquired the legal "security" of (ideally) life-long marriage. There seems to be a shift in perception once the bonds of marriage have been put in place. Working on the relationship disappears,

desiring to look attractive for one's lover wanes. Couples strive to maintain the relationship while it is developing and, for many reasons, stop this wonderful process once the paperwork has been filed making the duo "legal." Such an attitude contributes to the high rate of divorce. How do you think your everyday thoughts, words and deeds would be altered if you knew your partner was free to walk away from his/her relationship with you in four years, three years, two years, one year, next month, tomorrow?

I like the idea of having to earn your spouse's love every day. It may be disingenuous of me to say at this point, but I believe I would have already taken a chance on marriage, had it come with an option to renew. Like many of the men I spoke with, I am smart enough to know I do not know it all, including what I or any potential spouse will be like years down the road. We do not want to commit to something *forever* that we do not know enough about. Marriage, as it is structured today, makes us choose perfectly, the first time, when we see evidence all around us of how difficult that is to do. The renewable marriage works, because it not only simplifies the dissolution of a marriage, but it may actually make the partners work harder to keep each other. And I suspect working harder at marriage has more to do with it lasting forever than anything else. As I thought about it further, it occurred to me that the prenuptial agreement is a big step on the road to the renewable marriage because it contains the same two principles: it acknowledges that the marriage may not last forever and provides for legal guidelines in the event of dissolution. The renewable marriage cannot be far off. It was not a shock to me to find Dale was not alone in his thinking about renewable marriages.

Donald, a forty-eight-year-old owner of an electronics retail business in Arizona and a single father of a grown daughter, agrees with Dale about renewable marriages. Very competitive from his college athlete days, Donald was heavily influenced by his parents' unhappy marriage. He is honest with himself and his views on marriage and relationships. An idealist at heart, like many of the men, Donald now occupies that gray area where he is still attracted to some aspects of single life, such as new sexual partners, but is tired of being single and is resigned to the fact that he must change if things are going to change. He is just one of a number of men who reside in that chasm between being driven almost exclusively by their sexual desires, and understanding that sex is just an enjoyable part of a good relationship. Donald appeared to be on the cusp of a committed relationship when he spoke about his feelings toward marriage. He stated, "I don't really believe in it. I have always joked that a marriage should somewhat be like a presidency where you serve a four-year term and you evaluate it after four years. If it's working, you continue on; if it isn't, you don't. I base a lot of that on friends who are divorced or unhappily married, and a lot of it comes from my parents who have been unhappily married for a long period of time."

"*Have you always felt this way about marriage?*"

"Yeah. You get in a relationship sometimes and it's going really well, and I think in the back of my mind that it's going to hit a bump somewhere, and right or wrong, it appears after a period of time. I've been engaged once, when I was about twenty-five, but that's the closest I've been to getting married."

"*What is your biggest fear about being married?*"

"Divorce and being loyal."

"*Explain that.*"

"I think divorce means failure at something and I don't like to fail. I'm pretty competitive in everything I do, and my biggest fear is to be married, and you want to make it work, yet you lose attraction to her, and then you stray and cheat and you feel really bad about doing that. I just never wanted to put myself in that position."

Is it possible our never marrying is a strength, not a weakness, as it is perceived? That it can be a strength of foresight and honesty, of knowing ourselves, our wants and desires, and understanding that our being married would only hurt people (and we don't want to do that). Perhaps by not making promises we are not yet prepared to keep we are making a sacrifice so that others can find greater happiness elsewhere. Perhaps it is something for which these men should be admired.

I continued by asking Donald, *"Do you think you have a commitment problem?"*

"I would say so. When I date a woman, I'm often asked, 'Can you commit to anybody?' I think I can, but as I get older I'm thinking maybe I'll have more flaws than they do, and if I do want to get married and have a long lasting relationship, I'm just going to have to make some adjustments. I've been very independent my whole life, and own a business, and travel, and do pretty much what I want. To make someone happy, I'm going to have to adjust and give a lot more than I have in the past and that scares me. Trying to say I can't go to the country club and play golf everyday, and I can't go out with the guys, and I can't go to the ballgame, it all scares me giving some of that up."

Where do we get the idea that marriage is about "I can't" and giving things up? Is it something we imagine marriage to be or is that what marriage really is? Even if it is about giving things up and sacrificing, surely we get things in return like love, sex and companionship. When we make the sacrifices of marriage the focal point of our decision, when we give greater weight to the bad over the good, we make it difficult on ourselves to move forward. It is a classic example of the glass-is-half-empty mentality. Anybody who emphasizes the negative over the positive in any transaction is not likely to go forward with the transaction, be it marriage or a new job offer. Maybe that is what these men (and I) have in common: our disproportional weighting of the sacrifices of marriage over its benefits.

I finished by asking Donald, *"How would you feel if you got to the end of your life and you'd never been married?"*

"That's a tough question. How would I feel about that? That's a choice. We've all had opportunities to get married and be involved and if I go on and I'm single, then that's what I've chosen to do. I'm pretty happy [with] what I've done so far. So, I think I'd be okay with that. I mean, why settle and get married and be unhappily married just to be married. I don't think I'll ever go that route."

Finding the Right One

Of course, the best way to combat the stringent requirement of having to stay married forever is to be highly selective the first time. Jason, a fifty-six-year-old accounting manager originally from the East Coast, is one man who thinks finding the right one gives the best chance for marital success. Originally moved to Los Angeles sixteen years ago for a job, Jason prides himself on his East Coast values and believes he probably would have been married already if he still lived there. With just a trace of the East Coast he has left remaining in his accent, he conveyed to me that while he is content with life, he longs to have a partner and would like to be married someday. As for marriage, he stated, "I'm very much in favor of it."

"Where do you think that comes from?"

"I think it comes from values and commitment. It comes from flexibility and being in a partnership and doing whatever it takes: growing with each other, doing things together and sticking it out, as opposed to bailing out."

"Have you always felt that way?"

"I feel more about it now than I have because I don't want to be alone for the rest of my life, but I don't want to be with just anybody either."

"What is your biggest fear about being married?"

"I have none."

"None?"

"If it's the right person, I'm for it. I'm not commitment-phobic. I want to be with that person for the rest of our lives together. I don't even want to think about divorce. All my friends that are married on the East Coast are still married, even after twenty-five years."

"How does that make you feel?"

"It doesn't make me feel that great, because I probably would have wanted to have been married, with a family. [I] feel like I haven't accomplished what I want to."

"You have been dating twenty-plus years. Why do you think you have not met the right person?"

"Out here [in Los Angeles], the dating scene is very superficial. I just find it very difficult. I can't figure people out here; I really can't. I think if I were back on the East Coast, I would've met somebody by now."

I cannot help but wonder what Jason's life would have been like if he had met the right person: marriage, kids, the white picket fence? Was meeting the right woman the only thing that could have kept Jason out of this book? Is it just bad luck? Fate? Is it the kind of thing where some of us are just destined to get it and some are not? Or is that just an excuse we use to ease the pain of the consequences of our decisions? Jason was engaged a couple of times and he could have married one of those women and maybe not gotten divorced. Is it possible he could already have everything he longs for today? Maybe presuming divorce was just a crutch, some latent fear he has yet to acknowledge that has kept him from what he truly wants. Whatever it is, he is not alone. Echoing almost identical sentiments to Jason is Mitch, a forty-year-old self-employed single father from Oregon who is soft-spoken, laughing easily. As a result of an unplanned pregnancy from a one-night hookup, Mitch is a single father. His single life was heavily influenced by his parents' early breakup. He is above average at articulating his thoughts and feelings and is disarmingly honest in his assessment of himself, including his own questionable behavior in the past. As I spoke with Mitch, I got the impression he was on the verge of maturing into a more reliable father and man who is ready for a committed relationship. Starting to get "a little anxious after that barrier of forty," he is contrite about his past dealings with women and admits he has a commitment problem, but still hopes to be married someday.

"It's good if you can get it," he said regarding marriage. "It has a certain idyllic perception and I hold it in high esteem."

"Have you always felt that way?"

"I have. I saw my parents break up when I was very young and a single father took care of me, and a lot of that has been influenced by my father and the relationships he had. You don't make that commitment until you know you've got the right one, and that has a pretty high standard."

"Do you hope to be married someday?"

"Yeah."

"So you are not against it?"

"I'm not against it. Love can be fun."

"What is your biggest fear about being married?"

"Having to live with the choice."

"What is your nightmare scenario?"

"Being talkative and unmotivating. Wanting a consistency of life—things always being the same. That doesn't appeal to me."

"How would you feel if you got to the end of your life and you had never married?"

"I'd be sad, but I'd be okay with it. I have a daughter now; that helps soften the blow. I think marriage and children were always equal in my mind. Having the kid lessened the impact of the whole marriage thing."

Another man who believes it is *the right one or no one* is Gordon, a fifty-year-old real estate investor from Atlanta. Gordon comes from a large family with nine siblings, which forced him to become self-sufficient as a young child. Believing he is more handsome than sociable, he had some entrepreneurial struggles early in life that resulted in his never being married to this point. With his slight Southern accent, he leads a contented life and has a practical view of his situation, accompanied by a slight streak of cynicism. I asked him what he thinks about marriage. "I don't have a bad feeling about it," he said.

"I noticed you did not say you have a good feeling about it."

"When I was young, I didn't feel like I belonged there. You go to the weddings and you say I don't want to stand up there and do that. I'm not ready for that. But in your heart, you felt that your day will come, you [just] don't know what age that would be. I never put pressure on, 'I have to be married at a certain age and have the house with the picket fence.' I never felt like I was missing out or even needed it."

"Why is that?"

"I think it's because you just don't meet the mate that you want to be with at your side forever and ever, so you don't think [along those] lines. I do have friends that are dead set to get married and they keep running into the wrong ones, and I'm not like that. If I don't meet the right one, that's fine. I'm perfectly happy with that."

What separates those men who get married from those who don't?

Many of the unmarried men I spoke to claim it is simply a matter of not having met the right person. They want to marry the right one, but so does everybody, even the men who actually *do* get married. So for those men who do marry, were they just lucky enough to meet the right one—or at least they thought they did—or was it something else?

No single subject fascinated me more while writing this book than the notion of *finding the right one*. I believe that when the men I spoke to claim they would get married if only they could find the right one, what they mean by *the right one* is the one that will last forever. The conundrum is that, as they have postulated the problem, finding the right one is impossible to achieve. The fallacy in that logic of choosing the right one is predicated on the marriage lasting forever. But if these men judge the right one by the marriage lasting forever, they will not know it is the right one until they get to the "end" (hopefully many years from now). And if they do make it to the end still married, it probably will have had more to do with wanting the marriage to last and working at it, than with finding the right one in the first place. I can tell you this from my own observation, a big part of finding the right one is *being* the right one. There is an old expression that says when the student is ready, the teacher will appear. I believe that also plays a role in matters of the heart. When we become the right one, the right one will appear for us, and not because they are the right one, but because we see them differently. Perhaps it is not about finding the right one so much as it is about *seeing* the right one. And seeing the right one has a lot to do with expectations.

I have given a lot of thought over the years to the role that expectations play in the happiness we experience in our lives. I can best explain my observation with an example. If you expect to score a 100 on a test and only get a 95, you are disappointed. If, on the other hand, your expectation is for a 90 and you get a 95, you are delighted. In both cases you got a 95. The only thing that changed, which impacted your mood, was your expectation. I wonder if it is the same with men who marry. Do they get married because they are only expecting their right one to be a 90? If that is true, possibly the thing us never-married men over forty have in common is our unrealistic expectations. If we want to marry eventually, that is something we have to consider.

There is another man I spoke to who is looking for the right one, but his beliefs are so dramatically different from all the other men, I felt compelled to highlight George for his, and I hesitate to use the word, *antiquated* perspective. George, a fifty-two-year-old bookbinder from Canada, speaks with a deep voice and has an accent reminiscent of the characters in the movie *Fargo*. Often speaking in run-on sentences, I had a hard time pinpointing his moral compass based on the answers he gave. Oftentimes, his answers did not directly address the questions I asked, causing the conversation to stray from its original direction. Getting close to retirement, and with his financial worries behind him, he is generally happy with his life as he continues to build his dream house by hand. I asked George, who definitely has a traditional view of male-female roles in a relationship, what he thought of marriage. "I'd like to be part of it," he stated.

"Really? Why?"

"It expands your social life immensely. The older you get and you are single, it makes it harder. Where do I find other single men, fifty years of age, that aren't married, and never have been married, and don't have any kids?"

"You're saying you would like to be part of marriage. Have you always wanted it?"

"Yeah. I've always been prepared to get married, but I don't know, maybe you meet the wrong woman or maybe I'm being too critical of them. I'm disappointed in a lot of the women I've been meeting over the years and what I call their life skills."

"What do you mean by life skills?"

"My parents, more or less, operated as did many other people back in that era. They had the division of labor: my dad fixed everything around the house, he repaired the car, mowed the lawn and cleaned the gutters and my mom took care of the inside of the house. She cooked the meals, did the laundry and whatnot. My mother trained my sister to be a good cook and housewife, as far as preparing meals and keeping the place clean. My father prepared myself and my brothers for home maintenance and fixing our own cars. Even to this day, I hate anyone else working on my car, my motorcycles or working around the house. I'm totally qualified; I'm building my own house from a hole in the ground."

"So, these women are missing life skills?"

"Yeah. You can't find a woman that can cook a meal or really takes care of a house. They seem to be very social and very nice people, but they just don't have the part I'm looking for, like somebody that can cook and clean."

"Are these women who do not have these life skills typically divorced or never-married?"

"Well, at this stage of the game, they're typically divorced."

"And they do not possess life skills? That's interesting."

"Well, not up to my liking, and this goes back to a girlfriend that I was dating back when I was twenty-five and she was eighteen. I can fully remember her when she invited me over for my first dinner at her place back then. She got chicken from the Colonel's and she boiled a bag of corn. That didn't make a good impression."

Some men just do not accept Kentucky Fried Chicken from their dates. It would be easy to dismiss George as a male chauvinist with outdated views on gender roles, and I am sure the feminists are forming a protest rally as I write this, but that is how George feels. And somewhere out there is a woman for him, although she may be difficult to find. I suspect his views on husband-wife roles have dramatically shrunk the pool of women he finds acceptable, which may be why a man who would like to be married never has. He may not be the right one yet, even at fifty-two, and that is something he will have to address himself, as will all of the men (including myself) who are even entertaining the thought of marriage. What role do we play in all this? What can we do to not only find the right one, but become the right one?

A Preference for Bachelorhood

Some men just prefer to be unmarried; it's that simple. They have looked at the alternatives, weighed the pluses and minuses and made their selection, without hesitation or regret. Myron, a fifty-seven-year-old librarian from New York is one such man. Myron speaks like a professor with a slight accent that is classically New York. He is articulate, self-aware and speaks dispassionately in his assessment of himself and the world around him. Hanging out with hippies and spending time on a commune in the sixties influenced his thinking. It is clear he has already given some thought to the subjects we discussed and offers a practicality that comes with fifty-seven years of life.

Of all the men I spoke with, perhaps none affected me as much as Myron. Maybe it is because he is ten years older than I am and I see myself becoming him, which makes me sad for some unacknowledged reason. Or possibly it is because he is so honest with himself in analyzing his situation and I fear he speaks for me too. He sees all the benefits and costs of a committed relationship and has decided his freedom is more important than all the compromises he would have to make. This struggle, which should have resolved itself by now, remains at the heart of the issue for many of the men. The tug-of-war between wanting all that comes from being in a committed relationship and still not wanting to let go of that freedom. We began our conversation the way I started all of them, by asking Myron what he thinks about marriage. He said, "I feel neutral about it. I think it's neither good nor bad. I think many people like it and enjoy it very much, and that's good. It's not in itself a bad thing or a good thing. It just is very good for some people and not for others."

"How does it relate to you?"

"It's not good for me because I've always enjoyed being single. I've had experience living with women in my life for extended periods of time, and I realized that I was always happiest when I was living alone or with a male roommate, but mostly alone."

"Where does that come from, being happily single?"

"It comes from not wanting to be accountable for my time and feeling constrained when I was living with someone. I felt freer, happier, more relaxed. I was able to feel that I could do what I wanted more. I could even just enjoy my apartment more or my house where I was living. I could control the temperature my way, and could come home when I wanted. I didn't have to explain my thinking or endure any criticism. I think it comes from not having to anticipate or experience anger—being away from negative emotions."

"Have you always had this feeling?"

"I lived through the 1960s and that had an influence on my thinking. I was in college from 1967 to 1971, and during that time the way people socialized was very informal, and we hung out in groups. [We] were also very informal in our social relationships, and people didn't have the sense of ownership or jealousy that was part of mainstream society, and I was influenced by those attitudes. I lived on a commune for a while with people who considered themselves radicals or hippies, who didn't conform to mainstream values at the time. It was one of the formative influences of my life, feeling that people could relate to each other in ways different than just monogamous marriage."

I feel certain, when it comes to the question of marriage, Myron got the answer right, for *him*. Another man who feels the way Myron does about the value of his independence is Wayne, a youthful fifty-eight-year-old draftsman from Houston who speaks matter-of-factly with an easily identifiable Texas accent. Even though he has only had a few deep relationships, Wayne answered my questions directly and succinctly. His Southern Baptist upbringing left him with good moral fiber, and yet with a practical view of the way things are today.

"I think it's good," he said about marriage. "First of all, I believe children, should there be any from a marriage, are better served when there's two parents. My parents were married a long, long time, and while I don't know if they had the happiest marriage in the world, I certainly think they complimented each other."

"What if you don't have children? What about marriage then?"

"I don't think everyone is cut out to be married, but I think that for some people marriage is a very, very good thing."

"Have you always felt that way?"

"I have, and it's probably because of the way my entire family structure evolved. All my aunts and uncles were married. Most of my cousins have been married or are married. It's probably just my good Christian Southern Baptist small town upbringing."

"Do you have any fears about getting married?"

"Of course."

"What is your biggest fear?"

"My loss of independence. You're looking at a man who has been, for most of his life, responsible to no one but myself and my job. If I wanted to go somewhere, I generally did. I didn't have to worry about if I made it home, or what time or anything like that. When I listen to other guys, they have to keep tabs with their wives. If they go someplace, they have to call her and say, 'Hey, I'm going to go out with the guys and shoot some pool.' I realize that part of that is common courtesy, but having very few close relationships, I think that loss of independence is my biggest fear."

"How would you feel if you got to the end of your life and you had never married?"

"I'd be okay with that."

Wayne would be okay if he never married, but that does not mean he doesn't want to. It might seem as though asking the men what they think about marriage is akin to asking them why they have never married, but it isn't. Certainly most see marriage as a less-than-perfect institution, one that is in dire need of an overhaul. But as you will read in coming chapters, many are still open to operating within the confines of a flawed structure because they do want to marry. And just because it hasn't happened doesn't mean they don't want it to happen.

CHAPTER 3

Divorce, Infidelity and Children

We have all heard the statistics: 50 percent of marriages end in divorce. And depending on who you believe, 26 percent of men and 21 percent of women have had extramarital affairs. There is even a book titled, *The 91% Factor: Why Women Initiate 91% of Divorce.* What does all this mean? At the very least, it means a lot of marriages fail, and a lot of men *and* women have affairs. But what about the men in *this* book? They have never been married. Therefore, it follows that they have never been divorced and have not cheated on a spouse. It does not mean, however, they have not witnessed it or been affected by it. Certainly, they all have strong opinions about it.

When I began this project, I made the assumption—right or wrong—that if the men had never been married, then somewhere along the way divorce, infidelity and/or children must have played a role. In particular, the fear of divorce, the inability to remain faithful and the lack of desire to have children would all seem to be contributors to choosing a bachelor lifestyle. And in some respects, they all have.

During our discussions about divorce, the men had no difficulty separating the idea of divorce in general, from divorce as it relates to themselves. With regard to divorce for others, they had varied opinions ranging from "it's bad" and "you should try to work it out" to "divorce can be a healthy thing." But when it came to discussing divorce as it pertains to them personally, they had a more or less unifying theme: the fear of divorce is a significant influence on why they have never married, and that is because they only want to marry once. Of the men responding to the survey, only about one quarter are afraid of marriage, while half are afraid of divorce. As for the causes of divorce, they cite everything from choosing the wrong marriage partner to societal mores that make it too easy and acceptable to get a divorce. For those who see divorce as a good thing, they mention the benefit to women and how the women are no longer stuck in loveless marriages.

For the men I spoke to, coupled closely with their idea of only marrying once is the belief that if you do get married, you should be faithful. Almost without exception, the men believe that if you marry, being faithful is part of the deal. They even consider themselves as cheating if they have a relationship with a married person. One of the men even mentioned intellectual infidelity, which means looking for something other than sex outside of marriage. It is highly likely that the seriousness with which they take marriage and the desire they all have to avoid divorce and infidelity are the main contributors to why they have never married. They have immense respect for marriage's sanctity and its "forever-ness." It is ironic that these never-married men, with all their fears about divorce and infidelity, honor the institution of marriage by the decision they have made to not marry.

On the topic of having children, the men I spoke to ran the gamut from "no way" to "undecided" to "still want them". This is in line with the men who responded to the survey. Of those who responded who do not already have children, 42 percent have no desire to ever have children while 30 percent still do, with the remainder undecided. There were two results from the survey that I found surprising. One is that almost three in ten respondents have accidentally gotten a woman pregnant. That number is higher than I would have guessed. The other surprising result is that approximately 15 percent already have at least one child. The good news is that most of those who do have a child are actively involved in raising them. Whether it is divorce, infidelity or children, they all have a story to tell in regard to how it impacted who they are today.

Divorce: Bad

Divorce is bad; it is a failing, to some degree, great efforts should be made to avoid it. There are those who feel that way and believe the primary cause of divorce is picking the wrong person. Greater effort to get to know themselves and their partner would go a long way toward avoiding divorce. A man who thinks that way is Samuel, the forty-seven-year-old soft-spoken teacher from Colorado. He states, "In general, I don't think divorce is a good idea, but there are always exceptions. Obviously, if you've got a case of spousal abuse, then that's a bad thing and you can't look at it lightly."

"Why don't you think divorce is a good idea in most cases?"

"A couple reasons. One is I think too many couples make bad choices. Okay, you made a bad choice, now you have to live with it. I think if we would do some homework up front to say this is a good choice or not, then I think some of that could be eliminated. I also think that in some ways, divorce is a cop out. There was a trend in the late nineties among young people to have what they call a 'starter marriage.' What that means is people got married in their early twenties, and by the time they were in their late twenties, or [early] thirties, they were divorced. Quite often there might not be kids involved and they said, 'Oh, it's a trial marriage.' We'll go through it and the second time will be the one where we really figure it out. I'm like, 'what's with that?' When I look at other people who have been married three and four times, I just scratch my head. They're not taking it seriously in terms of what they're doing. They're not taking it seriously because it's too easy to get out of it. It's symptomatic of a throw-away society in some regards."

Samuel made an astute observation and I agree with him. If marriage is, in some regard, a reflection of society in general, and we have become a throw-away society, why should we expect marriage to be any different? The bigger question is what has caused us to become a throw-away (and divorcing) society? Is it merely a consequence of the sheer affluence that we enjoy? We have so much abundance that it affords us the luxury of throwing things away, including relationships? Is the institution of marriage, as we have come to know it, under assault from our wasteful way of life?

Divorce: Too Easy

A number of men feel it is too easy to throw a marriage away and divorces should be harder to get. "I think it's too easy," stated Jason, the fifty-six-year-old accounting manager originally from the East Coast. "In our parents' generation, folks stuck it out. If I'm going to be married, I'm going to be married for the rest of my life. I know there [is] no guarantee, but I'm not going that way. I've been engaged a couple of times. In both situations, they would not have worked; it would've wound up in divorce. [I] chose not to marry those two individuals."

He chose the weight of "never married" over what he felt would be a certain divorce. I wonder how many married, and subsequently divorced, men were faced with Jason's predicament and made the other choice? They certainly are different choices, and who's to say which is better.

Kyle, the forty-eight-year-old massage therapist from Texas, thinks like Samuel and Jason when it comes to divorce. Remarkably, Kyle, who has progressive views on marriage, gave a more traditional response when asked what he thought of divorce. "My parents have been together since '55 and, frankly, I don't understand how they were able to survive it all, because so many people that I know, their parents have separated or divorced."

"What do you think their secret is for staying together?"

"Who the hell knows, because to me, it seems like so many relationships are basically a symbiotic matching of dysfunctions."

"That's brilliant," I said with awe. "What does that mean?"

"It just seems that each other's maligned intentions tend [to] complement each other, and maybe that's enough. As far as divorce is concerned, for me, it's almost like, if you're going to get divorced, why did you ever get married? To me, this seems like a contradiction in terms.

I understand the situation that two people come together, they get married because [it's] the thing they're supposed to do and then figure out they're not for each other, then separate. I understand all that. It just seems that marriage is taken, quite frankly, like so many other things in this culture, very lightly. There is within our culture a certain pressure to get married, and a certain kind of ostracizing that is felt if you're not doing the thing that you're supposed to be doing, which is finding a partner and getting married. Maybe divorce is too easy, and it's unfortunate that people get divorced. It's unfortunate that people can't work out their differences, but to a certain extent, maybe those people shouldn't have gotten together in the first place."

These men take marriage seriously, in spite of the pressure and in spite of being ostracized. Their feeling is marriage is a serious commitment and they're just not sure yet, and they have chosen to abstain until they are more certain. That is not a commitment problem, that is courage. And for those who have made that decision to remain single, it should be worn as a badge of honor.

Divorce: Good

Just as there are men who see divorce as a bad thing, there are almost as many who view it in a positive light. As reasons for why divorce can be a good thing, they cite the empowerment of women, the liberation from bad marriages, as well as improving bad family situations. Myron, the fifty-seven-year-old librarian from New York, thinks divorce can be a good thing. "There's been a sharp increase in divorce and my feeling is that it's probably a good sign as opposed to a bad sign. It means that large numbers—especially women—don't feel they have to be constrained in unfulfilling relationships because they have more economic power than they used to because of their increase in access to education. They don't have to suffer in silence, and the increase in divorce probably in many cases represents a liberation for many people. So it's probably a healthy sign in some ways."

Dwayne, the sixty-three-year-old retiree from Oregon, had a different reason than Myron for why he thinks divorce can actually be a good thing. His opinion is heavily influenced by his parents' divorce during his early adolescence. He said, "I think it could be a very healthy experience for dysfunctional families. I come from one and I think if there had been a divorce earlier in my life, in my parents' life, the outcome might have been different in terms of my deal with marriage."

"What were some of your memories of this divorce that had the greatest impact?"

"I never knew my parents had separated until months later. My father, prior to that period of time, was always busy with his occupation and slept over at the office occasionally. I didn't know what was going on. I was kept in the dark for months afterwards, and when it finally dawned on me, I think I went numb. It was a real dark period, not being aware of what was happening. That also colored experiences in relationships. Just the fear of the dark period would come about and people would just disappear into silence."

"So, going forward, has that dark period reappeared?"

"Oh, yeah."

"In other relationships?"

"Yes, the fear."

"How would you describe that fear?"

"Abandonment, rejection."

It is easy to blame the parents, but I don't feel it is fair to do so because rarely is there malice involved. Dwayne's parents did not set out to intentionally hurt him by getting divorced. They merely did what they felt they had to do. But there is no denying it has impacted his world and his views on marriage *and* divorce.

The Best Reason to Get a Divorce

Of those who see divorce in a positive light, the majority mention one reason over all others as justification: that the two people are wrong for each other. This aligns perfectly with their desire to hold off on marriage until they meet the right one. In their way of thinking, divorcing the "wrong" one only expedites the process of meeting the right one. It all serves the same purpose. And whether they realize it or not, if their objective is to avoid divorce, their patience serves them well. According to the *Monthly Vital Statistics Report* (March 22, 1995), published by the Centers for Disease Control and Prevention, of men and women who marry for the first time between the ages of twenty and twenty-four, over 35 percent end up in divorce, but of those who marry for the first time between the ages of thirty-five and thirty-nine, less than 7 percent end up divorced. I don't know whether the lower divorce rate from older first timers is because it took them longer to find the right one or because older (and presumably) more mature people are better equipped to deal with marriage. Either way, if these men really do want to marry only once, they are not hurting their chances by being never married into their forties.

Gordon, the fifty-year-old real estate investor from Atlanta, thinks it is okay to divorce the wrong one, even if he or she started out as the right one. "I feel if you're in a marriage and it worked out well for a while and two people have grown apart, divorce is great, if it's because of the right reasons."

"What would be some reasons that would legitimize divorce?"

"I know financial struggles [are] why they shouldn't get divorced. If it's strictly emotional, where they don't feel that connection anymore, that's hard to regain. I would look to get divorced. You know you can make a mistake getting married. That's the way I look at it. I've seen so many people get married to the wrong people."

"And having seen all those people marry the wrong people, how has that affected you?"

"Not in the least. I don't believe I'll make the wrong choice."

"Obviously, picking the right person is paramount to you."

"I feel that the older you get, the [more] mature you get, the more time you take, and you do have an understanding of what you want, what you need and what feels right."

I only know of one way to be 100 percent sure you do not make the wrong choice when selecting a marrying partner, and whether he knows it or not, Gordon has done just that: he has abstained. Maybe he is right to do that. I sure hope so, because that is what I have done too. Maybe you can never be 100 percent sure, but you can increase your chances by getting to know yourself, and for some men (like Gordon), that takes time, even into their fifties. It does, however, make me wonder about the men who get married at a much younger age and actually manage to stay married. Was it simply a matter of discovering themselves at a younger age? Was it dumb luck? Or was it something else? How did they pull it off?

Sandy, a forty-two-year-old hypnotherapist from Cleveland, also thinks divorce is okay if they are the wrong people, although he has reluctantly come to that conclusion over time. Sandy is fiercely independent with a dry sense of humor. Somewhat of a rebel with no problem speaking his mind, he is a spiritual person who considers himself a truth seeker. He is well-educated with multiple Masters Degrees, and while he did well financially at one time, he is struggling somewhat at present and lets his situation dictate his relationship decisions. Because his parents were divorced, but ultimately remarried each other, I was curious to know what he thought about divorce. He stated, "My attitudes about divorce used to be that it's a pretty bad thing and you should probably stick through it. I think that just comes from my parents' marriage, which wound up ending in divorce after me and my brother left the nest, and then shortly after that they remarried each other."

"You said you used to feel that way. How do you feel now?"

"The way I feel now, without considering kids, is if it ain't right and the people aren't willing to get some counseling and commit themselves to that, then just move on."

"What changed? You had this one feeling and now you are open minded."

"Sticking with relationships, thinking that they were going to get better and half-ass counseling."

"And what do you think about infidelity?"

"It goes beyond just sleeping with someone."

"What does it involve?"

"I'd say it gets to the point of being in a committed relationship and yet seeking out something from somebody else on a consistent basis because you're just not getting it at home. I believe in the concept referred to as intellectual infidelity. I think it's every bit as dishonest and damaging to a relationship, if not more so, than sexual infidelity."

"Have you experienced that yourself?"

"Yeah. I've experienced that in a few women who were in relationships, seeming to want to get that one something from me, some sort of intellectual something, someone to talk to."

"So, women who are in other relationships, but have not gotten the intellectual thing they need there, they come to you?"

"Right, and the minute I figure it out, I cut it off."

"Where do you think that comes from, women wanting to do that?"

"They married the wrong person."

At a certain point, I stopped being surprised how numerous stories came back to the idea of finding the right one (and the consequences of choosing the wrong one). Nevertheless, I feel this way of thinking is a little naïve, that if somehow you could find the right one, all of the other problems would go away. I imagine avoiding divorce has less to do with choosing the right one and more to do with the tenacity and desire of the two parties involved to keep it together.

Gabriel, a young forty-seven-year-old media developer from Canada, feels similarly to Gordon regarding the validity of divorce. Gabriel was heavily influenced by his Catholic upbringing and rigid military father, and although he no longer considers himself a Catholic after years of rebelling against it, there is no denying its lasting influence on him. Gabriel still believes that when you marry, you marry for life, which is why he has yet to marry. By all accounts, he is of high moral and ethical fiber, but with a streak of pragmatism. According to him, when he was younger, he was unsure about marriage and is now open to it, but only if it is the right woman, and he would still like to have children someday. He said, "I think divorce can be a really good thing. It should be as simple as possible, but it should be for the right reasons. I've definitely met people who really don't know themselves and maybe don't know their partner that well, and I always wonder what's going to happen down the road when they have to face issues they haven't faced yet. I went to a thirtieth high school reunion this spring. I met two guys who had both just gotten divorced—one after ten years and one after twenty years. I was curious as to what led them there. I suspect that some of it was the issues that they didn't deal with when they got married and had to deal with later on, which eventually caused the divorce."

"If you think divorce can be good, what do you think about infidelity?"

"Very, very low in that I look at that as a personal failing, that if someone is cheating then they seriously have to look at why they're doing it, and if they're not happy, I don't think they should be there with the person. Essentially, to me it's an indication that the current relationship has failed and either you fix it or you get the hell out of it, but you don't cheat."

"Interesting."

"I even view it as cheating for me, being single. But if I had an affair with a married woman, I would still view that as cheating on my end, meaning that I'm still cheating. I'm single, but to me, I'm helping this woman ruin her marriage. I even had some married women who had approached me and I just said no thanks, I don't go for that."

There is Gabriel's integrity perfectly blended with his practical view of things. He only wants to marry once, would never cheat, but accepts the possibility of divorce. That line of thinking was not unique to Gabriel; the combination of idealism and pragmatism showed up repeatedly during my conversations. I really enjoyed interviewing Gabriel and I identified with him because I too am a strange mixture of idealism and pragmatism. I, too, only want to marry once, never want to cheat on (or with) a woman and accept the possibility of divorce. Perhaps it is this unique combination of supposedly incompatible beliefs that keeps us never married. There is always risk in relationships, and it seems a lot of us are not willing to take on that risk. We don't have a fear of commitment, we have a fear of uncertainty, and perhaps it is the fear of uncertainty that paralyzes us into being never-married.

A Sign of the Times

One man who I interviewed sees divorce and infidelity as inevitable, given the world we live in today. Wayne, the youthful fifty-eight-year-old draftsman from Houston said, "I think it's sad that people get divorced, but I also understand [it] in today's society. Not only is society changing at a rapid rate, but people are too. People are living longer and they're having more careers. Maybe it's just an extension of the fact that people have two or three careers now and move around a lot and I just think it's almost inevitable."

"Really?"

"If you stop and think about it, a hundred years ago, people lived and died in the same town or city they lived [in]. Where now they are scattered all over, and with women in the workforce, they're going to meet men. I read that two thirds of divorces are initiated by women."

Actually I think it's closer to 91 percent.

The Fear

There is no denying that, when it comes to divorce and infidelity, fear plays a big role. In a society where it is more unique to be never-married than divorced, I was curious to discover what lies behind the fear. There are those who are afraid because they have gone through it (as a child) and do not want to risk putting anyone else through it. Others are afraid because they have witnessed a friend or family member go through it. You only need to witness one bitter divorce to recognize it as something you want to avoid. Then there are those who fear both divorce and infidelity because they know they are not ready to be married. And, of course, there is the money. For those, the fear of divorce is really the fear of the financial disaster it can bring about. Danny, a forty-eight-year-old nurse from Washington state, fears divorce because he experienced his parents' as a child. With an accent that is more Canadian than American, Danny comes across very matter-of-fact when talking about relationships and matters of the heart. Growing up in a broken home with no father around has also had a significant impact on why he never married. He has only had a couple of long-term love relationships in his life, has never lived with a woman and claims he would marry the right one, but always seems to find something wrong. He loves kids and would love to have them someday, even if they are somebody else's. At the time I spoke to Danny, he was recovering from a recent breakup with a woman, who has come in and out of his life for over a period of thirty-four years. She captivated him with such intense infatuation, it has hindered his ability to form meaningful relationships with other women. What I really wanted to know was what impact his own parents' divorce had on his life.

"I don't want to be divorced, but almost everybody I know is," he volunteered.

"Has that affected you?"

"That's a fact of why I didn't get married."

"Really?"

"Because I grew up in [a] family with no dad, so I didn't want to do the same thing."

"Do you fear divorce?"

"Yeah, because I didn't have my dad around. That definitely is a big influence—the number one influence. Getting married because I felt like I had to get married (because that's normal). If I don't find somebody to love, I don't want to get married."

His fear of divorce is strong enough that he would rather remain single than risk it. But there are no guarantees; there is always some risk of divorce. And if finding a "risk-free" situation is what it will take for Danny to marry, I suspect he will remain single (and that's okay too). Like Gordon, who has not married for fear of choosing the wrong one, Danny has opted for the same foolproof way to avoid divorce.

Paul, the fifty-three-year-old CPA from Texas, feels the same way, only it was not his parents' divorce, it was his aunt's. Regardless of the relationship, one bitter divorce is all it takes to have a lasting effect on a child. He stated, "It's a tragic event, because you see it played out so viciously against each other, and it's like, how could you love someone so much that you got married, and then when you divorce be so absolutely bitter about it? Like my aunt, for example, is going through a divorce and it's going on a year and a half right now and it's still not over. She has no money. She's thrown $30,000 into the divorce so far and it still isn't final. I just think it's sad that when two people divorce, it can't be on an amicable basis."

"What impact do you think that has had on you?"

"I think it's had an impact on me. I've been stabbed in the back so many times that I just feel like I don't get it."

"What does that mean, stabbed in the back?"

"Taken advantage of or used."

"Financially?"

"Either used financially or emotionally or whatever. It would probably be the money thing, and that's terrible to say, but it's happened not all that long ago, where I knew damn well that all she wanted was a husband so someone could take care of her financially. I think once I got to this age, that's even become more of an issue."

"How far did you get into that last relationship?"

"Not very far."

"It sounds like your antennae are up and looking for this stuff."

"Oh, they're up big time."

"I know what you think about divorce. What do you think about infidelity?"

"That's probably another reason why it'd be hard for me to marry because I think it would be very hard for me to be with one person for the rest of my life."

"Why do you say that?"

"I just think it would. I get bored very easily, and I just think I would be bored with the same person for a multitude of years."

"Have you seen that in your past relationships, getting bored?"

"Yes."

I recall the old anecdote of the bachelor explaining why he never married. He offers up that he enjoys eating lobster, but not every night. Is that the problem, are we expecting a lifelong marriage free from boredom? Is marriage supposed to entertain us? I was always under the impression you make your own fun. Is this merely another example of misguided expectations about marriage? Whatever it is, Paul is not the only one who feels he cannot remain faithful. Donald, the forty-eight-year-old owner of an electronics retail business in Arizona, echoed Paul's sentiments regarding infidelity almost exactly. He said, "That's probably my biggest hang-up in not getting married, because I certainly don't want to get married and cheat, and I haven't gotten to the point sexually where I can feel like this is going to be my last partner. Hopefully, that will happen with me some day, but right now that has not happened, so that's one of my reasons why I've never gotten married."

"Since one alternative to infidelity is divorce, what do you think about that?"

"In a sense it's a bad checkmark against yourself if you've been married and divorced. And then on the other hand, I think, well, at least people have gotten married and tried it. I haven't. But my goal is at some point in my life to get married and live happily ever after."

"Even though you don't believe in it?"

"I do and I don't. I think as I get older, I'm tired of the dating game and the excitement of meeting a woman and dating and sex and all that stuff. I think as I get older, I see there's a light at the end of the tunnel. I just haven't quite gotten there yet."

Donald is right on schedule, for *him*. He wants to get married some day, just not yet. He knows it, he accepts it, he has acted accordingly. For a number of men, especially those with no desire for children, forty or fifty *is* the right age. With an extended life expectancy, it is not unrealistic to think you can get married for the first time in your forties or fifties and still have a forty-plus year marriage. For some, that scenario represents the best of both worlds.

Manny is also controlled by the fear of marriage. A forty-three-year-old software developer from Raleigh, NC, Manny has a voice which makes him sound more mature than his age. A social person by nature, he has a strong need for independence, even though he is currently living with a woman. He mentors children and is generally happy with his life, and while he seemed to lose his place occasionally while answering my questions, that may have been because our conversation was actually part of *his* self-discovery process—as if by answering the questions he was getting to know himself for the first time.

"What do you think about infidelity?" I asked.

"I believe a married couple should be true to each other. I think that would be hard for me."

"Why do you say that?"

"Just because I've learned [that about] myself. I never really cheated on anyone until I was about thirty-five, and then once I did it once, it seemed like it was kind of easy to do."

I was glad to hear at least one of them say it: you can cheat on a woman even though you are not married. I happen to believe cheating is a violation of trust between two people who care about each other and does not depend on a marriage certificate. Nevertheless, merely by identifying his action as cheating, Manny has, in some small way, started thinking like a married man.

I continued, *"Why do you do it (cheat)?"*

"I guess because I'm a guy."

"What are you looking for when you cheat?"

"I think the answer is just sex. I've always been promiscuous to some degree. That plays into it after I'm in a relationship for a couple of months. I always wonder what else is out there sexually."

"Why do you need sex if you are already in a relationship?"

"It's new, right?"

New sex? That's the answer? It is not a particularly Earth-shattering explanation from a bachelor on why he has never married. He needs a little variety? What is compelling about that? Nothing. But what is informative is how few of the thirty-three men I spoke with said the same thing. Most were sexually content if they were in a relationship. I expected to hear that answer (i.e., new sex) more frequently than I did, but the research confirms what I heard during my conversations. In the online survey, when asked what is the most important thing in a long-term relationship, only 15 percent chose sexual compatibility. When asked if they could be satisfied with one sexual partner the rest of their lives, almost six in ten said yes, while only 15 percent said no. And in a 2004 online survey for *Best Life* magazine, only 5 percent of the men responded that they were no longer sexually attracted to their wife when asked for reasons for why they got divorced. For all of our fears about sexual monotony, the research indicates it is not a major factor in why relationships fail.

Possibly with Manny, the reason new sex is important to him is because he is "only" forty-three. I do not think men ever lose their desire for sexual variety and newness, but as Donald alluded to, I think what changes, as we grow older, is we have neither the desire nor the ability to do anything about it. It can almost be viewed as a simple finance problem: the return on investment no longer seems worthwhile. The day we come to that epiphany, it liberates us and we can feel it. Donald senses it coming and I have already felt it. Something trips within us, and suddenly sex with one woman we really care about seems a lot more satisfying than sex with a bunch of women we don't. It happens at different ages for different men, but for some men, the return always seems worth the investment.

Children: Undecided

Of the men surveyed, as well as those to whom I spoke, more are still undecided about children than those who feel strongly either way. I suppose that should not be surprising coming from a group of men who, by and large, are still undecided about marriage. When it comes to considering parenthood, they are sensitive to their age and understand the realities of raising a child at their stage in life. They also believe the odds of attracting a woman of child-bearing age are not very good, and consequently a few are open to adopting or raising other people's children. Quite a few of the men had wanted children at an earlier age, but have abandoned the idea as the calendar moved on or as other circumstances dictated. An example of that thinking came from Wayne when I asked him if he ever wanted children.

"There have been times I wanted some, yes."

"What made that change over time?"

"I don't know that I can honestly say. I know a few years ago when my mother was very ill and I moved her in to live with some relatives, I was going through a lot of her stuff. I had all these old family photographs of her and her parents and grandparents and I thought to myself, how sad it's going to be that when I die all these photographs will be chucked in the trash, and that's when I thought, it's too bad I didn't have any kids. But for the most part, I don't miss having kids because I don't have a lot of patience, and kids take a tremendous amount of patience. As a matter of fact, I just had a young woman tell me a couple of weeks ago that she thought I would make a good father, especially for a little girl."

Andrew, a forty-six-year-old DJ from Florida, is also undecided about children but arrived at his indecision differently than Wayne. For a long time, Andrew never wanted children and is now at least toying with the idea. Andrew, who speaks with the deep, confident voice you would expect from a professional DJ, was dramatically impacted by his parents' break up at an early age. A man who has definitely lived the party life of a DJ, he speaks with a greater frankness and honesty about sex than any of the other men. His sexual desires are a constant theme running through our conversation and his life. Still searching for answers and beginning to find them, he told me why he is now open to having children. "I go back and forth. One side of me would like kids, one side of me wouldn't. I didn't want kids for the longest time and just recently, in the last couple of years, I thought that maybe having kids would be a good thing. Obviously, if I'm going to do it, I would want to start very soon. Otherwise, I'm going to be the grandpa with the kids graduating high school."

"What changed over the last couple of years to make you want to have kids?"

"A newfound relationship with God, and for some reason it just seems like the thing to do. I can't really explain myself. For some reason, having children seems like a normal progression of things."

A man who used the same exact words to describe his feeling toward having children is Dylan, a forty-year-old in hotel management from South Florida. Originally from New Jersey, Dylan still has not lost his South Jersey accent after twenty-two years. The oldest of four children from a happy, healthy Irish-Catholic family, he has positive feelings about marriage and family. He is conservative by nature, and even though he is particular with whom he dates, he is open-minded, and I got the impression he is going to get married eventually, it's just a matter of time. With such a wonderful upbringing, I was curious to know what Dylan thought about having children of his own. "I love children. I know I'd be a great dad and father," he shared.

"Do you want children?"

"I go back and forth. It would be nice. Before you have children you need to find a good woman, preferably in her thirties. I think under thirty is a bit too young; I draw the line at twenty-eight. It would be nice, don't get me wrong, I love kids and if it happens, great, and if it doesn't, it wasn't meant to be."

"Why do you draw the line at twenty-eight?"

"A lot of people in their early twenties are into partying and into drugs, they have a job and not a career, they rent, they don't own and I'm not comfortable with that."

"It sounds like you are looking for an adult as opposed to a child."

"Yeah, that's why I'm more comfortable dating women forty and older. It's just my preference. I bet 99 percent of the men would rather pick somebody younger, but I'm the exception."

"Would you be open to being with a woman who already has children?"

"Yeah, that's not a problem."

When it comes to his indecision about children, Samuel, the forty-seven-year-old soft-spoken teacher from Colorado, has the same tug-of-war going on in his head as Dylan and Andrew. "I like kids, but kids can be a pain in the neck. When people say that parents have the toughest job, that's very true, because parents and families have to give up a lot of what they do to enhance the child, and some people are willing to make that commitment and others are not."

"How about you? Have you ever wanted children?"

"That's a hard question. I don't know. I know there [are] tremendous rewards from seeing a child every day, so I wouldn't rule it out. As far as me having kids, at my age, the scientific realities of it are probably not very good, simply because the research coming out showing the odds for a child to have mental illness or be born with a disability, they increase with the age of both parents, especially the man. So, that makes it a little difficult, because that's a pretty big risk. And as far as doing what I call the 'add water family,' where you marry somebody who has kids, that's difficult as well. I don't think you can say blanket yes or no, because you have to look at the kids and you have to look at the other person involved. If it's a good fit, then you say yeah, it's a good deal. I think some men have a great reluctance to take on that role simply because they're not looked [at] as a parent. They're looked on as some source of income, and I think a lot of men have some trepidations about being used that way. When you go into a step-parent situation, you have very little control over how the kids are disciplined. You have to really work at that, and if you don't, you've got problems."

"Would it be fair to say that, at forty-seven, you are still open to the possibility of having children?"

"Yeah."

Kyle, the forty-eight-year-old massage therapist from Texas, is also undecided about having children, but his influences are much different from the other men. Because he was an adopted child, he views parenthood with an admiration that is unique among the group. He also told me a chilling tale of the role fate played in his life. He said about children, "Well, without them we're dead in the water, in terms of continuing to survive."

"That is a good big picture view, but what is your own particular bent on things?"

"I think it's probably the ultimate responsibility that people could choose, and that most people are ill prepared for. I was actually an adopted child, and my parents adopted four of us because my adopted mother couldn't have children. I've come from a very unique family dynamic because whereas a lot of families kind of begin unintentionally, my parents made the conscious decision to get one kid, then another and then another. As far as myself, I'm open to having children. It's interesting because there seems to be a trend of both men and women waiting until they're older to have children. So if I'm to have a kid, I would definitely be in that category, but I don't think having a child at this point is a saving grace to my validation of being a human being."

"Would you be okay if you got to the end of your life and you never had a kid?"

"Yeah, I think I'd be all right with that, because I've viewed myself in my own personal history. I was an accident to begin with, and then there were the circumstances that happened. My birth mom gave me up for adoption when I was born and six months later she was killed in a car wreck. If she would have kept me, there was a good chance that I would have been in that car with her. So it seems like I'm obviously supposed to be here."

"So are you fatalistic because of that?"

"No, I don't think so."

Well I am, and his story made me shiver. I could not help but search for the greater meaning in the story of a man who is still here because his birth mother unselfishly chose to give him up for adoption. I think if it were me, I would read something more into it and feel an even greater sense of obligation to have children, as if somebody was sending me a message: I am going to spare you, but you owe me. But not Kyle, he sees no such message in any of it.

Children: Indifferent

Unlike the men who are undecided about parenthood, there are others who are simply indifferent to it. Some men go back and forth, these men can take it or leave it. One such man is Justin, a forty-one-year-old attorney from Washington, DC. Of all the men I spoke with, I think I had the least in common with Justin. An only child from a conservative Christian family, his Biblical lessons are a constant theme during our conversation. A self-proclaimed mama's boy, he was shy and started late in life sexually, but managed to sow his wild oats in his late thirties. He is well-spoken, still optimistic about life and was the first man to talk about having a sense of obligation to have children. He said, "I'm not uncomfortable with children, in fact I end up being kind of the good, fun uncle to my friend's kids, which is of course different from actually being a parent. They seem to like me in my capacity as an uncle, but I guess I don't really know much about children. I was an only child, so it's not like I had brothers and sisters around who have kids."

"You said you are not uncomfortable with it, but you did not say you are looking forward to it either. Do you have a desire to raise children of your own?"

"I've often felt the urge to be married, more or less strongly at different times in my life. But I've never really said, 'Gosh, I want to have a family. I want to have kids.' I can take it or leave it. I think it would be fine, but it's not going to break my heart if it never happens. Because I'm an only child, I feel a certain amount of pressure because my parents want grandchildren, and I'm the only game in town at this point. The biological line dies out with me if I don't. That's the only pressure I feel. Otherwise, I could take it or leave it."

"Where do you think that indifference comes from?"

"Being raised an only child, it was never a particularly friendly environment. I was always sort of raised as a little adult; I always had to amuse myself. I think it's a very different experience than someone who grows up in a boisterous family of five or six kids. There's a whole kid culture, as opposed to the parents in the family."

Evan, the forty-one-year-old mathematician from Virginia, has similar feelings of indifference when it comes to the subject of children. He stated, "I don't have anything against them. They're a lot of money; they're a lot of responsibility. If I'm going to be a parent, I'd like to be a good one and certainly you'd like a good partner to help you in childbearing. But ultimately, I have no burning desire. If I died without ever having children, that would be okay with me. I wouldn't feel unfulfilled in any way."

"Where do you think that comes from, that indifference toward children?"

"Ultimately, it just isn't me. I'm very confident with what I have— I have enough. There is enough in this world to occupy myself and yeah, maybe I just don't want to be distracted with them. And my family life wasn't that great growing up, so if I were going to do it, I would want to be a more responsible parent and a more available parent than maybe mine were."

Whether they are undecided about children or indifferent to them, they have made peace with it and are comfortable with it, no matter how things turn out.

Children: Not Too Young

They would like to have children, but not babies. These men like the idea of raising a child, they're just not crazy about the thought of dealing with them before a certain age. I can see their point. When I think of having a child, I think more about little league than I do about changing diapers. For years, I used to say, sarcastically, the problem with children is they're not adults. It is reassuring to know there are other men who think the same way, such as Dale, the forty-five-year-old mortgage analyst from Seattle. "I like children," he stated. "I think they bring a lot of joy into people's lives, and I think they bring a lot of frustration. I just think they're an enormous responsibility."

"Would you like to be a father, or have you wanted to be a father in the past?"

"Yeah, absolutely. My attitude is, bring them to me when they can talk. I don't like them when they're little shit monsters. They're okay, I just don't want to take care of them. I don't want to hold a baby and I don't want to change a diaper, but when they can start talking around age two-and-a-half to three, then I can interact with them and they can count on me as a dad."

"Do you think that first two-and-a- half to three years of child-rearing has maybe had an effect on your not having children?"

"Not consciously."

Nathan, the fifty-two-year-old student counselor from New Hampshire, feels the same way, but he thinks even three-years-old is too young. "I work with them," he stated. "I think they're the most wonderful things in the world. I've worked with them since the day I got out of college. I don't have any, but for me, I feel like I have a family of children all the time."

"What draws you to them most?"

"Their enthusiasm for growing up."

"Do you still want any children?"

"You think about it, and it would be nice. Believe me, I like my solitude when I'm at home. Truthfully, I like kids after the age of ten."

"Why is that?"

"Because you can talk to them, and they don't scream all the time. I'm not a big fan of younger kids."

"And it's because of the screaming?"

"It's because they're not adult enough until they get older. I've always liked older kids. When I first started, I worked with all teenagers, and then they put me in charge of a unit with six-year-olds. I was like, 'Oh God, this is awful.'"

"So, you really only start to like kids after about the age of ten. Has that had any impact on your having kids?"

"I never got married, so it didn't really matter."

Children: Too Late

There are those men who have always wanted children, but life didn't work out that way, and now they reluctantly accept that it is too late for them for differing reasons. Several had not met the right one;

while for others, life seemed to slip away as they made other things a priority, such as education and career. Now they feel constrained by their age, and feel powerless to attract a younger woman to give them children. These men wanted to be fathers, but as the random acts of life played themselves out in response to their choices, it simply hasn't happened. From my own personal experience, I do not believe it is too late for them. My father was forty-four when I was born and my brother-in-law was fifty when my nephew was born. But these men think it is too late for them, and that's all that matters. A man who fits this category is Randy. Randy, a forty-eight-year-old engineer from Southern California, has a quiet, gentle voice but with a quick, easy laugh. The product of a difficult upbringing by an abusive father, he enjoys tennis, golf and is generally content with his life. Our conversation at times was challenging, as he would frequently offer two disparate answers to my questions. Originally from Virginia, he has four siblings who are all unmarried as of our conversation. We talked about having children of his own. "I love children," he stated.

"Did you or do you want any?"

"I do not want any. I love everybody else's, as long as they go home and somebody else changes the diapers and listens to their screaming."

"Why don't you want children even though you love them?"

"I'm too old to have children."

"Did you feel that way even when you were younger?"

"No. I think when I was younger, if the right person had come along, like a soul mate, and everything was perfect, I could see myself settling down, being married, having children back then, not now."

"At this point it is just an age issue?"

"Yeah."

"So if you found the right woman today, you still would not want to have kids?"

"Absolutely not."

He is forty-eight. I am forty-eight. I know exactly what he is saying. Unless a man has a burning desire to have children, forty-eight is too old. We do not think in terms of having a baby, changing diapers and watching them take their first step. When you are our age, you do the math: forty-eight plus eighteen is sixty-six and that is too old. That is the age we should be touring the country in our motor homes, not yelling at high school students to turn down their music. Yes, we do the math, and the number is too overwhelming and too intimidating. The journey of a thousand miles may begin with a single step, but when all you focus on is the length of the journey, it is easy to avoid taking the first step. We surrender.

Dwayne, at sixty-three, told a similar story when I asked him if he ever wanted children. He replied, "Oh, yeah. It's been one of the sad parts of my life, not having children. It's always been in the back of my mind, the desire, but it's been overshadowed by other events in my life, and it wasn't until midlife that I've come to realize that it's really been missing."

"Can you talk about those events which overshadowed it?"

"The way I lived [in] different parts of the country, travel and especially education."

"Can you explain that?"

"Going to school, college, post-graduate work, establishing a profession, and then health issues like arthritis."

"These are all the things that overshadowed it?"

"Yeah, family and children. Whenever the potential was there, the events and fears would come to the forefront."

"How does that make you feel?"

"I think about it sometimes, but overall, I just have to look at it as it wasn't meant to be."

Gerald continued the theme of thinking it's too late for him. Gerald is a fifty-two-year-old bus driver from Seattle who was raised by a cold father and an indifferent mother who were divorced when he was fourteen. Being a painfully shy young boy has impacted his confidence and self-esteem to this day. And even though he thinks he is an attractive guy, he feels he has nothing to offer women in the way of financial security as a result of questionable career choices. Although he admits he has never really been in love, he has always wanted the traditional family, but is resigned to his current situation. With his desire for a traditional family, I had to ask Gerald what he thought about having children. "I like children," he stated.

"Do you want some for yourself?"

"Not at fifty-two, no. Mostly because as much as I like kids, I don't think it's fair to the kids. My belief is young parents, young children. By the time you're fifty-two, I'd be too old to play with them."

"You wanted children though?"

"I wanted kids, oh yeah. I wanted the traditional marriage and two point whatever kids, and the picket fence, and all that, but it just never happened."

"When did your feelings about children change? When did that I'm-too-old thing kick in?"

"Probably as I was getting into my mid-forties. That's when it changed, because I realized that now I'm getting a little bit too old for kids. The women my age are no longer of child-bearing years, and if I wanted kids I'd have to find one of child-bearing age, and there's a fat chance of that happening."

"Why do you say that?"

"Just that I don't have anything to offer. I can't offer security or anything like that."

The walls we build around ourselves limit us far more than anything life imposes on us. Maybe Gerald can attract a younger woman and maybe he can't, but he does not think he can, so it is *fait accompli.* Thankfully, my father did not think like that because he was broke when he married my widowed mother with two young girls. My mother used to joke in later years that if she had known how poor he was, she would not have married him. He was in his forties, he wanted children and he did not let his financial situation deter him. Maybe he was foolhardy, but it did not stop him, and together they pulled it off and managed to raise three semi-normal children. I wonder if today's pragmatism about marriage, family and money, keeps at least a few from taking the plunge. Are we too smart, too perceptive? I used to joke with friends after I graduated from college that had I known how hard college was going to be, I never would have gone. That kind of thinking would serve us well when it comes to marriage and family. It might be better if we did not know how hard it was going to be before we start. Years ago, all aspects of life were a struggle: money, food, health. There was nothing particularly noteworthy about marriage, it was just another struggle along the way. Now we live lives so free from inconvenience, the mere thought of a potential challenge—like raising children without the financial wherewithal—can keep us from something we truly desire.

Children: The Wrong Life

When life does not turn out the way you had hoped, it is easy to be fatalistic about it, and that is what happened with most who never had children. They may have wanted them, but their life did not allow it to happen. Sometimes it was financial issues, possibly the way they were raised, or perhaps it was the vagaries of life. For the most part, they have accepted the way things turned out and are okay with it. Myron shared his feeling about wanting children and why he did not have the right life to make that happen. "I think it's a wonderful thing. I never had children and that's something I think I might have liked, if I had a different attitude and lifestyle. I think I've missed out by not having children. I think in order to have children, to be fair to the children, you have to have stability and monogamy, and you have to base your life on the needs of the children, and I wasn't willing to do that. So I never had children for that reason, but I can see why it would have been a wonderful thing."

"Where does that come from, that not wanting to agree to all those things?"

"In my case, most likely, it's because I grew up in a home where the marriage was without love. They didn't get divorced, they didn't hate each other, but there was a kind of deadness about the home."

"How did you know it was without love? What were the indicators?"

"When I was a little boy, I probably intuited or sensed something was different in my home than in some of the homes I visited. My other friends may have been nine or ten, and I visited their homes, and people talked to each other in a nicer way, and there seemed to be more a group feeling, group camaraderie, group decision-making. My parents didn't really talk to each other much, or if they did, it was in a way which wasn't supportive. So, I believe that observing that and living with that had an influence on my attitude. I'm sure that my development was affected by the environment in the home."

Sandy, the forty-two-year-old hypnotherapist from Cleveland, shares the sentiments of Myron in that children are great, but it just did not work out for him. "My attitude toward children is that there's a lot that is sacrificed in the raising of children, and there's a lot of rewards. Besides just the reward of watching a child grow up, there's a tremendous amount of reward in having a young adult who's your child. And if you can't make the sacrifice, if you can't do a good job raising the child, you shouldn't [have one]."

"How about you personally, are you ready to make that sacrifice?"

"I'm not in a financial position to do that."

"If you were, would you?"

"Yeah."

"So, you would like to have children some day?"

"Yeah, but I'm not going to have children and go into debt. It's going to take a considerable amount of money up front. I almost see it as paying for the child up front, and when I say that, I'm referring to [you] better have the means to clothe him and educate him and all that."

"You see money, or lack thereof, as actually a hurdle keeping you from having kids?"

"Absolutely."

I once asked my mother why she and my father decided to have me when they already had two children, knowing they did not have a lot of money. She said you never have enough money for children, you just have them and somehow you make it work. We could learn a lot from her.

Ryan told a similar story to Sandy and Myron. Ryan is a forty-two-year-old sculptor from Wisconsin who wanted to be an artist from a young age, which distracted him from forming any real long-term relationships in his life. He is also extremely shy and introverted, which has left him passive and timid in pursuit of relationships with women. Consequently, he has had limited relationship experience and is still developing his relationship skills, skills which should probably have been developed at a younger age. Somewhat of a loner, he has even lost interest of late in his art, and despite being relatively young, he is beginning to give up hope on having a woman in his life. He told me he did not have the right life to have children. "I guess I wanted to avoid children because I didn't want the responsibility of raising them, again going back to being an artist. I knew that most artists were poor and struggling, and I knew it wouldn't be fair to either myself or to the kids or to a wife, to be selfish and pursue my art if it wasn't generating any money. If I did get into a situation where I had some responsibility, I would have [had] to change the direction of what I was doing. I would have to find a way to start earning a living to support these people. So, I like kids, I just didn't want the responsibility myself."

Children: Too Selfish

These are the ones I wanted to hear from most. They do not want children now, the majority never wanted them, and they all have the same basic reason: they are too selfish. I respect them for not giving into societal pressure and doing what others expect of them. In some ways, I feel as though these men are the most unselfish men of all. It takes an unselfish person to recognize and admit they are selfish, and to not lay that burden on an unsuspecting mother or undeserving child. For my own selfish reasons, I wanted to hear from them because for as far back as I can recall, I never wanted children. Paul never wanted children, as I discovered when he shared, "I just don't think I was ever meant to be a father. I would be too selfish. That's terrible to say, but I've wanted my car, my pool, my this, my that. At an early age, if I would've had children, maybe my attitude would've been changed, but definitely, at this point in my life, I just think I would be too selfish."

"What do you think makes you that selfish?"

"I'm set in my ways, used to being able to buy whatever I want."

Telling a comparable story is Martin, the fifty-four-year-old writer and actor from Missouri. "I think children are great," he stated. "I've never had a strong desire to have children of my own, although I can say that I do miss that sort of relationship of having children."

"Why have you never had a strong desire?"

"I think I've been, to some degree, pretty selfish. I don't know if having a child and making the eighteen-year commitment—or longer—is something that I ever really felt ready for."

"When did you realize that you were a little selfish?"

"I think about twelve years ago it started to be more apparent to me that I was selfish. For the past ten years, from the time I was about forty-two, I was thrown into a situation where I had to take care of some elderly relatives, and for the first time in my life, somebody else was the center of my life rather than me, and so it changed my way of thinking about things. I've always known that I was a selfish person, but I never realized the extent of it."

"How did it manifest itself, this enlightenment about being selfish?"

"It manifested itself in that my time wasn't my own. There was somebody else that had a claim on my time. It wasn't something I really objected to. In some ways it convinced me that maybe our purpose is more to serve others, whereas I wasn't necessarily convinced of that before."

There are those who want to be able to buy whatever they want, while others simply want their free time. And for others like James, the forty-year-old software technician from the South, there was never any interest. He said, "I love my nephew, I love him to death. He's great. I love to hang out with him, but I'm glad when I get to leave. I'm always the cool uncle and I'll just have it that way. I think I'm too selfish to have kids of my own and I just never really had a desire to do that."

"Where do you think that comes from, that sort of selfishness?"

"I'm not sure because my brother had a kid and my parents had two siblings each, and they always wanted kids. I think some people are set for that and some people just aren't. Just a lack of interest, I guess."

Manny is much like James in that he never wanted children either. "I've never wanted them," he stated.

"Why is that?"

"I had a vasectomy about four years ago."

"That is kind of a consequence, but why have you never wanted them?"

"I think it's my independence; I like my independence. I like to be able to do what I want to do. I don't even have a dog because dogs tie you down. I think it's my being able to be as free as I want to be. I've always been one to want to be able to do whatever I want to do and kids would certainly change that lifestyle."

"Where does that desire for independence come from?"

"I started working when I was thirteen. We didn't really have any money and I always helped out around the house. I guess I was raised to think that you got to pull your own weight."

"So, you were forced to grow up young?"

"I think so, yeah."

You start working when you're thirteen, it forces you to grow up fast, which makes you desire your independence. So, you never want children. Every man's story is unique, and every bit as real and valid to them.

CHAPTER 4

Women

Even before I had my first conversation for this book, I assumed the men's feelings about marriage would not be indicative of their feelings toward women, and for the most part I was right. They may have mixed feelings or uncertainty regarding marriage, but they feel strongly about women. With little exception, these men love women, and the trait that more respondents (50 percent) seek than any other is a sense of humor—more than intelligence, physical attractiveness or even sexual compatibility. I suppose laughs carry the day. That is not to say they think women are perfect; they see the flaws, too. But they make allowances for them, as they do for themselves. Overall, their feelings are positive.

These men not only love women, they have been in love. Over half the respondents have had three or more serious love relationships in their lives, while less than one in ten claimed to have never been in love. And at the time of the survey, almost one in four of the men claimed he was in a love relationship.

During our conversations, when I introduced the subject of women, I usually began by asking them to complete this sentence: "I think women are..." I intentionally wanted to ask an open-ended question to get a deeper response. I was hoping this approach would get me closest to the truth. Many of them dodged the question by saying they did not think women could be summed up in one word or phrase, but that too was a revealing answer. To force the issue even further, I would often follow up by asking them to tell me the best and worst things about women. I did not want them tip-toeing around the question, and every one of them had a strong opinion in response to that solicitation.

Then I got to the subject that I really wanted to explore. Such a large number of the men claimed they would have gotten married if they met the right one that I had to know what they meant by the right woman. I asked each of them to describe his ideal woman. In response, I got what I now affectionately refer to as the *shopping list*. Each man had his own unique combination of attributes he looks for in a woman. There were common qualities the men cited frequently, such as intelligence and a sense of humor. The shopping list, once again, led me to consider what role expectations play in finding the right one, because it seems we *all* have a shopping list in our head.

In the online survey, I equated the *right one* with the idea of a soul mate. The respondents were almost equally divided in thirds about their feelings regarding soul mates. About a third do not believe in them; about a third do believe in them, but are not waiting to meet her; and about a third believe in them and *are* waiting to meet her. The percentages changed somewhat during the conversations. I asked the men if they were waiting to meet *their* right one. Most are not. I suppose that is a practicality that comes with age. For those who are waiting to meet their right one, I asked if they thought they deserve her, which led to unexpected responses. And finally, I inquired where these men actually go to meet women today. Very few are barflies and most have tried online dating, albeit with mixed results.

The Shopping List

Quite a few of the men had a shopping list that included intelligence. Aiden, the fifty-year-old mortgage and real estate broker from Southern California, was one of them. "I love 'em," he stated in regard to women. "I think women are very nice. They're fun to be with. They're my opposite. It's nice to have them around. [It's] good to wake up with somebody in the morning."

"Describe your ideal woman."

"Someone who is intelligent. Somebody that's intelligent and can hold a conversation. Someone that's caring and loving and can cook. What I have to do is describe what I don't like."

"What don't you like?"

"Vegans," he said, punctuating with a big laugh. "I don't like women that are in an extraordinary amount of debt. I don't like women that are financially needy. I don't like women who can't trust you."

There's that word—*trust.* This would be a constant theme running through my conversation with Aiden. I have repeatedly seen that we are affected in the present by what happened (or did not happen) to us in the past. It dictates what we want and what we want to avoid. It occurred to me, as the conversations developed, quite a few of the items on the shopping lists were attributes the men had *not* gotten in their previous relationships, or at least not in sufficient enough amounts. But with Aiden, even though intelligence is on his list, it's what cannot be on the list—what he absolutely wants to avoid— which is paramount. As men hit a certain age, it may be less about finding the right one and more about avoiding the wrong one.

A man with a slightly longer shopping list, which also included intelligence, is Martin. "I think women are wonderful," he shared. "I have always enjoyed the company of women. Most of my best friends have tended to be females. In fact, I probably have a more difficult time relating to men than to women."

"What is it about women you enjoy the most?"

"Their emotional access."

"What does that mean?"

"Their access to their own feelings. They wear their emotions on their sleeves. That's not my experience. I see myself as kind of an emotionally closed-off person."

"Describe your ideal woman."

"Probably the things that everybody would look for: beautiful, intelligent, someone I have things in common with."

"What unique characteristics would you look for?"

"I consider myself a Christian and someone who I had that in common with, similar spiritual values."

"Are you waiting to meet your ideal woman?"

"I was at one time, but now I've kind of given up on the idea. I do believe there is somebody that's right for me and that I'm right for, but then there were several times in the past where I thought that as well, and it hasn't turned out that way."

"Do you think you deserve this woman?"

"Probably not."

"Why do you say that?"

"Because, in my past, I had a lot of sexual issues, and I found a lot of women, when I told them things about my past, they [made] judgments about me based on that."

"When you say sexual issues, what are we talking about?"

"I can tell you that, in my twenties and thirties, [I was] very experimental sexually."

There are those walls again; the ones we build around ourselves. Still trapped by his own interpretation of his behavior over twenty years ago, fifty-four-year-old Martin, the spiritual Christian, does not believe he deserves the woman he seeks. There are a lot of reasons why some men never marry. Critical self-judgment is one of them.

Another man who would like a woman who is both intelligent and religious is Dylan. He said, "I think women are beautiful. God put them on Earth for a reason."

"What's the best part?"

"Most women are opinionated. Most of the ones I meet are strong, confident, so those are the ones I appreciate. I respect women."

"Describe your ideal woman."

"Age twenty-eight to forty-five, single, responsible, independent, close to her family, Catholic is nice, educated would be great. I think intelligence is number one or number two in my book. I need somebody who is going to challenge me. Most of the time, women who I've met or dated, I go out on the first date and they're just not my cup of tea—there's no chemistry. A lot of women have told me they are intimidated by me."

"Why do you think that is?"

"Maybe I like to speak too much, but I treat them well. It's finding that one that complements you. You want to find the perfect one for you."

"Talk to me about this chemistry thing. How do you know when you have it?"

"I think you feel it either on the phone or chatting online, and you go out with them a couple times and you get a gut feeling. Whether it's one date or three dates, you kind of have the chemistry or you don't."

"You have described your ideal woman to me. Are you waiting to meet her?"

"It'd be nice. I don't think I'd move from South Florida, but like millions of men and women who date online, you just never know. I have family here, I own a home, but I never say never. I'm waiting to meet [her], but I don't rush. I'd like to meet somebody and get married. If it happens, great, but let time take its course. I know women who want to bear kids, and if they want to meet right away, I ask them what the difference is if we meet today, tomorrow or next week. What's the rush?"

"How do you meet women? It sounds like you use online dating. Is there anything else?"

"No. I'm not a big drinker, so I [only] go out occasionally. I'll go to a sports bar with the guys. I see them at the book store, the grocery store and through friends. When you work a lot, your down time is normally home and people go online. I've had success with online dating."

Dylan is not in a rush to meet a woman. Perhaps it is because he is forty years old and figures he still has plenty of time, which he does. It got me thinking, though, about the role time plays in finding the right one. After all, the game of finding the right one is not an infinite game. It ends, and as we grow older we become more and more aware of it. In the pursuit of finding the right one, there are two opposing forces at work on us as we get older. On the one hand, we become more discriminating. Our understanding of ourselves and what we want becomes narrower and more focused. Our days of self-discovery are, for the most part, behind us and we know what we are willing to accept and what we are not. This, in theory, should make it more difficult to find the right one because we are more restrictive in our search and what we will even consider. But then something happens: a switch trips in us and we begin to consider the limitation of time.

Like some relentless, plodding creature pursuing us ever so slowly from behind, it is a constant reminder that we may have to make concessions and expand the search if we truly want to find somebody. This compromise that we are ultimately forced to negotiate calls into question the practicality of finding the right one as we get beyond our forties. Perhaps the *wrong one* today might become the *right one* a year from now and not because they have changed, but because we have. We change what we are willing to consider as a viable partner. We no longer judge the women we meet by the boxes we can check off on the shopping list, we begin to compare them to the alternative—being alone. Almost without exception, the men I spoke with do not fear being alone, which has had some influence on why they never married. But it is enlightening to see how the definition of the *right one* changes over time. It would be sad if the men who postponed marriage in hopes of meeting the right one felt as though they ended up "settling" for their current one because she beats the hell out of the alternative of being alone.

Gordon, like Dylan, wants an independent woman to match his own unique sense of freedom. I asked him to complete the sentence, *"I think women are..."*

"Wonderful," he stated.

"What makes them wonderful?"

"Mostly because I don't have a problem with them because I try to understand them at their level. I don't try to understand them at my level as a male. I just try to get into their mind, into their understanding and how they act and respond. The more you understand the female species the better off you can relate to them at any level."

"What kind of understandings have you come to about women?"

"The idea of how communication is their major force. If you can communicate on their level, you pretty much can get along with anybody. Of course, they have to do the [same] thing for males, too. They have to realize that they don't understand the male either."

"What is the best thing about women?"

"Beauty. A beautiful woman makes a male melt, just to feel good about her being around, looking at her, touching her."

"And what is the worst thing about women?"

"Their not understanding how to handle a male. They don't handle situations properly. It's their way or no way."

"If you were going to give women advice about understanding men, what would it be?"

"Just understand our thinking. Get a handle on [the fact that] we're going to think differently than you. It's not always the extreme opposite, but it is different."

"Describe your ideal woman to me."

"I'm definitely more into the independent woman, career woman, athletic, healthy, adventurous."

"Has it always been that way or have your tastes changed over time?"

"It changed, because in my twenties, I didn't even know what a career woman was, and I wasn't looking for a mother-type because I don't need another mom. I'm totally domestic, one hundred percent. That's probably why I'm not married. I've washed my clothes, bought my clothes and fed myself since I was fourteen years old. Nothing has ever changed and no woman has ever tried to cook, clean or take care of me. They don't have to."

"Are you domestic because you had so many brothers and sisters?"

"No, I'm domestic because I think I had a vision [of being] in there, in the kitchen, helping my mother set the table, wash the dishes and cook the food. I have never changed, and I think that has a lot to do with why I don't even think about marriage as a priority. I like women, I like them around when I'm in a relationship, but as far as needing one, I don't need one."

"It sounds as if that has played a big role in your life, not needing one."

"Right."

"You have just described your ideal woman. Are you waiting to meet her?"

"Yeah, definitely."

"Do you think you deserve her?"

"Yeah, 100 percent."

"How do you go about meeting women nowadays?"

"I depend on the Internet right now, the dating services."

"Has the online dating thing worked for you?"

"Not yet. I've been on Match.com for five or six years. It's nothing but struggle, not that I'm trying that hard. I wait to see if they're going to wink and I'll see if I can pick a conversation with them. Then you meet them and, of course, you run into the ones that aren't telling the truth, sending the right pictures. I've never dated anybody off Match. I've met maybe ten—never went anywhere. Most of them weren't what they said they were and the other ones will just disappear. You try to have an e-mail conversation with them, or phone conversation, and they just don't return your calls. That's how I found most people are, disrespectful and [I] just moved on."

Gordon is fifty years old, and while he would like to meet a woman, he is quick to point out that he does not need one, which made me curious. What role does his *not* needing a woman play in his never marrying? He insisted he wants to find the right one. What if one of the prerequisites of finding the right one is you have to *need* the right one. For independent men like Gordon (and me), that is sometimes hard to admit.

Just as there are those who are attracted to intelligent women, there are others who are every bit as attracted to women's caring and nurturing side. Randy, the forty-eight-year-old engineer from Southern California, is such a man. When I asked him what he thinks about women, he simply said, "Great."

"Why do you think they're great?"

"I love women."

"Why do you love women?"

"Because they're just so opposite of men. They're verbal and romantic, soft, sexy, and men are not."

"What is the best thing about them?"

"Probably their nurturing aspect: their nesting, mothering instinct."

"Do you look for that in a woman, that nurturing instinct?"

"Yeah. It's nice when you're dealing with somebody and you have a bad day, they're usually sympathetic, or you have a sore lower back and [they] rub it down."

"All right, give me the flipside. What is the toughest part about women?"

"They all seem to want to be married. You don't find too many women who are happy [to] just cohabitate, although I'm sure they're out there. My younger brother's lived with three separate women. The last two left because they wanted to get married, have children, and he didn't. There was no way he was going to compromise."

"Have you ever lived with a woman?"

"I have. Not for long. I like my own space. I like [it] to be quiet."

"Describe your ideal woman."

"She's probably mute." (big laugh) "I like the whole android idea. Cook, clean, always in shape." (another big laugh)

"Any characteristics from a woman who would be on planet Earth?"

"It's funny, because the woman that I got along best with, and could probably see myself either living with or married to, unfortunately happened to be a lesbian."

"Interesting. Are you waiting to meet your ideal woman?"

"Yeah, absolutely. I know she exists."

"How do you meet women?"

"The tennis court, the park, hanging out, friends, friends of friends."

"Ever used online dating?"

"Yeah, I've tried it."

"Didn't work for you?"

"No. I certainly tried; subscribed to two different ones. If you do your search, you have fifty hits. If you contact all fifty, the list never grows, unless you're willing to travel a hundred miles, which I'm not willing to do."

Nathan, who also appreciates their caring side, said that women are "good friends, wonderful people to chat with" and "they're just nice people."

"Why do you think that?"

"Because I have a lot of women friends that I do a lot of things with, and we have a good time."

"I noticed you didn't say anything about lovers or sexual partners. It all had to do with friends and conversation."

"That's because I don't think I've had a sexual relationship in years."

"Is there a reason for that?"

"I hang around with the same people. I've hung around with the same women, same men for thirty years, and so pretty much, we do the same kind of routine all the time. We're boring."

"Everybody over forty is boring, so welcome to the crowd. What is the best thing about women?"

"They're caring, they're honest, they listen, they're available."

"What do you mean by that?"

"You can call them and chat and things like that."

"Describe your ideal woman to me."

"Somebody who would make me laugh all the time."

"That's it?"

"That's the most important thing for me, somebody to make me laugh."

"Are you waiting to meet this ideal woman?"

"No, I think I met her and she went somewhere else."

"How do you meet women today?"

"The only time I would meet them is through other people, and that would be people in school or my friends."

"So you are not actively out there?"

"No, not really."

Confusion

When asked about women, there are those who feel confused. They just do not understand them. George, the fifty-two-year-old bookbinder from Canada, who has an extremely traditional view of man-woman roles, declared his confusion over women in one word: "Different."

"Explain that," I pressed.

"I stopped trying to analyze it. You just can't explain women and why they do things. I like to think of it as an emotional versus a practical solution to every problem. They do things emotionally."

Justin displayed a similar confusion when I asked him to complete the sentence, *"I think women are..."*

"Generally speaking, wonderful," he said.

"Why did you put a qualifier in there?"

"Well, I like women and I'm attracted to them, but they really do seem like a different species sometimes. Their brains work in other ways. They complement us, but they're hard to understand. You also have to do this thing in relationships where you're trying to think what the other person is thinking. We come from different places and it seems we don't always communicate with each other."

"Why is it so hard to communicate with women?"

"You've probably read the same articles I have. Women like to verbalize things, they like to complain, but they don't like to seek solutions. Whereas men come home and want to stare at the TV, and if we tune them out as they yack on about their day, except to say here's the solution, they find that kind of abrupt."

"What do you like best about women?"

"They're tremendously sensual and attractive, and they make very good wives. There's nothing like a dame, right?"

"What is the worst part about women?"

"Women expect men to be mind readers. It's a cliché, but it's true. They'll get mad about something and they assume that we know what they're mad about. We don't, they have to spell it out for us."

"Describe your ideal woman."

"I'd like someone who's fairly intelligent, someone who shares my religious beliefs and outlook on life. I'm thinking Angelica Houston for some reason; I've always found her attractive. I've always been attracted to women who are slightly older than me. My mother is seven years older than my dad, so maybe that's the reason. I tend to find women in their forties or even early fifties more interesting than women in their twenties or thirties, which has a bearing on the whole child question."

"Are you comfortable with older women?"

"I love them; I think they're terrific."

"What's the best part about the older woman?"

"I think their sex drive is actually higher. I think they're more relaxed about their bodies. They're not as hung up and as crazy in some ways as younger women tend to be. They're more sane, they've got their heads more screwed on straight, and plus, to be perfectly cynical, they're grateful for the attention."

"You have described your ideal woman. Are you waiting to meet her?"

"Yes, I guess I am. When you say waiting, I guess I'm intermittently active and passive. You can just sit and wait for her to drop out of the sky, but that's not really a proactive way to go about it. I'm active on several Internet dating sites and I try to do a certain amount of social activities, but sometimes work gets in the way, or I just lose interest and go to work and go home."

"How is that online dating thing? Does that work for you?"

"I've met some nice ladies through Yahoo! Personals, but nothing that's worked out long-term, obviously."

Samuel, like George, summed up his confusion in a single word: "Perplexed."

"You think women are perplexing?" I inquired.

"When I say perplexing, I look at it from a number of standpoints. I think they're disingenuous. I don't think they say what they mean and they don't mean what they say."

"Why do you think that?"

"Because their behaviors don't match their actions."

"Why do you think they do that?"

"Historically, they've had to because they've been on the lower end of the income scale, in a less powerful position than men, [so] they've had to resort to disingenuous behaviors. I also say that because I've come to the conclusion that there is a tremendous amount of disrespect towards men, and towards women."

"Give me an example."

"When I say disrespect, I see women and they're not asking for guys that are genuine. They come in with a laundry list of things: don't do this, do that, you must be this. It's like they're looking for perfection. I see that somewhat to a lesser extent with men."

The list doesn't feel so good when someone else is doing the shopping. I suppose it only makes sense that women are looking for the right one as well. I question whether the search for the right one is really about fulfilling the shopping list, or is it more about self discovery and finding ourselves? The search goes on.

Don't Need Perfection

A number of men have a laundry list, but they keep it manageable. They know women are not perfect and try to keep the list short. Additionally, they acknowledge they too are imperfect and take a reasonable approach to their search. Perhaps the best example of this group is Donald. He said about women, "They're all so unique. I can usually find a good trait in almost all women. On the other hand, I can usually find a bad trait in almost all women, but I think they're very interesting. I love women."

"Describe your ideal woman."

"Looks-wise, she'd look something like Pamela Anderson. She would be into sports. She would allow me to do my own thing— play golf—and have a life somewhat separate at times. She'd be totally secure with who she is and who I am, and not be the jealous type."

"Are you waiting to meet this girl?"

"No."

"Why not?"

"All women have warts. You can find a flaw in all of them, as I know I have many flaws. But I think it's about adjustment, and you have to take the good with the bad. And hopefully a woman out there has more good traits than she does bad, and I can live with that."

"How would you know if she was the right one?"

"I think it's longevity. If you decide you want to date this woman and she really excites you, and that continues on [for] a period of four, five or six years, and you're still as interested as you were the first year, or close to it, that would tell me she's the one for me."

"Talk about the role that sexual satisfaction, or lack thereof, has played in your past relationships."

"I think it's probably one of the biggest parts, because I think initially you meet someone and have great sex, and hopefully everything falls into place. I can be pleased fairly easily, sexually. It's just the rest of it that you hope is as fun as the sex part."

"Have you ever been in a relationship where everything was great but the sex?"

"Yeah. [A] girl, that if I could figure out a way to be attracted to her [sexually], we'd probably be married."

"So, the lack of a fulfilling sex life kept you from moving forward?"

"Yeah, it did. And after we dated for five or six years, we would have sex once every two or three months. Then I became [dis]loyal, and as a result I felt bad about the relationship. I didn't like doing that to her and we stopped going out."

"Was the opposite ever true? Have you ever been in a relationship where there was almost no attraction other than sexual?"

"Yeah. Sure."

"And what was that like?"

"It lasted three and a half months. She drove me crazy in a lot of ways and the fact that she drove me crazy, [the] sex stopped being fun."

Donald was the man who came closest to actually using the word *compromise*, as it applies to women and relationships. He also pointed out he would not know if it was the right one until years later, because it is about longevity. His comments confirmed the conundrum that I suspected exists: not knowing it's the right relationship until years later.

Myron, like Donald, has a long list but accepts it is unrealistic to find somebody with everything on the list. "I think women are a diverse group. No two are alike and every person has a different, unique set of emotional characteristics that may or may not be complementary to my own. Sometimes you can find a woman that satisfies your emotional needs and sometimes you can't.

"Describe your ideal woman."

"My ideal woman would be someone whose particular sense of reality overlaps with mine enough so that we can share a lot of enthusiasm of life. My ideal woman is a woman that has similar emotional, political and social responses to the world the way I do, so that we're compatible. We can talk about things and we can get excited about the same things. And [someone] who's able to resolve anger easily and is able to deal with differences without going over the top; someone who can be sensitive and can express themselves and be assertive, without being accusatory and domineering."

"Are you waiting to meet her?"

"Oh no, I'm not waiting to meet her. I know that the reality is that you usually meet someone who is not ideal. You meet someone who's not too bad and you enjoy what you can. I don't expect a lot either. I expect a certain degree of comfort and warmth, but I don't expect the ideal. No, I'm not waiting to meet her because I don't expect to ever find her. It might just be an abstraction—the ideal."

"Can you elaborate on that a little bit? That concept of the ideal being an abstraction."

"When people talk about ideal anything—the ideal job, the ideal relationship, the ideal marriage—it's a construct. It comes out of someone's own individual view of the world. The ideal person probably doesn't exist because there are too many variables that would have to be met. If that's the case, human nature being what it is, no one can be ideal over time. There would always be conflict. There would always be negative emotional feelings at times in a relationship, even a very good one. The ideal is the kind of thing that exists in the world of the mind, not in the real world."

"Would it be fair to say the woman you are with right now is not your ideal woman?"

"No."

"But not because she isn't a good woman, but because there might not be such a thing as an ideal woman."

"Right. She's not my ideal woman; no one is. We have our bad days and our good days, and I expect both. So I don't get too rattled by them."

"I guess the good outweighs the bad."

"Yeah. I guess you could say that."

What he said fascinated me. Myron was the only man to acknowledge the possibility there may not be a right one—it's only an abstraction—something we long for but doesn't really exist. Hearing that made me recall a monologue from the movie *The Life of David Gale*, in which Kevin Spacey, playing the title role as a philosophy professor, discusses the concept of desire:

"Fantasies have to be unrealistic because the moment you get what you seek, you don't want it any more. In order to continue to exist, desire must have its objects perpetually absent. It's not the *it* that you want, it is the fantasy of *it* that you want. Or why we say the hunt is sweeter than the kill, or be careful what you wish for, not because you'll get it, because you are doomed not to want it once you do."

How much of this never-ending search for the right one is misguided aspirations? What if it is a search for the unobtainable, because even if we were to find the right one, they would cease to be the right one simply because we found them? Almost all of the men in this book (myself included) have had good women in their lives. What role has this search for the unobtainable played in our thinking they were not the right ones? And is that why married men get married? They understand there is no such thing as the right one?

My feeling is these two men (Myron and Donald) are a little further down the evolutionary path toward a long-term relationship than the rest of us. If the first step is making the shopping list, then the second step is coming to terms with the fact you will probably never meet someone who meets that criteria. And that's okay, because it wouldn't make you any happier even if you did.

An Unconventional View

There are a few men whose views of women and relationships can only be described as unconventional. A few even use that word themselves, such as Dwayne, as I discovered when I asked him if he was still interested in meeting women.

"Yes, I am," he said.

"Tell me a little bit about your ideal woman."

"Open communications, expression of feelings, a willingness to be spontaneous—being unconventional."

"What does that mean?"

"Not just doing ordinary things, but working at [being] different. Looking at the world and what's going on, being liberal, progressive, very left-wing."

"Are you waiting to meet her?"

"No, not anymore. I'm open to it but I'm not waiting."

"Why aren't you waiting?"

"I think that's part of the problem. When you're waiting, like waiting for a bus, you're looking for it. The more positive relationships I've had were ones I never expected, [they] just kind of happened. Whenever I find myself waiting for something to happen in looking for a relationship, it never happened."

"Do you ever use online dating?"

"Oh yeah. Since my arthritis has been severe, I think that opened up the world of online communications. I've had several relationships online, and it's too bizarre."

"What do you mean by too bizarre?"

"Unless you follow up meeting somebody in real time, it tends to be a relationship filled with fantasies and expectations and [it's] easy to succumb to that and make it real, and it's not real."

Evan has an unconventional view of attraction. He still has a shopping list, but it is not what drives him. He believes there is a different source of attraction. He said, "I suppose attraction ultimately is based on residual pathologies of your parents and your upbringing."

"Residual pathology?"

"It's like the works of Harville Hendrix."

"Maybe you could explain to a layperson like myself what residual pathology means."

"You gravitate towards someone who has certain characteristics of your main caretaker, and certain characteristics that you wish they would have had. I tend to be drawn toward more outgoing, friendly women. My mother was outgoing and friendly, but you know the flip side of that, they can be moody like she was, so it is dangerous in ways. I'm at the point where I'm a bit confused about my likes and dislikes because I realize that sometimes the women I'm attracted to are not particularly good for me. So I'm trying to readjust that. You don't get to choose what you're attracted to sometimes. Intelligence is important to me; I just can't converse with dumb people. I like to resolve conflicts without yelling. So a very calm personality, as far as resolution of conflicts is concerned, is an important thing for me."

"Anything else?"

"Honesty and trustability [*sic*]. I'm not really big into people who are deceiving and lie. I like people who have a lot of candor, and someone who's blunt, even though it might lead to some conflict. Personality tends to be more important to me than sex. Certainly if there were no sex, I'd question why there was no sex, but overall it's been okay. I've never cheated on a girlfriend with whom I was in a monogamous relationship."

Sandy, the forty-two-year-old hypnotherapist from Cleveland, also had an unconventional view based on stereotypes that may or may not be true. But, they are true for him, therefore it affects his decisions and his actions. I asked him to complete the sentence, *"I think women are..."*

"People," he said.

"Can you be a little more descriptive?"

"I really try to keep it right at that. Other than some allowance for PMS, I see women as people. I see them equally capable of opening that door for themselves or for me. I'll open the door for an old person, a young man, an old man, an old woman. I think it's important to open the door for other people period, and if I'm with a woman and she seems to have this attitude that she's going to wait in front of that door for me to open it, that sucks. I'm against gender bias."

"Do you make any allowances for women?"

"Just a little for the PMS."

"What do you think is the best thing about women?"

"I think they're more emotional and men tend to be more intellectual, so I think women can bring some emotional balance to the equation."

"Is that important to you?"

"Oh yeah."

"Why?"

"Because I'm a truth seeker and I just intuitively know that you're not going to arrive at the truth through a process that's purely intellectual or purely emotional."

"Wow, that's pretty enlightened. What is the worst part about women?"

"Their attitudes about being women."

"What in particular?"

"That would just be all the messages that society gives them: they're weak, they need to stay home and have kids. The fact of the matter is, the way I see it, these stereotypes are still being reinforced."

"They succumb to the stereotypes and that is what you do not find attractive?"

"Right."

"Okay, so what do you find attractive? Describe your ideal woman."

"Risk taking, aggressive, assertive, doesn't fly off the handle and get completely emotional when there's a crisis. Actually thinks their way through a crisis rather than just freaking out."

"This ideal woman, are you waiting to meet her?"

"In the earlier part of my life, my ideal woman was some sexy physicist or some extraordinarily intellectual person, and I've spent time with women like that. Things have changed, I don't focus on the physical that much. Their mind, their level of spiritual maturity [is more important today]."

"How do you go about meeting women today?"

"Online works for me."

"What do you like about it?"

"It starts off with words, and I'm confident in my abilities to communicate. My biggest problem online is they tend to become highly infatuated with me before they've ever met me. So I use it as a screening thing."

Another man whose view of women is driven by stereotypes, but even more so, is Winston, the forty-five-year-old corrections officer from Boston. He said, "I know it's going to sound chauvinistic, [but] the best thing about women is their domestic capabilities, because I don't even have a lot of great conversations with women."

"Why is that?"

"Women are more programmed for their immediate environment."

"What does that mean?"

"The house. I like to explore world issues, I like world politics, I like studying history, I like studying other cultures and I love to travel. I think women are a lot more content just to belong to a man."

"Have you ever met one who was more like you, who liked politics and travel and all that?"

"I have, and I enjoyed talking to them, but I never met one that I clicked with."

"Describe your ideal woman to me."

"Again, chauvinistic, I think an ideal woman would be what I envision a Southern woman to be like, very domesticated, behind her man. She would be employed, she could be employed, might not be employed, I don't really care. But [she has to be] a domesticated, submissive woman."

"Is that important to you?"

"Yes, it is."

"Why is that important to you?"

"To me, a woman will always get her way and I'm happy with that. But at the same time, I don't want somebody nagging me, telling me what to do. I want a woman that's going to be supportive of me, be happy just having a house, having a man and doing activities with me."

"What do you think of independent women?"

"I love independent women. I've had a stay-at-home girlfriend and their world becomes you, they live through you, and I don't like that. You come home and they've got no perspective of the world except for you. I want a girl that's going to go out, have their own perspective of the world, come back and share it with me, but at the same time, she is to be the wife and fulfill that role as housekeeper."

"Would it be fair to say that you are attracted to the more traditional roles of the family?"

"Yes."

"You have described your ideal woman. Are you waiting to meet her?"

"Not any more."

"Why not?"

"At this point in my life, I'll tell you exactly what's going on with me, and this is going to sound awful, but quite frankly I don't want to deal with American women. I don't have the time in my life to take a chance. I went to Thailand last winter for a month, and this winter I'm planning on heading to the Dominican Republic and check that out. I just plan on getting a third-world wife and possibly bring her back."

"And is the attraction to these third-world women the fact that they are more aligned with traditional roles?"

"Yes."

He wants an independent, domesticated, submissive housekeeper with her own perspective. I had to fight the urge to scream, "Good luck." I do not think what Winston is looking for is realistic, but it doesn't matter because he does, and plans a trip to the Caribbean to try and find it. Speaking with Winston highlighted one of the more appealing aspects of talking to thirty-three such diverse men about women and relationships. I got to hear them tell me things they believe with complete conviction that I may not happen to agree with. It is their reality and it affects who they are. It is eye-opening to see how people can come from such different beliefs and still end up in the same place: never married.

Perhaps the most unconventional and outrageous description of women was offered up by Andrew, the forty-six-year-old DJ from Florida. Not yet knowing what a central role sex played in his thinking about women and relationships, I asked him to describe his ideal woman. "I'm going to have to be brutally frank, and for some reason I almost want to explain myself, but I'm going to use the fewest words possible and the best way to describe this woman would be an *intelligent slut.*"

Almost taken aback, but with great intrigue, I asked him if he could expand on that.

"You know, she's a lady in the living room and a whore in the bedroom. Just so I know she's a slut in bed, not everybody needs to know that."

It would be easy to think Andrew is speaking for effect when he uses words like "slut" and "whore", but he isn't. He has really thought this through, and although I might have chosen a different way to describe such a woman—his way made me a little uncomfortable—he is simply demonstrating his own level of comfort and honesty with the subject.

He continued, "I'm going to take it a step further and say I only think a woman would make a good wife if she would make a good whore."

"Intelligent slut. Are you waiting to meet one?"

"Absolutely."

How many other men want that? It's not politically correct to say, but it resonated with me. I knew exactly what he was talking about and I want that too. I want a woman who both turns me on intellectually and in the bedroom, and there should not be anything wrong with wanting and hoping to find that.

I felt obligated to continue the conversation with Winston, no matter where it went. I asked him, *"Have you ever been in a relationship in which the woman was not sexually accommodating enough, and how did you handle it?"*

"Oh gosh, yes. I met her when I was a DJ in Pittsburgh and I was out at a nightclub. This one particular night I'm hanging outside the DJ booth and all of a sudden this tiny brunette with 32B's—I couldn't forget that because I love 32B's on a tiny woman—and she's got this shirt that's buttoned way down. I saw her walking up the stairs and we made eye contact and without saying a word, she walks up to me and we just embraced and starting kissing."

"And then?"

"So, we go out the next Sunday. [I] take her out to dinner and she's all buttoned up. She's prim and proper, but I'm thinking well she's still got this wild side to her, but she was great to talk to. I've never spent so many dates without having sex with somebody, but I just loved being with this girl. She was wonderful; I couldn't get enough of her. [We] went to the zoo and went to places that I would never go. It didn't matter where I went because I was with her, and it just felt so good to just be out of my comfort zone, just going anywhere and doing whatever, simply because I wanted to be with her."

At this point, I was wondering what this had to do with a woman who was not sexually accommodating, but it told me that Andrew could connect with a woman at a level other than that of pure sexuality.

He continued, "Well, after a few weeks, she shows up at the radio station and she says, 'You know I want to go home with you.' I said great. I drive her home and we end up in the bedroom and we start to talk about sex, and I say that I'd like sex twice a day every day, and she says she'd like sex basically once a week. I'm like, 'Oh, you're kidding' and she goes, 'No, I guess I'm not the right girl for you.' She goes on to say that she only likes the missionary position and won't do it any other way, case closed. Well, come to find out she wasn't kidding."

Often our first impressions are misleading, especially when it is from a woman under the influence of alcohol. Maybe she was more flirtatious than she would otherwise have been and Andrew took it to mean something else. I know it has happened to me. It changes expectations, therefore it changes the relationship. Andrew went on to have several unfulfilling sexual encounters with her, stemming from drastically different sexual appetites and expectations, and after a few weeks it ended. That it ended is not surprising. At the end of their last tryst, he basically kicked her out. After briefly going to her car, she returned minutes later, knocked on the door and said, "I hope you find the slut you're looking for."

He said, "Thank you," and that was that.

He knew what he wanted; that never varied. It was the same exact word he used with me. Only his expectations were off base due to an initial misreading from a first drunken encounter. But the bigger story here is, Winston really enjoyed this woman's company long before they ever got intimate. He connected with her on a non-physical level and even acknowledged how good it felt to be with her. Why was that lost on him?

Women Issues

Like a lot of men, a number of the men I spoke with have issues with women, issues which tend to be centered around those things that have affected them directly or recently. For instance, Manny thinks women "need to prove themselves more."

"Explain that," I inquired.

"On Saturday night, we went to a dinner where six couples all get together and everybody brings something. So, Sarah and I made something together, and we get there and everybody likes the food and Sarah takes credit for it. That's just a small example. We made food and she took credit for the whole thing, when really both of us put into it equally."

"How did that make you feel?"

"I like for Sarah to feel the way she was feeling when she said that. I didn't need any assurances. I didn't need to be able to say I helped out, but Sarah does and it makes her feel good, and for her to feel good about [it] makes me feel good. I know she wanted it to look like she made the dish and I was happy for her."

"Why do you think she needed to feel good about that?"

"To feel like she's contributing. That she's needed, that she's wanted—something like that, whereas guys don't need reassurances from society as much."

All I could think of at that moment was the *Seinfeld* episode with the big salad, where George gets mad at a female friend for taking credit for buying it. I suppose it's funny on television, but not as much in real life.

Wayne also has an issue with women that is obviously still affecting him. "Insecure," is how he describes women. I asked him why he feels that way.

"Because they're always thinking if you're not with them, that you're with another woman. If you don't call them every day or however often they deem necessary, they think by gosh you're chasing another woman."

"Do you have direct experience with that?"

"Yes."

"Tell me a little about that."

"I dated a woman for a number of years who lived, and still does, in South America. She would come up here three, four times a year and spend time with me and her sister and so forth. Every time she would leave she would say, 'Yeah, I know as soon as I leave you're going to find another woman.' And it just drove me crazy when she would call and say, 'Why don't you call me more?' Or, 'Why don't you write me more?'"

"Do you think that had any lasting effect on your relationships?"

"No."

"Okay, so describe your ideal woman."

"She would be intelligent; I'm a man who likes intelligence in a woman. She would be striking, not necessarily beautiful, but striking."

"What makes a woman striking?"

"It's hard to say. Generally, a woman [who] is a little bit taller, maybe unusual facial features, the way she carries herself. I think it's very important that a woman has very good moral values."

"Are you waiting to meet this ideal woman?"

"If she happens to stroll along, yeah, but I'm not sitting here thinking, 'Oh gosh, I've got to meet this woman or my life's incomplete.'"

"How do you go about meeting women today?"

"If I see a woman I like, I try to find a way to meet her."

"Have you ever used online dating?"

"That for me has been the most dismal failure."

"Why do you think that is?"

"It's just not a medium that works well for me. I stand a much better chance of being at a gas station, pumping gas, and meeting a girl than I do on the Internet."

I have to agree with Wayne because online dating never worked for me either. I think it brings out our worst prejudices (from both men and women). The biggest problem is it gives us the illusion of choice. As a result, we get into a mode of filtering people out, because they are the wrong age or we are not attracted to their photograph. But we want intelligence and a sense of humor, two exceedingly difficult things to discern in the two-dimensional online world. Consequently, we struggle to find what we think we want while looking through the wrong glasses. In spite of that, it does seem to work for some people.

Keeping with the theme of being directly affected by past relationships, Paul also has an issue with women. They are "looking to use me," he said.

"Why do you say that?"

"It's the money issue."

"How many women has that happened with?"

"Several. I tend to be an enabler, unfortunately, so I've had a couple that have been out-and-out drunks, that I had to play hard love with and ditch them."

"Why do you think you are an enabler? Anything in your past?"

"No, not really."

"What do you think is the worst thing about women?"

"They can be a damn bitch."

"Give me an example."

"I've been terminated twice in my life from jobs, and they've both been because of women sleeping their way to the top. That has always left a bad taste in my mouth about women. It's terrible to generalize and say that all women are like that, but women do have that advantage over men, especially when it comes to professionally."

"Describe your ideal woman."

"She would definitely have to have her own career. That would be the biggest thing. Her own successful career, where [she] and I could have our careers, but yet decompress together in the evenings and go on vacations and that kind of thing. But I would definitely have to have somebody that could hold their own."

"An independent woman?"

"Correct."

"What else is important besides independence?"

"That they're fun to be with. They have a serious side; they have a fun side; they have a party side; they are truthful."

"So, a balance of independence and integrity."

"Right."

"*This ideal woman, are you waiting to meet her?*"

"At this point, I doubt it's going to happen."

"*How do you meet women today?*"

"I'm not one to really go out to bars or things like that. Usually, it's professionally, at a professional seminar or something like that. [I] kind of like the type of woman that would be at something like that."

"*Do you ever use online dating?*"

"No, not really."

"*Why is that, because a lot of people try?*"

"It seems to me like you never get what you're really talking to."

Echoing sentiments similar to Paul is Perry, a forty-two-year-old sheet metal worker from Missouri. Perry is a single father raising a daughter on his own, even though he believes in the traditional family. Of all the men I spoke with, Perry wanted to be married the most; it just has not worked out for one reason or another. He admits it is difficult for a single father to meet women, which contributes to his disenchantment with women in general. When asked what he thinks about women, Perry completed the sentence this way: "In need of something."

"*Why do you think that?*"

"Well, most of them I meet, it seems they don't necessarily like me for me. They like me for what I can do for them, or what I have to offer. It seems like there's always some other reason besides just me that they like. It's like, oh, he's got a house, or he makes good money. One girl I know is disabled, and she is looking for somebody to settle down with and have stability and help take care of her. I don't need it. She is nice, but I don't really see myself wanting to do that in the future."

"*Describe your ideal woman.*"

"Probably brunette, less that 170 pounds, probably taller than 5'5", and attractive. Pretty in the face and nice body."

"*Anything nonphysical that you would be looking for?*"

"I would definitely appreciate someone who is intelligent, but not arrogant. Some people, I find it hard to believe, are close to forty years old and they never learned anything. I don't know how you can get that far without knowing basic math or how to read a ruler. I have met some people that just amaze me."

"Intelligence is obviously pretty high on your list."

"I would say fifty-fifty of being attractive and intelligent. If they were kind of fat, but smart, that would be okay."

Sure, they have issues with women. But I do not think it's fair to judge the totality of these men by their rants during my conversations with them. They were only giving me what I asked from them. I do not believe there is a great deal of difference between this last group and the rest of the men. They simply chose to focus on those aspects of women that were foremost in their minds at that moment. A couple of years and a good woman from now, I'm sure their responses would be completely different.

CHAPTER 5

I Would Have
Married Her, But...

Isuppose the other heading I could have used for this chapter is *Have You Ever Been In Love?* That is what it's really about, and it's also a question I asked each of the men. My thinking was, if you have been in love and never married, there is a reason (and a story) there. And there is also a question there: Why didn't you marry her? For the majority of men, love is a precursor to getting engaged and getting married—but not these men. Instead, I heard all their reasons for why love never turned into marriage. I also discovered how close these never-married men came to actually taking the plunge.

It turns out that there are only a handful of reasons why a man who ostensibly loves a woman does not marry her. There are those who thought they were too young when they had the chance. Others had wanted to, but the woman didn't. And some never faced that decision because they claimed they had never been in love, which is a good reason for not getting married. And of course, there are some who said they had not met the right one yet. I discovered there was also a hopeful group among these men, who were in a relationship that felt like it could be the right one.

For the men responding to the survey, more than two-thirds had lived with a woman, while more than one-fourth had lived with at least three women. I find it fascinating that such a large percentage of men engaged in co-habitation—several more than once—in essence living the married life, but with no desire to get married legally. Did they learn from previous experience that marriage is not for them? Or perhaps it's not married life they object to (and its lack of freedom), it's just marriage itself. For those who have lived with at least one woman (three out of four), more than a fourth had lived with someone for at least five years. Five years is longer than a lot of marriages. These men had experienced both the married life and the longevity normally associated with marriage. Despite living as married men, with every aspect of married life except the piece of paper, they chose not to marry. This again raised the question: Why didn't he marry her?

Not the Right One

By now it should come as no surprise that the most frequent reason given for not marrying a woman they were in love with was that she was not the right one. In that regard, I suspect these men are no different than the majority of men today, both married and unmarried. It has been a long time since simply being in love meant automatically getting married. What I find intriguing is how long it often takes to come to the conclusion that the woman they love is someone they do not want to marry. For men like Gabriel, it takes years.

Gabriel is definitely not the guy you think about when you envision the playboy-bachelor stereotype. He is careful with his emotions, still suffers from early childhood shyness and has had only two long-term relationships: one for seven years and one for ten. He works at home, which severely limits his ability to meet women. He did try online dating for a month, but found it extremely frustrating for a multitude of reasons, not the least of which was the age prejudice he experienced for being over forty. And it was clear to me that Gabriel had already given previous thought to my questions. He was extremely insightful, oftentimes having consulted his close friends for feedback. At the time of our conversation, he was dating a woman he met two weeks prior, but I wanted to know about his previous relationships and why they did not end in marriage. He said, "I sort of knew what they meant by chemistry, but it never really sank in for me until the last ten years. My last relationship ended because of that. We dated for about seven years. I wanted to move in together in the first year, but she's a fairly conservative person. She has a Japanese background and she wanted to wait. So, we actually dated for seven years, which is kind of crazy when I think about it now."

"Yeah."

"We lived together for three years and then I just sort of had my mid-life crisis when I started to think, unless I do something about it, this is gonna be the last relationship of my life. I started to think about it and it sort of freaked me out, in that I didn't have the relationship I wanted. I started to think about all the things I've missed. Part of it was physical—she was pretty inhibited sexually. She didn't like sleeping in the same bed. If you want to spoon with the person, it's nice to hold them while you fall asleep. I couldn't have that. We were on different sides of the planet."

What do you do when you are seven years in and you don't have the relationship you want? One thing you can do is ask your friends, which is precisely what Gabriel did. He asked, "Is there enough that works in this relationship that I can settle for this and say this is good enough?" And he got his answer. "Most of the guys I talked to, they all pretty much said, 'Yeah, just settle. Settling is good enough as long as you know you're happy.' But most of the women I talked to, they all said, 'Don't settle for a second. If you think you're settling, that's a giant red flag, get the fuck out of the relationship. It's a disaster if you're thinking of settling.'"

"So, what happened?"

"In the end, I sort of agreed with the women. I was the one that prompted the breakup, because I started thinking, 'God, I've got to do something.'"

That was a unique twist on the commonly accepted belief that women want the relationship and men have a commitment problem. In this circumstance, it was his female friends who warned him not to settle. Still, I had to know why it took that long to figure it out. He said, "I didn't put my priorities first or my own happiness first. I had this silly idea when I was younger that I could be compatible with just about anybody in a relationship. I could make anyone happy with me, but I wouldn't be happy. That was the missing part of the equation, which I kept ignoring until I was older and realized, well, you've got to be happy for this to work. If you're not happy there is no way in hell this relationship is going to work."

I have experienced that too. It is almost a code of honor among men, a male toughness that says you don't quit until you succeed. We can make anything work because we're tough, we're men. But what if we are truly unhappy in the relationship? We become torn between this primitive urge to succeed—to make this person we care for very deeply, complete—and our own fulfillment. Two forces pulling in opposite directions, and then we begin to bargain. We think maybe this is the best it will ever be and I am lucky to have her. We wonder, how much happiness am I entitled to? We doubt ourselves and rationalize that conceivably this is happiness and we just don't know it. Maybe we are really happy after all. It's not surprising that it takes years to resolve. Unlike a true-false question on a college exam, there is no correct answer. We follow our instinct and our heart as the years roll on.

An additional reason why it is difficult to end a long-standing love relationship without marriage is because in doing so, we are inclined to believe we wasted our time (and hers). By putting off the pain of that admission, we support the status quo. It is only when we reach our forties and beyond that the ticking clock gives us the fortitude to make quicker and braver relationship decisions. I don't think it would take Gabriel seven years to make that decision today.

Jason also took years to figure out the woman he loved was not someone he was going to marry. I asked him to tell me about being in love.

"When you're in love with somebody, you're willing to go that extra mile—to do whatever; you want to be there for that person. You're willing to go above and beyond because you want to please that individual—be their someone to lean on. Somebody who you'd want to spend the rest of your life with."

"What was the best part of being in that relationship?"

"Just sharing each other and having fun together."

"What was the worst part?"

"Always complaining, always upset, never happy with what I did or never happy with me as a person, and no matter what I did, it wasn't good enough."

"What kept you from marrying her?"

"Those issues. I cannot be [with] someone who's going to be miserable and unhappy and upset with me all the time. It's like, 'Me, me, me!' Very self-centered."

"How long were you with her?"

"Four years."

"That raises an interesting question. You were in love with her, but she was not the right one. How soon into those four years did you start to get an idea she was not the right one?"

"The last year of the relationship."

"Did something change?"

"Yeah, it did. I had some major health issues. I had a job that I was working eighty hours a week and she was not very compassionate about it. When we went away on our trip, she didn't like the hotel room because it didn't have a view. I planned the trip, paid for the hotel, airfare, the rental car, where we were going to go, where we were going to stay and she wanted to end the trip. She cut the trip short because we couldn't get reservations for a restaurant on Christmas Eve, that I didn't do a good job of planning for the trip. I don't want to be in a situation where I'm doing everything. I want a partner who's going to contribute and help out and assist in that situation."

"Was she a partner for the first three years?"

"When I met her she was separated and she had just come out of a twenty-two-year marriage, and I think the first two years was an adjustment for her and me both."

"You had a couple more years. Was she a contributor during the last two years?"

"I would say no."

Four years of dating a woman who did not contribute to the relationship for a man who clearly values contribution and partnership. Why do we do this to ourselves? Why does it take that long? Is it because we want love so badly that we become blind to its shortcomings? Is it any different from someone who marries the wrong person and holds on for four years because they want to remain married? In addition to hanging on in hopes of fulfilling our needs for love and closeness, people suffer from inertia. We avoid change and usually find it easier to stick with what we know, at least until it becomes intolerable. Possibly what separates the men in this book from the married men isn't that they have never been married, but maybe it is that they have never been divorced. After all, having never married is their status quo.

Theodore is in that small collection of men who loved multiple women who were not the right ones. Theodore, a fifty-year-old living in Florida, was recently laid off from a job in the telecom industry. While his thoughts would diverge during our conversation, he spoke respectfully and yet with brutal honesty. Greatly affected as a teenager by his father's death from cancer and his mother's bouts with depression, he has done a lot of personal growth work and as a consequence, was the most introspective man with whom I spoke. Although shy as a young boy, he broke through his shyness as he matured, which led to his having an above average number of sexual relationships with women. Unlike other men who were directly affected by their parents' marriage, Theodore was affected more by his own interpretation of childhood events. As we spoke, other reasons also surfaced. Theodore's stories were enlightening because in each circumstance, breaking up with a woman caused him to confront himself, his behavior and his beliefs, which ultimately led to breakthroughs in his self-discovery. With Theodore, it is less about not marrying the wrong one and more about personal evolution. The women were merely steps on his journey of self-discovery.

I asked Theodore why he did not marry Megan, a girl from his early thirties who gave him an ultimatum. He replied, "I'll give you the answer at the time that I gave her, and then I'll give you the answer that

I think applies today. The answer at the time that I gave her, which I believed at the time was the real answer (and keep in mind that I was thirty-one, thirty-two years old) was at that time I had *not* decided conclusively, on a conscious level, *not* to have children. She could not have kids, and I didn't want to be placed in a position till-death-do-us-part with someone who couldn't have my kids, if I made that decision. That's what I told her, and at that time that was absolutely true for me. What I came to realize was that as time went on, that was not the real issue. The real issue was that I was not ready for a ready-made family[1]. If you look at the kinds of relationships I've had recently, they don't reflect ready-made families."

"Were there any other women?"

"I got involved with another woman and I thought that this woman was the one. I was just so sure, and yet this relationship was not working on any level. Every thirty-nine-and-a-half days, like clockwork, we were breaking up."

"You said this was the one, and yet it wasn't working at all these levels. How is that possible?"

"One of the biggest reasons it wasn't working was the sex absolutely sucked, I mean for both of us. I thought it was the one because she had a beautiful spirit, she was a lovely person and she was gorgeous, and that always helps, but it just wasn't working. We weren't communicating, and so one of the things that happened was after about four months, she and I split for good. I was crushed about it, because I'm usually the one that ends relationships, but this one ended because she couldn't stand the sex. Anyway, this motivated me to take this course, and that's when I really started looking at these belief systems. One of the things I realized was how much anger there was in my previous relationships, how much anger there was [in me], and how much that impacted my previous relationships."

"So, why do you end relationships?"

"One of two reasons, or a combination of the two. One is that women inevitably want to go to the next level, the next level being the white picket fence and I'm just not there. Or, in some cases, I'm just bored—I bore easily. I don't bore in martial arts or challenging things like skydiving, but I bore easily. It could be a combination of boredom and the next level."

While Theodore had to deal with his own anger, Dale had to deal with his partner's anger. I asked him to tell me about a relationship that could have led to marriage but didn't. He said, "I think what kept me from wanting to get married is that the relationship wasn't strong enough, or I didn't feel comfortable committing my entire life to this person."

"Why didn't you feel like committing 100 percent to it?"

"Because she drove me crazy."

"What about her drove you crazy?"

"There were lots of rules. I wasn't allowed to do things; I wasn't allowed to hang out with my friends. She was just an extremely controlling individual. There were some good things about this person as well and I was very much in love. The controlling thing was one thing, but there was this kind of uncontrolled anger that would come out every once in a while. It scared the hell out of me because it was just like everything's fine one minute, and then the next the eyes are red, smoke's coming out of the ears and I'm in trouble. And I don't like being in trouble. I don't consider myself to be the type of person that does things wrong, and I'm sure I do things wrong, but I don't intentionally do it and getting mad is not going to help."

"It seems as though she almost had two personalities. Is that what kept you from going forward in the relationship?"

"Yeah."

"How long were you with her?"

"Three years."

"When did the dual personality thing rear its ugly head?"

"It was a few months after we started going out."

"So, you knew about it early on?"

"It was about four months in and then the ugly side of her would come out. I think it had something to do with her cycles, her periods."

"So, after four months you said, ' I cannot do the dual personality thing; I have to hit the road?'"

"Yeah. At the same time I couldn't find a job in Austin and I think that had a lot to do with it. Then I started getting some pressure from her, so I said, 'Fine, I'm leaving.'"

"At any time did you think about marrying her?"

"I thought about it."

There are numerous things that keep someone from being the right one. Sometimes it is us, and sometimes it is them. Mitch, a forty-year-old, self-employed single father from Oregon, admits the problem with his finding the right one was him. He did not pursue the opportunity to marry the mother of his child, a woman he was attracted to and cared for very much. Deeply intrigued, I asked him what kept him from marrying her.

"I did want to marry her."

"What happened?"

"I guess I kind of threw some destructive behavior into the mix."

"Tell me more about that."

"She pretty much dumped me on Thanksgiving last year and I can't blame her in hindsight. I was doing some pretty stupid stuff."

"Like what?"

"It had to do with the Internet and e-mail, to meet what you need on the Internet. She went into my e-mails and saw some of this, and I think part of it was the bachelor in me trying to get out of the relationship."

"What were you thinking when you were doing the Internet thing?"

"Looking for that woman, that ideal woman, I guess. I had recognized early on that the mother was a great candidate for marriage, but she represented about 80 percent of what I really wanted."

"She had 80 percent of what you were looking for. What was she missing?"

"Liveliness of thought."

"What does that mean?"

"[Being my] intellectual equal, being able to stimulate my thoughts, be an equal partner in the development of my ideas, my entrepreneurial ideas, my political ideas. That's a big part of it. She is a beautiful gal; she's a great mother."

She is the mother of his child, and a great mother at that, and beautiful, but she does not have *liveliness of thought* (the missing 20 percent). It's different for everybody, and I refuse to pass judgment on whether 80 percent should have been close enough for him to marry her. Mitch is not the only man to use 80 percent to describe a woman he wouldn't marry. I think when used in this way, 80 percent is a metaphor for *close, but not close enough*. Maybe 80 percent is a rationalization and there are other, perhaps unacknowledged, reasons why he would not marry her. In the end, it does not matter. It represents a disparity between what he wants and what she is, and it is big enough for him to look elsewhere. I have previously touched on the role that expectations play in relationships, but expectations are not static, they change over time. When we were younger the 80 percent seemed terribly small, the (missing) 20 percent seemed awfully large and forever was a long time to do without it. And when we were asked if we could live without the 20 percent *forever*, invariably the answer came back, *No!* What happens as we get older, into our forties and beyond, as the 80 percent starts to look more appealing, the 20 percent seems more manageable and forever is not such a long time anymore. It would not shock me if Mitch reconsiders and ends up marrying the mother of his child. It is a logical conclusion and one that would make for a happy ending.

Too Young

Maybe the most acceptable reason for not marrying someone you love is that you were simply too young when you had the chance. There were a handful of men who felt that way, and surprisingly they all seemed to have one thing in common: an emotional detachment from marriage. They rarely suffered from idyllic childhood notions of romantic love, being swept off their feet or living happily ever after. They understood, at a young age, the realities and odds of making a marriage last. For example, Evan once loved a woman, but knew he was too young to marry her. "I think we were probably too young and we realized that we were going down different paths ultimately. She would have wanted children earlier and I wanted to go back to graduate school. I didn't really want to be married with children and in graduate school, and we had religious differences. She was much more religious than I was and I think it would have made conflicts in the end."

He knew they were too young and knew it wouldn't work. Does he get any credit for that, or just the label *commitment phobic*? Dylan told me a similar story about a young girlfriend when I asked him if he had ever been in love. "Yeah, a couple of times," he said.

"Tell me about the most important one."

"Dated her five years; we were young. She was an attorney and she just graduated from law school and moved down here. There was a connection right away because within a couple of months, we were living together. My parents didn't approve at the time, but we dated for five years. We were so young. She worked a lot; I worked a lot. Our careers took off and we just kind of went our separate ways. We broke up at twenty-eight and now I'm forty, so that was a long time ago. At that time, she wasn't willing to have kids. At that time, she wasn't willing to settle down and neither was I. I don't think either of us was ready."

They were twenty-eight and they weren't ready. Everyone is on a different schedule, but one thing is for sure: we are all on different time tables than our parents. Today, if you are still unmarried at twenty-eight, nobody thinks twice about it (or writes a book about it).

Like Dylan and Evan, Gordon also felt it was too soon to marry a young love. He told her he was willing, just not yet, and he paid a price for that. He said, "I fell in love with my high school sweetheart, but we didn't call it love back then at eighteen years old. Dated her for four years and she wanted to get married and I said I needed a bit more time. Then she marries my brother. I got blown right out of the water."

"Is she still in your family?"

"No, it didn't last the first year, and I knew that because I knew them both very well. My brother is the exact opposite of me, and I said, 'You love me, you're certainly not going to love him because he's nothing like me.' She found out the hard way. She married him and she couldn't wait to divorce him."

"You told her you needed a bit more time. What made you say that?"

"Work, work, it's always work. I had two great jobs: I was a chef and a groundskeeper at a country club, but I just felt it wasn't where I was supposed to be in life. I said I can't settle down on a marriage because I don't feel right where I am."

I question how many other men declined to move forward in a relationship because they did not feel good about where they were career-wise. Gordon was relatively young, but I understand what he felt. We want to be strong, we want to be good providers and we want to be ready to take care of our women. We want to bring strength, stability and certainty to a marriage, and if we do not feel we can do that yet, it is difficult for us to proceed. At its core, we do not feel worthy of marriage.

Paul's story of being too young is even more unique. When I asked him if he had ever been in love, he responded, "Yes, actually. It was my very first love in college. I met this girl and just fell madly in love with her. She was the one that ended up getting pregnant. I just always thought that she would be the one. When we were in college, I was one year ahead of her and was in a fraternity. I kept trying to get her to join a sorority and she never would. Then I went ahead and graduated and moved for my work. She was still a senior and she finally did join a sorority. And when she did, it was like all of a sudden, [she] flowered, so to speak. She decided that she didn't need me anymore, and that was just the biggest crush in my life. I just couldn't believe it happened. Here I had talked her into it, and then when she did, she didn't need me anymore, so that was a real blow. Then a year or so later, she decided she wanted to get back together, [but] by then I had moved to a bigger city. I was having fun with people at work, so I said, 'Okay, we'll give it a try,' and she moved in. Now, this will sound bizarre, one day she was in the shower and she had a notebook laying there, so I just happened to pop it open. Written over and over and over again was 'Mrs. Paul Brown, Mrs. Paul Brown, Mrs. Paul Brown.' You will never know how that just turned me off. I didn't want her to be Mrs. Paul Brown. I wanted her to be her own person, and that, for me, ended it right there."

"What kind of residual effect did that have on you, seeing that in the book?"

"It just absolutely changed [for me] as far as she was concerned. When I say that, it's like this isn't going to work. I don't want somebody that's going to walk in my shadow all the time. She could buy a pair of pantyhose, then I'd have to help her pick the damn color. It was just ridiculous."

Knowing that incident was the primary reason he chose not to marry her, I asked him, *"Do you think seeing that in the book has had a lasting effect on why you have never been married?"*

"Maybe, subconsciously. I don't think so, but anything's possible."

Wasn't Meant to Be

There are those men who are more fatalistic about why they did not marry a woman they could have. To hear them tell it, sometimes you love a woman and you just can't marry her. They rationalize it by concluding it wasn't meant to be. It does not diminish what they had, nor does it mean they loved her any less because they could not marry her. Manny felt that way, as I found out when I asked him if he had ever been in love. He said, "Yes. It was at the office, and quite frankly she wasn't all that attractive, but she was quite boisterous and very social. So, we met at work and she was always laughing, always grabbed everyone's attention, but not because she was attractive. Most people probably would not have put her with me. I don't think she did either, but we went out for about three months and I got sent away to Detroit for nine months. So, we put it on hold and when I came back, she did not want to get back together."

"Did she tell you why?"

"I think she really didn't think I wanted to be with her."

"Did you?"

"I absolutely did. About a year-and-a-half later, we got back together again and she thought I lied to her, so we split. Then we got back together in 1998 for like a year, and we both admitted that we always loved each other. After six months or so, we started realizing that, even though we loved each other, we just couldn't live with each other, but she definitely touched my heart more than anyone ever had."

"You had the courage to say, 'I love you, but I cannot be with you?'"

"That's right."

Gabriel also loved a woman, but claimed there wasn't anything he could do about it. I suppose there are people who aren't meant to be married, only in love. For Gabriel, it was his first serious relationship and it affected him considerably. In retrospect, there probably wasn't anything he could have done differently to make it work. He said, "We were together for seven years, but I knew within the first couple of months that she had a serious problem that I foolishly thought I could help her get over. The problem was that she was molested as a teenager by her father. That really did a number on her, and I think I was the first man she was able to have a relationship with. We actually had a sexual relationship, whereas she'd never had sex with anyone else before [me] because of what had happened to her. So, at the time, I thought I could help her work through this and eventually she would get over it and things would be great. What happened was kind of the opposite. As the relationship went on, it became more and more of an issue and essentially, by the end the relationship, we were living like roommates, and so what happened is she broke up with me. One morning she said to me, 'I realize I can't be in an intimate relationship with anyone at all.' She broke up with me and moved out and I was destroyed. I probably cried for three days. I remember a few months later, going to my family physician and I wanted him to prescribe me Prozac because I was so depressed."

She Didn't Want Me

It's not always the men who do not want to get married. Occasionally, it's the women. There are a number of men who have experienced this, so it should not be too surprising. In matters of the heart, it is just as likely the woman doesn't feel a sense of connection. Nevertheless, because they were not the ones to make the choice, these men are possibly the ones most affected by the consequences of that failed long-term relationship. Randy falls into this category. As he stated, "I've been in love several times."

"Tell me about the most significant one."

"The most significant one was probably the earliest, when I was extremely young. You know how puppy love is, and the crush. It was very ideal and romantic and sweet, you know, everlasting."

"What was the best part of that relationship?"

"Her family. She had the greatest family."

"It sounds like you were in love with her family."

"Probably, yeah. We got along great. Her parents loved each other, unlike mine. Her father was doting. Her parents were deeply in love and you could see it."

"How did that manifest itself?"

"They would openly hug and kiss each other and hold hands. She'd sit in his lap, they joked with each other, she'd put her hand on is arm, those kinds of things."

"And you never saw that from your parents?"

"Never, not at all."

"What kept you from marrying the girl?"

"She broke up with me to go back to her high school track boyfriend. I would've married her."

"Sounds like a broken heart waiting to happen."

"It was. That was awful."

"Sometimes when we are young, we have these significant events. What role did that play in your never getting married after that?"

"I think that was the start of it."

Myron experienced a similar situation, but he brought a perspective to it that was unique among the men. He said, "Yes. I've been in love in the romantic sense that we see in the movies and in the literature, especially when I was younger, like in my twenties and thirties."

"Why younger and not more recently?"

"When I was younger, I may have romanticized the relationship. I was young and I hadn't yet experienced that in its full glory. I may have, at the time, seen the relationship as being more important, or more wonderful, that it really was. As I got older, I began to learn that when you spend a lot of time with anyone, the romantic ideal begins to fade a bit in the reality and abrasions of daily life. So, when I was in my twenties, I may have met some people that I thought I was in love with in the romantic sense and, later in life, I met people that I loved in a less romantic way. There are different kinds of love. The romantic love of the twenties was replaced by a more sober, let's say pedestrian, but good love of later life."

Myron was the only man who talked about different kinds of love. The romantic infatuated love of youth and the more pragmatic love we discover as we grow older. I suppose the people who get married and stay married have learned to adapt their expectations of love as their love changes. As we continued, I asked Myron to tell me a little about the most important love he had. "I think the most important one I had was probably the second, when I was about twenty-four. The reason it was the most important love is because we achieved a higher level of emotional and physical intimacy than I had with anyone before that. It was important at the time [because] I would not have known that such a degree of emotional closeness even existed, that such a feeling of comfort and safety with another person could have been experienced. It increased my understanding of what it means when people are in love, and we were together for several years. It increased my appreciation of how loving and close two people can be. It set the standard by which later relationships were judged."

"Would it be fair to say that the best part of the relationship was the closeness?"

"Yeah. The closeness was much greater than I had ever known in my life before. I was able to talk to women better after that. It helped me grow emotionally and, therefore, approach women differently."

"What was the worst part of the relationship?"

"The breakup at the end, after about two years. I was twenty-six when it ended and she was about twenty-four, and her parents very much wanted her to marry somebody who was the same religion as they were. They were Episcopalians and I'm Jewish. She eventually gave in to parental pressure and went back to live with them, and that was sad for me."

"Did you want to marry her?"

"That's a good question. At the time, we may have wound up married because I liked her so much. I think that had she been able to resist the feelings of parental obligation, we might have wound up being married because it was a very good relationship. We were talking about it. My attitude had not yet been fully formed. So, there's a good chance I would have wound up married."

Nathan, too, would have married a girlfriend who set the standard for all the rest, but he lost her to someone else. Eventually, he became resigned that it was for the best. When I asked him if he had been in love, he said, "Yeah. It was somebody who I worked with when I was in the residential treatment place, but she was caught up with this guy who was an Army person. [She] had met him in college, even though she never saw him and he treated her like crap. For three or four years, we spent a lot of really good time together, but she married him."

"She married this Army guy who she did not know very well and did not treat her very well?"

"Right."

"Why is that? That had to be bugging you."

"I think it's because she had some family issues, a father that didn't treat her very well and things like that. But she has four kids now with him and I think she's happier."

"Would you have married her?"

"Absolutely."

"What kept you from asking her during those three or four years?"

"Because she was determined she was going to eventually marry him."

"So, the whole time you are with her, she was thinking about this other guy?"

"All the time."

"How did that feel?"

"It was horrible, but you can't do anything about it."

"After that kind of torn relationship, what effect did it have going forward in your future relationships?"

"Obviously, it's very difficult to put yourself back out in the world after that situation because you're not sure it'll ever happen again. She was just the best, and you're not so sure you want to fiddle for anybody else."

"So, she was the standard you used to compare other women to?"

"Yep."

"And you have not met another one like her?"

"No, not at all."

"I would say that has had a long-term effect."

"It has."

Wayne had a similar story to tell. Like Nathan, he also loved a woman who did not love him back, but he also admitted there had been women in *his* past who loved him and he did not reciprocate. That became a common theme among the men: wanting women they couldn't have and not wanting women they could.

"I have been in love, yes," Wayne stated.

"Tell me about the most significant one."

"The most significant love I ever had was unrequited."

"Tell me about it."

"I went to a nightclub one night and saw this beautiful, striking Latina dancing on the dance floor and I wanted to marry her the minute I laid eyes on her. I went over and asked her to dance and she said yes and I almost had a heart attack. So, we got out there and danced and I really liked her. Just something about her. I spent two years of my life chasing this woman and trying to convince her to fall in love with me and it just didn't work out."

"Were there any women that loved you back?"

"Not that I can think of."

"Why do you think that is?"

"I don't know. I meet a lot of women that ask me why I've never been married and I've said well, the women that have wanted to marry me, I didn't want to marry, and the women that I wanted to marry, didn't want to marry me."

"Do you have any insight into that?"

"I have no insight. I'm not a person that asks a lot of questions, and women, I've found, rarely tell you the truth anyway when it comes to why they don't like you or don't want to go out with you or won't marry you."

"So, the feedback you have gotten from women you cannot really trust as being true?"

"Right."

It's simply human nature: we place greater value on things that are more difficult to obtain. There are men who only want women who don't want them. I question whether that is merely an excuse though. It's easy for these men to say they would have married a woman they knew would not marry them. There is nothing at stake. I do not know if that is what happened with Nathan, but I am certain about one thing: None of us will ever get married until we get that under control—not wanting what we can have.

Of the thirty-three men I spoke to, Danny, the forty-eight-year-old nurse from Washington State, was most affected by a woman who didn't want him. First meeting her in the ninth grade, she has come in and out of his life over the years. While Danny grew up and dated and never married, she had two children, one from a tenuous marriage that was on shaky ground when they finally reconnected years later. During the time of our conversation, he had recently broken up with her after dating her for four months—even though she was still married. Since this woman held such fascination for him from the first moment he laid eyes on her, I questioned why he had not done something about it back then. He told me about meeting her for the first time. "I've known her for thirty-four years. When I first laid eyes on her in ninth grade, I was instantly in love with her. I was just, 'Oh man, she's the cutest girl I've ever seen.'"

"Why didn't you do something about it back then?"

"I did. But I never felt she felt as intense about me as I did about her. I feel so intense about her. If she looks at another guy and smiles, it causes all kinds of anxiety inside me. So, I went out with her a few times and kissed her a few times, but I just never felt she had the same feelings for me. So, I broke up with her. That was in ninth grade. Then I saw her again when I was twenty-five. Same instantaneous infatuation, but she was with somebody else. Now I met her in the hospital four months ago and she looked just great—[looked as] beautiful to me today as she did thirty-four years ago. No change whatsoever—instantaneous infatuation. This time she gave me her number and it lasted four months."

"Why did it end? Do you think you have a commitment problem?"

"No. I'd marry this woman in a heartbeat. I would have married her three months ago. She has two kids. I said [to her that] I accept them fully."

"*Why wouldn't she marry you?*"

"Because she's separated and I think she still wants to give her husband another chance. I asked her why she doesn't divorce him, because they've been separated for four years and she just gives me lame excuses."

"*Are you still holding out hope?*"

"Well, yeah and no. My greatest fear is that I hook up with another woman, and then she calls me back, and I have to hurt somebody else because of her and I don't want to do that. I don't just want a rebound to take my mind off her. It's getting better, but I'm having trouble sleeping at night."

"*Do you think this woman has had an effect on your life since the ninth grade?*"

"Oh yeah. After all these years and no change in my feelings for her. I always felt so unworthy of her, so inadequate. I don't know why."

"*Do you think she's your soul mate?*"

"I don't know, but I'll tell you this, [it was] the best sex I ever had in my life."

"*If you could tell her one thing right now, what would it be?*"

"I'd probably tell her, 'I can't change you, I can only change me, and I want more than anything for you to be happy in life, and if being with me would make you unhappy, I don't want you to be with me. I want you to be with someone who'd make you happy.'"

"*Anything else?*"

"I can't force her to like me. So, I just have to accept her and accept the fact that I am powerless to change her."

"*Where do you see yourself, relationship-wise, five years from now?*"

"I don't really want to get into a deep relationship. I don't want to hurt anybody, you know, in case she calls back."

He is waiting for a ghost. He can see it, but he cannot touch it. It holds him like the leg irons that held Ben Hur on that Roman galley. I hope some other woman comes along and sets him free.

Andrew had his own story of a woman he loved who did not love him back, and as usual, sex permeated the entire conversation. To him, sexual compatibility is such a strong precursor to any other deep feelings, including maybe even love, that I was curious to know if he could even tell them apart.

When asked if he had ever been in love he replied, "I have. It seems like the women that I truly care for and I love, don't love me back. Maybe it's a game they're playing, maybe I'm not getting it or something, but I've had a handful of relationships that I think were keepers. One in particular I met when I was in Ohio. We would go out, have a good time and we'd get back to my place and she said, 'You know, I don't want anything to happen this evening, however, I would like to cuddle.' So, we go upstairs and one thing leads to another and we have some great, wonderful sex. So, we started seeing each other more after that. She, for whatever reason, figured, 'Well fine, I don't want to get serious, but I don't mind coming over for some fun on Friday or Saturday night.' So, it was a regular thing on the weekend that we'd see each other, and needless to say, she was phenomenal in bed. To me, she was a keeper. Oh, she was a keeper."

"*And then?*"

"That relationship kind of fizzled out. But for a time it was wonderful."

"*You said the women you fall in love with don't seem to love you back. Why do you suppose that is?*"

"I think part of it is guys know what they want from a woman very quickly. A guy knows whether he likes a woman, and knows how much he likes a woman, after a date or two. Whereas women take a lot longer to decide what they think of you. So, I knew I liked her right off the bat. I knew I wanted her to be around and I couldn't hold my emotions back. To her, she was still in that I-don't-know-how-much-I-like-you phase, and I'm showing too much emotion. One of the things she'd say to me is, 'I don't know why you like me so much.' By the same token, there have been women that I didn't care for that much, but I dated. They at some point really started to like me, but I didn't like them any more than the level I liked them after two dates. So, I didn't want to be around somebody that cared for me much more than I cared for them."

It is easy to create generalities about women that we formulate over the years as a result of our (limited) relationships with them. Rarely are they true—few generalities are—but they are exceedingly important because they impact how we relate to women in the future. For Andrew, the generalities he has formed about women might as well be true, because it is how he sees them.

No Need

Having conversations with thirty-three men, I did not think there would be one story unique enough that it would stick out from all the others. I was wrong; Dennis' story is that story. Dennis, a sixty-four-year-old retired computer programmer from North Carolina, is the exception. Originally from New York and the oldest of three bothers, Dennis has been in a loving, mostly monogamous relationship with the same woman for thirty-eight years—never married. I was almost taken aback by how profoundly he could articulate why he had never married, without hesitation, without doubt and without regret. He is well-spoken, objective and has a sense of certainty about his life and his relationship that I rarely found with the other men. I wanted Dennis to tell me about Tracy, his partner of thirty-eight years, and why he never married her. "Tracy and I have been together as a loving couple for thirty-eight years. We dated, and for the first ten, twelve years of our relationship as a loving couple, we did have some relationships with other people, so it was not always monogamous. But since the early eighties, for more than twenty years, we have been happily monogamous. Now, some people say gosh, that's almost being married, but it's not really. For one thing, Tracy is a fiercely independent woman who had always insisted on living her own life in her own house. She will not live with me, and so she and I had always lived separate but near to each other. We are well-matched in terms of education, intelligence, religion, hobby interests, basic philosophy—it's really difficult to point to anything that's a source of friction between us. And in particular, we don't fight—it's just not in our nature. There are disagreements and we work them out, but we don't fight. We have never had any real fights in thirty-eight years."

"*That is really interesting.*"

"All through the years we've had a custom that works well for us, and that is two days out of the seven day week we go our separate ways. We might be in contact by telephone or e-mail during the day, but two days out of seven we're separate, and that's been just the right amount of togetherness versus having a measure of independence."

"*Has jealousy played a role in your relationship at any time?*"

"No. As a matter of agreement, we were always honest about going out with somebody else, when that happened. But also as a matter of agreement, there were never any specifics divulged. So, I don't know if she had sex with the other men or not, and she hasn't told me and won't tell me. And we're comfortable with that degree of what you share and what you don't."

"*Did you offer to marry Tracy?*"

"No. I made it clear to everyone that I had any close relationship with that marriage simply wasn't a part [of it]—I wasn't going to do it. It was not in my life plan. There were some who thought, 'Well, all guys say that and he'll change,' and certainly some young men might say that and then they do change their minds, but I was sincere and did not change. Tracy had somewhat different ideas for me. She always felt that she wanted to be a career woman. She did not want to have children. She was interested, at least early in her life, in getting married, but she did not want to follow the typical path of having children."

"*What keeps the two of you unmarried, but together?*"

"The same forces which pull married couples apart act on the unmarried. One important difference for us is that we are not shackled to each other. We don't have children. We don't have jointly-owned real estate. Most important, we don't have that legal formality of a marriage contract. In theory, we could walk away from each other any day. If I were ever to seriously mistreat my partner, she could ditch me and vice versa. We can never take each other for granted. We can never exploit our partner. Think of it as a marriage contract which must be renewed every day. Seems fragile, destined for failure, but we've been together for thirty-eight years and our relationship is stronger than ever."

How many married people can say that? I have preached for years, to anyone who would listen, my questionable logic that a couple who is only dating actually has a stronger relationship than a married couple, because it is easy to end it. There is nothing external keeping them together. I am confident there are a number of married people who stay together simply to avoid (or postpone) the hassle of divorce. But when two people are dating, who have nothing keeping them together except for their desire to be together, continue to stay in the relationship, they must really want it. I was curious, in this unique situation, if Dennis and Tracy were close after all these years because they never got married, or would they be just as close if they had? I don't know the answer, but I do know the relationship Dennis and Tracy have created for themselves works for them, and it's hard to argue with that.

Never Been in Love

There are men with a ready-made excuse as to why they have not married a woman: they claimed to have never been in love. I suppose these are the men most justified in having never married. Naturally, I was curious as to whether they had never been in love, or had they been in love and not known it. Love can be elusive like that. And there was one other thing these men had in common: short-term relationships. Samuel answered without hesitation when asked if he had ever been in love, "I don't think so."

"Really?"

"No."

"Why not?"

"I've had a couple of people I've been very infatuated with."

"What kept it from being love?"

"I wasn't with the person long enough. When you've only been with somebody a few weeks or a month, you can't call it that."

"What is the longest you were with somebody?"

"I'm probably an aberration. It's been a very short period of time. I would say a month or so."

"What causes it to be short typically?"

"I honestly don't know."

"Really?"

"You'd have to ask the females."

"Do you typically end it or do they typically end it?"

"It's always the woman."

"And you have no insight as to why?"

"No, not really."

"Not even a guess?"

"I'm not even sure I would hazard a guess. I knew one person I was [seeing] recently, she started seeing somebody she had been seeing before."

"I have got to tell you that I am fascinated by the idea that you have had these one month relationships, and they end on the woman's part and you do not really have a lot of insight as to why."

"No."

"Because I know if it were me, I would have to find out why."

"I look at it this way, people make choices and I have not been the choice. It's okay, I'm just going to move on. In some ways, it has been very good. I have other things I enjoy doing and so I just go and do them."

Women make choices and so far Samuel has not been on the shortlist. It's hard to find fault with that, but it does make one wonder. Perhaps there is something there that needs to be addressed, but Samuel is not going to find it unless he is willing to dig a little deeper into his own psyche. Justin related a similar story of not knowing whether or not he had been in love. "I'm not sure. I've certainly had infatuations. I don't know that I've ever really been totally head over heels in love with a real person."

"Why do you think that is?"

"Maybe I just haven't met the right person. Maybe I'm emotionally inhibited somehow."

"What is the longest relationship you have been in?"

"This is pathetic; it's about six months. There have been several about that duration, but I've never really been in relationship longer than a year."

"Is there anything magical about six months, if they all seem to end around there?"

"They tend to fizzle out for one reason or another. I'm thinking of a recent relationship [that] was a long-distance relationship. She lived about three and a half hours [away] from me. There was a lot of driving back and forth, a lot of long-distance calls, but it just got old after awhile. And I think she wanted a commitment from me, which I was not willing to give, and things kind of fell apart."

"Do you think at this moment in your life, if you met the right person, you could fall in love?"

"I certainly hope so."

"But you are not a 100 percent sure."

"I don't know. Like I say, I don't think it's ever happened before."

Another person who feels the same way is Trent, the fifty-two-year-old retiree from Vancouver. When asked if he had ever been in love, he said, "No, I wouldn't say so. Close, where it was really important, but there was the fear. It only lasted about nine months or so."

"Why have you only come close to love, but not all the way?"

"I really don't know."

"What was missing that made you fall short, because it sounds like you were close?"

"We were very close, but it required a whole shift change in what I did and where I went and I just couldn't maintain it. It wasn't just me and it wasn't just her. We were just sort of playing this game. It was really enjoyable, but we just went through this phase of just being really hung up on each other. Of course, it wasn't permanently workable."

"What kept it from being permanently workable?"

"It took time away from ordinary, day-to-day stuff: the ironing and going shopping for groceries."

"It sounds like you never made it to a level of normalcy."

"Never did, really. We were just really enjoying each other for that period, but there's no way we could maintain that sort of relationship for a long time. It was very obvious. I actually moved to San Francisco and that was the end of that."

Considering It

A few of the men were in a loving relationship at the time of our conversation, and when asked about marrying them, they responded, "We're considering it." One such man was Sandy. Even though the relationship was far from perfect—how many are?—I think there was enough there to make it work. He readily admitted there was a good chance he would marry her. I do not know if he will, but it was certainly his thinking the day we spoke. When I asked Sandy if he had ever been in love, he gave a refreshing response, "Well, I think I am now."

"Can you tell me a little bit about her?"

"She's pretty different than what my ideal was."

"In what ways?"

"I think she comes from a lower-middle class upbringing, didn't really have a good opportunity for education, just a blue-collar type of background, very different than mine. Physically, she didn't seem to be what my physical ideal had been in the past."

"What is it that draws you to her?"

"She's like a diamond in the rough. Turns out she's really very smart. She really is very spiritual. When I met her she [had] a lot of potential and, physically, we have a good relationship."

"What is the best part of the relationship with this girl?"

"The spiritual connection."

"What does that do for you, that spiritual connection?"

"It's a common ground; a way of looking at the world and what's going on and what we're meant to do."

"How long have you been in the relationship with her?"

"Three or four years."

"To give a counterbalancing opinion, what is the worst part of being in the relationship with her?"

"When the pressure is on, she becomes very abusive to me."

"In what way?"

"She started out being physically abusive to me. I was living with her and I had to leave. Then it was emotional abuse, just the typical, 'If you really loved me, you'd do this,' and that type of crap. Silent treatment and all that. At this point, she's in Cleveland and I'm in Columbus and I told her, 'You keep pushing away from me, and you move away one inch at a time, and [pretty soon] I'm about 150 miles away,' and she doesn't have any power to hurt me. I've taken that away. So, basically when she starts flying off the handle, I can just walk away from it."

"Do you still love her?"

"Yeah."

"Do you think you will marry her some day?"

"I think there's a good chance of it."

"What would cause that to happen, because you have been dating her for four years now?"

"About a year or two of emotional stability in our relationship."

"Is she getting any help for that?"

"Not professional help, but she's growing and changing."

"Is she getting better?"

"Yeah, she's getting better."

Sometimes it's one thing, one character flaw, that keeps the ball from crossing the goal line. It's that way for Sandy and his girlfriend. He wants her to win and he is rooting for her, so there is hope they could succeed.

Perry, the forty-two-year-old sheet metal worker from Missouri, is a man in an almost identical situation to Sandy. He is with a woman he would marry if she will only make one change in her life. I asked Perry to talk about the mother of his daughter and why he did not marry her. He said, "I got together with a woman with two children, and we decided that we would have a third. We were supposed to get married and low and behold, she became pregnant, and we did have a third child together. Then she decided she had been married twice before and she didn't want to get married. So, we never got married."

"Are you still with her?"

"No. She started drinking heavily and we split up. Basically, I kicked her out and so I am raising a girl by myself."

"So you do not have any contact with her now?"

"No. I just talked to her a little while ago. She moved out, met a guy and moved in with him. That didn't work out too good for her [because] he has been beating her up and she put him in jail. I've been telling her to come back."

"Do you want her back?"

"Well, in the meantime, I haven't really met anybody, and she is the mother of my child, and if she could be a decent mom, yeah, I'd want her back."

James felt his best love relationship was the one he was in when we spoke, and as a result, is open to the possibility of marrying her. When I asked him if he had ever been in love, he said, "Absolutely! I've been in love lots of times."

"Tell me about the best one."

"That's the relationship I'm in now. I didn't realize how crappy some of the relationships I've had in the past [were] until I met her. We just hit it off, and we were friends long before anything else happened. Then when it finally did happen, I just headfirst into it and there was no looking back. It's great! We're best friends and I have no desire to stray or do anything. I miss her when she's not around. It's a good feeling."

"What is the best part of being in this relationship?"

"Not going through life alone. Knowing that someone's got my back, and it also feels real good knowing that I can do the same for her."

"Are you going to marry her?"

"I'm planning on it."

Recalling from earlier in our conversation that James did not really see a need for marriage other than for children, I followed with, *"So, all that stuff you said about it (marriage) being a label."*

"I still believe that in theory."

"Have the two of you talked about going forward and what's in the plan?"

"We have. It's really hilarious because we both felt the same way. We both felt that marriage was just a label. We have no good reason for getting married. It just sounded like the right thing to do."

There are people for whom it takes a bunch of bad relationships to help them realize what they have right in front of them is pretty darn good. It's called perspective, and clearly it takes longer for some to get it than others.

CHAPTER 6

So Why Have You Never Been Married?

So, why have you never been married? If you are an over-forty never-married man (or woman), you have probably been asked that question. It's an easy question to ask, but one that is sometimes complicated to answer because there isn't always a single reason and sometimes we are not exactly sure of the answer ourselves. There are influences from the past and fears about the future. There are incidents from early childhood, adolescence and even recently. Some have never wanted to be married and some have never given it a second thought, while others have wanted it and it simply hasn't happened. And are these men glad to be over forty and unmarried? They may not be miserable about it, but they certainly aren't celebrating it either. According to the survey, while the largest collection (representing 26 percent of the respondents) are indifferent to having never been married, only 8 percent are happy about it. There is also a small number (6 percent) who are sad about it and 15 percent actually admit to being lonely.

There are a few common themes that permeate this group of men as being reasons, in part or in whole, as to why they never married. Several were influenced by their parents' bitter divorce, while others were impacted by their parents who did not divorce, but probably should have. Almost half of the men surveyed claimed their parents' relationship had at least some effect on their never marrying. There are those who viewed their parents' relationship in a negative light, which caused them to seriously question married life. Still, for others, their parents' marriage served as such a positive representation for them, they simply refuse to marry someone who they feel cannot produce that same quality relationship. A few even cite their parents' "normal" marriage, with its typical marital interactions, as a reason why they have shied away from marriage. For these men, it is less about having witnessed a bad marriage and more about not wanting a normal marriage. And there are a number who were influenced by early child-hood events that had nothing to do with their parents' relationship.

Almost seven in ten men pointed out that their past relationships had at least some influence in their decision. I asked each of them what their biggest fear is about marriage. As I discovered, fear is a major factor for many, but there are different sources of fear. From the survey, the fear of marrying the wrong person far outweighs the fear of never marrying at all, by almost ten to one. And the reason given more than any other (48 percent of respondents) as to why they have yet to marry is because they have not found the right person, compared to 13 percent who do not think marriage is important, 9 percent who have not been ready and 7 percent who enjoy being single. Those who were negatively impacted by their parents' relationship typically have fears about marriage. Commonly, they feel their parents were wrong for each other, which explains their intense preoccupation with finding the right one. The idea of being careful because they only want to marry once came up repeatedly during my conversations.

For several men, the decision to remain single was influenced less by what happened to them earlier in life and more by who they are, or who they have become. They don't blame their parents or any other circumstance in their past for not marrying. For these men, it's who they are. It might be shyness, lack of confidence or lack of financial wherewithal that keeps them from pursuing a mate. And there are also those who claim to have no fear of marriage because they want to get married. A few want to, just not yet, while the remainder have actually pursued marriage, but for whatever reason, it simply has not happened.

The Parents

There is little doubt there are men who were sufficiently impacted by the profound affect their parents' relationships had on their decision to not marry, regardless of whether Mom and Dad are divorced or still together. For a few, it was the exact opposite: it was their parents staying together (or staying together too long) that influenced them. One man even pointed out that had his parents divorced sooner, he may have turned out differently. For all of those in this group, together or divorced, their parents' marriage serves as a model for what they definitely don't want. It is usually about fighting, bickering or the lack of affection, and these men simply do not want any part of it. However, there was one man impacted by a parent in a way that had nothing to do with fighting or divorce, but rather the untimely death of his father when he was a young boy.

Regardless of the specifics, quite a few men in this book remain unmarried to this day because of their parents' influence. Like Evan, as I found out when I asked him what the single greatest influence was on why he had never married. He said, "I'd be fooling myself to say that my parents' marriage, and their subsequent divorce, didn't have a lot to do with it. My parents had a bad marriage and I remember that. In fact, these memories come back to me more now that I think about these things. As I've aged, I look at my own relationships and I try to think of my parents' influence on them. You see how things can unravel and go downhill."

"What is your biggest fear about being married?"

"I guess maybe just growing apart as the years go by and being married to someone who changes into something I don't want to be attached to anymore. That's one big part of it. The other part is financial. If I were to be married to someone, and they divorced me, and they didn't make as much and took a lot of my earnings, retirement and so forth, I would worry about being hurt financially. Just growing apart and then waking up and saying alright, are we into this relationship anymore? It's the permanence of it that I take very seriously and I suppose that's why I haven't done it. Because if I do, I would want to be sure about it."

When I asked Evan if he thought he had a commitment problem, he said no, because he takes it more seriously than other people. I continued, *"Thinking back to your early twenties, where did you think you would be relationship-wise today, in your forties?"*

"I really didn't think much about it. I guess I never saw myself as a married type of guy, even when I was that young."

"Why is that?"

"Ever since I was a child, I just never felt it was my calling, at least not the traditional relationships that I see. I look at them and I think, I don't see myself in that. I could be wrong; I may change my mind tomorrow. I see other people have girlfriends and they have this great drive to have a girlfriend and then I would think, why do you want to have a girlfriend just to have a girlfriend, or have a wife just to have a wife, as some abstract concept. I don't need another person to validate myself. If I found someone who I really felt complemented my life and would make a good partner sexually, business-wise, emotionally, then I would think about it. But I never saw that as a goal to attain. If it happens, it happens."

Evan represents an interesting combination: he exhibits serious-ness about the marital commitment, and also has direct experience seeing what can happen in a bad marriage from his parents. I think his belief in the permanence of marriage, coupled with his knowing the reality of what can go wrong in a marriage, has left him unmarried.

Andrew told a similar story about the break up of his parents at an early age. "My parents were divorced and I think that has a lot to do with it. If you're raised in a broken home, you're gun shy of marriage. My grandparents were married for fifty-plus years, till they died, so I could see how a long-term relationship was. If I'm going to get married, I want to do it once, and I want to do it for good."

"Do you think your parents were the wrong people for each other?"

"Oh absolutely; without question."

"What in particular made them wrong for each other?"

"I'm into astrology to some degree and there's certain astrological signs that should never get together. My dad was a Sagittarian and my mother was a Cancer and they say that's one of the worst mixes. The two children, myself and my brother, are Pisces and Gemini, and those two should never get together. So we had four people in the house that shouldn't be in the same house and it was a nightmare. [So,] it was actually a good thing (I hate to say it this way) when my dad did leave finally. The house kind of calmed down a little bit. It was a very volatile situation. There was fighting, but my dad never struck my mother to my knowledge, so it wasn't like that, but they were just arguing. It just wasn't a pretty situation."

Donald had a comparable experience to Andrew, but with Donald, it was his mother's behavior that opened his eyes to the potential consequences of a less-than-ideal marriage. He said, "I think what affected me [most] is my parents' bad relationship and them being separated their whole life. I know my mom wasn't a hundred percent loyal to my dad. I spent a lot of time with my mom and I think in the back of my mind that floored me a little bit, thinking women are potentially like that."

"What made it a bad relationship?"

"He traveled a lot and she was lonely, and she developed some bad drinking habits, and that's what made it bad."

"Anything else influence you?"

"My experience with other people that are unhappily married. Knowing that it's going to be [a] really tough situation to make a marriage last and be happy. I'm pretty content in what I do. I have a kid who's raised; I don't want to have kids. I have success, I can do my own thing and I'm just pretty selfish. I don't want to give up a lot of things, and I haven't quite found the mate that I can coexist with and still have fun with."

"Thinking back to your twenties, where did you think you would be today relationship-wise?"

"I didn't really have any goals back then to be married and have kids. I had goals as far as where I was going to be sports-wise and financially, but as far as relationships, I've never really had a goal. I think I'm setting goals more [now] that I'm older. I don't want to be eighty or ninety years old and not married."

"Why didn't you have any goals to be married when you were younger?"

"Probably just my parents and seeing how unhappily married they were, and fighting too much, and my mom drinking and cheating on my dad. Things like that just turned me off to the whole marriage thing."

More than any other man I spoke with, Dennis (the man who had the same girlfriend for thirty-eight years) knew exactly why he had never married. It had to do with his parents who did *not* divorce. By his own admission, it was his parents' "normal" marriage that affected him. He said, "I have a very clear idea of why I stayed single. I made a choice in adolescence; I may have been fifteen or sixteen. I made two life decisions at that relatively early age. The first was that I wanted to live in a place that had a low population density. My parental home was in New York City and I decided I don't like living in a big city. The other decision was that I would stay single always, and I have a clear idea as to why I did that. My parents married in 1940. It was the first and only marriage for them. The marriage lasted until this year when my dad passed away at age ninety-one. [My] mother is still living. They have always said they had a wonderful marriage, a loving marriage—everything positive. They both said that, and from my point of view it simply was not so. In particular, they tended to bicker all of the time. They'd pick on each other and from my point of view, [it] was Mom picking on Dad mostly. These were not big fights; they were not ugly fights. There never was a marital separation, never any contemplation of divorce, nothing like that, but constant friction, and I didn't like that. I didn't want that. I didn't want to live that way. My parents' marriage is perhaps the prototype for me and I decided, pretty early on, if this is what a good marriage looks like, then I decline to participate. I'm not going to do it. I made that decision early in life and I have stuck with it and have not had cause to regret it."

Rarely is it a single influence, as it is with Dennis, that keeps these men unmarried. The great majority have multiple influences, of which their parents' relationship is a contributing factor. A good example of this is Justin. Unlike the previous men who were affected in a negative way by their parents, Justin was impacted by parents who were in an almost perfect marriage—if there is such a thing—proving that even when everything is ideal, parental influence can still change the course of a person's life. With Justin, it was his mother's influence, although that too was merely a portion of a larger recipe that has conspired to keep him unmarried. *"So, why have you never been married?"* I asked him.

"Well, the short answer is, I've never met the right person. Another factor is, to be perfectly candid, I'm a bit of a momma's boy. I have a very close relationship with my mother, in part I think, because I'm an only child. I think she looms large in my life and her approval or disapproval counts for probably more than it should. Maybe I find a certain degree of emotional, though not physical, intimacy with her that might have kept me from actively pursuing other women."

"Has she ever disapproved of a woman you were interested in?"

"She hasn't met a lot of them, but I think she has very high standards. After a while, I know what her reaction is going to be."

"Have her high standards become your high standards?"

"Well... no. I'm a little bit more flexible. I like what I like."

"But do you think her standards have kept you from moving forward in a relationship?"

"I think they probably have. I know she would have hated this woman I was in a long distance relationship with for six months. They never did meet, but at this point I just knew what her reaction was going to be. They might have gotten to like each other eventually, but it would have been awkward."

"So, her approval in the back of your mind actually kept the relationship from going forward."

"Yeah. I know I'm an adult and I can do what I want, whether Mommy says so or not. But because I'm close to her and my dad, I just can't completely write them off either. Their opinion counts for a lot."

"How would you describe your sex life as a never-married man?"

"Would you believe, I lost my virginity at the age of thirty-four?"

"I believe it."

"My religious beliefs played a certain role in that. I tend to believe that premarital sex is wrong, but at the age of thirty-four, curiosity, if nothing else, got the better of me. I just wanted to see what all the fuss was about, and for a while there in my thirties, I made up for lost time. I got a lot out of my system."

"And how did you reconcile your religious beliefs with the fact that you experimented with sex?"

"I knew it was wrong, but it was an itch that just had to be scratched."

"Are you back to your more religious ways now?"

"Pretty much, yeah. I'm not really dating a lot right now, and that, as much as anything, explains why there's no action. Mostly, I have very little sex."

"What role have these beliefs about premarital sex played in your never getting married?"

"Well, theoretically that should drive you to marry early—if you believe that's the only legitimate outlet for sex. I suppose I would have been very happy being married earlier. I guess I was never really self- confident with women, certainly not in high school and not very much during my twenties."

"Why didn't you have self-confidence before your thirties?"

"I guess I've always been shy and introspective. I went to an all boys private high school, so I had very little exposure to the opposite sex during my teenage years. Didn't have any sisters, so really I don't know what girls were about most of that time."

"Do you think that had an effect on you?"

"I think it definitely did. My life would probably be different had I grown up in a co-educational environment."

"What is your biggest fear about getting married today?"

"I'm very careful to make the right choice the first time, because I don't want to end up in divorce. Therefore, I'm very picky, probably too picky. At this point though, it's only now occurring to me that it's going to be such a change from being single all these years that I don't know what it's like to be married. I've never done it before and it's a big change of life."

"Are you worried that change is so big now that it may actually keep you from taking a chance on it?"

"No. I haven't given up. I'm still waiting to take a chance on the right person."

"How would you feel if you got to the end of your life and you had never been married?"

"Well, I'm certainly not the only person that's happened to."

"But how would you feel?"

"I guess I'd feel disappointed. But then again, if I met the right person at the age of eighty, I'd get married then. I never give up hope."

"So, the right person is more important than the right time?"

"The right time was probably fifteen years ago."

The fear of change can be a powerful force, especially the fear of giving up the single life. In speaking with Justin, I recalled that scene from the 1994 film *The Shawshank Redemption*, right after Brooks Hatlen (the character played by James Whitmore) discovers he is going to be paroled. The cons are all sitting around in the yard when Red (the character played by Morgan Freeman), philosophizing about Brooks' erratic behavior, says something to this effect: "Funny thing about these walls, at first you hate them, then you get used to them. Enough time passes and you depend on them." For some of the men in this book, perhaps myself included, the same could be said about the walls of bachelorhood. We may be miserable inside those walls, but we have been living there long enough it has become all that we know. And we may not be able to make it on the outside, just like Brooks. We have been unmarried so long we are paralyzed to try something different— even if it is a better way of life. Therefore, we rationalize it by saying we haven't met the right one yet. And the walls get higher.

Childhood Influences

A number of the men were powerfully impacted by early childhood events that had nothing to do with their parents' relationship. Theodore, the fifty-year-old, recently laid-off telecom worker living in Florida, is such a person. As was often the situation, his self-discovery process was at work when I asked why he had never been married. He said, "I grew up in a two-parent family until the time I was twelve, and my father died of lung cancer. My mother was a very successful lady, but she also had a lot of health challenges, including depression, and all that occurred through the time that I was growing up. I had some great relationships, but there's no question that our adult lives are influenced, not by the circumstances of our childhood, as I've learned in some of the personal growth work I've done, but I do believe our belief systems—what we make circumstances mean about us, have a lot of influence on what we do later in life."

"Can you elaborate on that?"

"As a child, my mother was removed from the home for treatments of mental illness and my father died in 1968, the same year Martin Luther King and Bobby Kennedy were assassinated. Different people make things mean different things about them, but in my case I made those events mean about me that men abandon, women abandon and the world isn't a real safe place. If you look at the life that I've designed for myself, forget the fact that I've been unemployed since last June and have some financial issues, I have a paid-off four-bedroom home, I have a paid-off car. Yes, I've had lots of great relationships and lots of great sex, but I would suggest that this has probably had some influence on my overall marital direction."

"You are in a great relationship with great sex. Why not marriage?"

"It goes back to what I was talking to you about. My inability to commit based on my belief systems around women, men and safety. Another thing is that a lot of people in my life that I was close to, that I thought were cool, were single. Do you remember the old show *Route 66*? *Route 66* was about these two cool single guys that tooled all over the country in their Corvette. I always thought that was cool. I thought my uncle, who never married until he was forty was cool. Some of that influenced [me] as well. So, I just never took the additional step. I take full responsibility, but I do value my independence."

"Do you think you have a commitment problem?"

"Some of my relationships certainly would reflect that. I've done multiple relationships, and multiple dating [of] different people at the same time. The other piece in me, and I've gotten this from women who never dated me and some that did, is that I have another mistress: and that's my life. I do martial arts six days a week. I've taken skydiving lessons. So, I have a lot of other things going. In terms of commitment, my last relationship proved to me that I could commit to one woman, but what tends to happen is that I get bored."

"You mentioned your uncle not getting married and you said he had a really cool life. What does a cool life mean to you, because it has obviously affected who you are today?"

"Even though I have a lot of financial challenges in my life, I've been very fortunate. If you looked at where I'm sitting right now, you looked at the way I live, at the things I can do, I have a lot more freedom than somebody that's married with 2.2 kids. I like the freedom I have. The fact is, I have had twelve significant others, and probably well in excess of a hundred flings in my life and I feel that I have a sense of freedom that maybe the average bear doesn't have."

"What is your biggest fear about being married?"

"I believe that there [are] probably unconscious fears that I have around the fact that marriage, for me, would be a death sentence."

"Is that because of what happened to your father?"

"I think that has something to do with it. I looked at my father, and I looked at my mother, and I looked at the fights over money. I made a decision, and it probably was early on, I'm not going to be that. I may be in a relationship, but I'm not going to be that. I've come close a couple times, but I just don't feel motivated to feel the fear and do it anyway with marriage."

Occasionally, events *outside* of family life can have a dramatic impact, such as a first love gone awry, as I learned when I spoke to Aiden. He has not found the right one yet either, but that stems from an early childhood issue—trust—which I uncovered when he told me why he had never been married. "I think the reason I've never been married is because I've never found anybody I can trust enough to get married."

"There is that word trust again."

"I don't want to end up in divorce."

"Where does that heightened sense of wanting trust come from?"

"I guess it goes back to the first girl I ever dated. She was from Texas. She said she got pregnant and my dad, who was a doctor, tried to have her checked out, and she finally just broke down and told me that she was just trying to use me to get married."

"How old were you then?"

"I was nineteen."

"Aha."

"That could be it."

"What would you say is your biggest fear about being married?"

"I don't have any fears about being married. I just want to be able to trust someone."

"It sounds to me that if you found a woman you could trust, you would be open to marrying her."

"I would."

There it is: A single, unresolved issue from an incident over thirty years ago; it can paralyze you at work, in life, in relationships. The random acts of growing up spread their seeds in unwitting and unknowing ways that may not become apparent until years later; in some cases, when it is too late.

Gordon was also significantly impacted by an early relationship. He told me what he thought was the single greatest influence on why he has never gotten married. "I can tell you my two early relationships have really interfered with my thinking and my direction. The first one was devastating to me. I was twenty-three years old and [had] dated her for four years. She disappeared [and married] my brother. So, I felt like I lost a brother and a girlfriend. I thought I was done. I was suicidal at a point because I lost the first thing that was close to me, and at that time you feel like you'll never date another woman. It's just a total loss in life."

"Why did she leave your relationship to marry your brother? You were with her for four years."

"She was impatient about me not committing to her. She just wanted to get out of her parents' house. She just wanted the ring on her finger. She didn't care where it was coming from."

"Why didn't you marry her, if you were with her four years? That's enough time to figure out if she's the right one."

"At twenty-three years old, I said, 'I want to marry you. I look forward to marrying you, but I'm not ready. The time is not right.'"

"What about the other relationship?"

"I think I went seven years before I met another woman. I moved to Florida and fell in love with this woman. But not knowing the strength of what love is, I realize that you don't know what love is until it's gone. When you're young, you're single, you're a bachelor, you don't know what love is until it hits you across the face. The only way I knew I was in love with this girl was because I left her and the pain was so great in my heart, my stomach, my mind, I said, 'What the heck is this?' I leave women all the time, so I knew I had tremendous feelings for this woman. The situation was so bad, I had to leave—she was still married."

"You were in love with a woman who was married?"

"She was married. She was my real estate agent and I was introduced to her by her husband. They didn't live together; they were separated for many years. They lived in separate houses and he had no problem with me dating her."

Whether the causes are well understood or not, many of these men were profoundly affected by what happened to them early in life. Another example of that is Myron, whose early childhood influences were more nebulous and are better understood by the fear they caused than what actually happened. Addressing why he had never married, Myron said, "I was always afraid that the intimacy of marriage would lead to a replication of the kinds of negative emotions I experienced as a teenager and a child in the family."

"What is that fear?"

"Having to experience dealing with the downside of intimacy, which has to do with negative emotional feelings like anger, confrontation, humiliation and jealousy. Now, in a good marriage, they would be controlled, but I found it easier to not feel those things by just not living together."

"Yet, you have lived with somebody."

"I have lived with three different women. One for nine years. That was in my late thirties and early forties. That's a long time and that was sort of like a marriage. But after a few years, we were more like roommates. So, the first two or three years was a romantic relationship and the last six of it was more like friendly roommates."

"And so..."

"It faded away."

"How would you feel if you got to the end of your life and you had never gotten married?"

"That's very likely. As a matter of fact, since I'm fifty-seven, I don't feel like I'm all that far from the end of my life. It doesn't scare me or frighten me, and I don't have any negative feelings about it, [but] I don't expect to get married. What I would like is to experience a relationship during my last years that had the kind of closeness I really want in my life, but haven't had much of."

Shyness and Lacking Confidence

In every relationship, somebody has to be the strong one, the confident one, the provider. In our society today, most men and women think it should be the man, for better or worse. But what if you are a man who has no self-confidence or you believe you cannot be a good provider? One of the things which can happen is that you don't get married. Of all the men I had conversations with, the ones who consider themselves shy or lacking confidence are the ones most resigned to their lot in life as never-married men. I suspect that is the result of a life spent carrying the weight of a self-perceived inadequacy. It saps their strength and they don't have the energy to do anything about it. Gerald, the fifty-two-year-old bus driver from Seattle, fits that mold. He answered with an empathic "No" when I asked him if he had ever been close to marrying anyone.

"Why do you suppose that is?" I inquired.

"Well, a combination of things. A lack of a decent career for one thing, which was a mistake on my part. I just drifted along from one job to another, just hoping something would click. I never really concentrated on any one vocation. I've never been able to offer financial security. That may sound a little cynical towards women. I'm not saying they're all gold-diggers, but nobody likes to be poor. It sucks. So, I don't blame them for that, at least not any more. Also, when I was younger, I was painfully shy and lacked confidence. I think insecurity had a lot to do with it."

"What were you insecure about?"

"It probably has to go back to things that happened to me in childhood: the parents' divorce, indifference, a very cold father. My mother was always well-meaning, but I don't think she really thought of the consequences of her indifference [to me]."

"Do you have any fears about marriage?"

"The only thing I fear about marriage right now would maybe be financial. I'm not able to offer much financially."

"Have you ever met a woman who did not care about your finances?"

"Yeah, but it didn't last. I met women in my younger years. When I think back about it, [they] could have been good prospects in that they were probably interested, but I never made the first move because of lack of confidence. I considered them way above me."

"Did your lack of career contribute to your lack of confidence?"

"I would have to say yes; that was a big factor. I'm a little more fatalistic about it now. Screw them if they don't like it. This is the way I am, this is the way I ended up. Yeah, I made some mistakes, but if you can't deal with it, then fine."

"Do you wish you had that attitude from day one?"

"Yeah."

Given that he lacked confidence from an early age, I wanted to know where Gerald thought he would be at age fifty-two, relationship-wise. He said, "I thought I'd be married. When I was in my twenties, I never really pursued women. I just went about my daily life, and I would date every now and then or go to parties. I thought I'd be married with kids, and the kids grown and maybe even grandkids. But it didn't work out that way."

"Back in your twenties, did you have a plan for that or was it just in the back of your mind?"

"It was just in the back of my mind. I never sat down to plan it. It might have worked out better had I done that. I feel strongly had I really focused on a decent career, getting an education when I was younger, it might have put me in different social circles."

"How would you feel if you got to the end of your life and you never got married?"

"Probably disappointed, but if it doesn't happen, so be it. I'm not going to fret over it. I'm not scared of facing old age alone. Nobody likes being alone. It would be nice to find somebody that I could share my life with. Every now and then I try to make some efforts toward that, but not as much as I used to. I would just resign myself to the fact that it never happened, so just be content with whatever I got around me."

Do you ever wish you could do it over? Have the chance to get it right the second time? Of all the men I spoke with, Gerald's resignation hit me the hardest. Sitting there at fifty-two with unlimited possibilities, he is trapped by a past that was not all it should have been. I wanted to coach him: "Get up! Get going! It's not too late." But I'm no coach. I have as many questions and doubts as he does. Why is it we can see things in others that we cannot see in ourselves?

Ryan, the forty-two-year-old sculpture designer from Wisconsin, also let his early childhood shyness and career decisions impact the rest of his life. I asked him if he hoped to be married someday.

"I don't really know," he responded. "I think about it, [but] I can't actually picture myself being married. So, I guess I would say no. I don't hope to be married."

"*Why?*"

"I have always wanted to be an artist when I was a kid, even in kindergarten, five years old and up. I was more of an introverted person; I was really self-focused. One of the things I rationalized in high school, and this just sort of worked out for me being introverted and shy, was I just wanted to avoid getting involved in anything that would distract me from pursuing my goal. This is my rationalization. I had seen how my friends with girlfriends really changed what they were doing. I didn't want to compromise. I didn't want to have to change my goals, whether that was a good decision or not. It might have really helped me to actually get hooked up with someone and have the support of someone, but I really just made the conscious decision to avoid getting into any relationship. Once that took hold, every year that went by, I just became more and more removed from actually getting into a relationship. In high school, everyone was going through that and learning that. I really wasn't developing those skills and, being shy and introverted, it certainly didn't help me with talking to women. So, as the years went by, it just became more and more difficult, even if I wanted to."

"How would you feel if you got to the end of your life and you had never been married?"

"I'm probably going to feel like I've wasted an opportunity."

"Tell me more about that."

"I had this life to live and I just intentionally diverted myself away from pursuing a relationship and was never really successful at actually getting one. So, I would feel like I missed out on a lot of stuff that I could have experienced."

Destined to Fail

There are men who view the marital commitment as something far too great for them. It overwhelms them, leaving them intimidated and certain they would fail to live up to its enormous demands. Ultimately, they feel they would have to deal with the consequences of that failure. Often, their primary motivation is the desire to avoid hurting anybody else. This hypersensitivity to the downside of marriage is common amongst the men, and I have experienced it, too. You can go back to the landmark book, *Think and Grow Rich* by Napoleon Hill, which points out that what we focus on becomes our reality. For the men who focus primarily on the downside of marriage, that is their reality, and it is the only way they know how to view it. Trent has chosen to focus on what can go wrong in a marriage. "I can't see the purpose of it," he said. "I can't see why that would be a good thing for me, and I just don't think I can give enough into a relationship like that."

"Why do you say you cannot give enough?"

"It's because I think it demands so much, and on a very constant, day-to-day basis. I just don't trust myself. I'm scared if I take on those responsibilities that I'll fail somehow, and then have to live with the consequences of that, and I don't want to do that, thank you very much."

"You don't think the rewards outweigh the risks?"

"Yeah, but the rewards are transitory and the consequences are permanent."

"Why do you think the rewards, like love, are transitory?"

"Because they are. You go skiing or something like that and you're having a great time, and that's transitory, but the whole permanent thing, settling down, taking on kids and education and all that sort of stuff. If you screw up on that, you don't have a second chance."

"What is your biggest fear about being married?"

"Letting people down. Misunderstanding of the consequences of what I do and then finding out that I really screwed up, and you can't go back. I just don't want to hurt anybody and have to live with that for the rest of my life."

"How would you feel if you got to the end of your life and you had never been married?"

"[I] think about that from time to time. You see people with their kids in the stroller walking along, and you go, 'Well, that's wonderful.' But I haven't experienced that. You either participate or you don't. If you don't, well, I can't see why the great importance on marriage. I think having friends when you get old is important. I can see people being really proud of their kids, having those great traditional marriages, but I see the opposite too. I've seen an awful lot of pain there and hurt and suffering. If it works, great; but if it doesn't, it's hell."

"I think what you are saying is that the downside seems a lot further down than the upside."

"I think the downside is permanent; you can't do anything about it. If your kids turn out to be an absolute horror story, what do you do?"

"What do you see as being the biggest downside of getting married and having children?"

"Disappointing them. I think that's the whole thing. My parents were European and we weren't really given that much exposure to what marriage is really about. And then suddenly, you graduate from the university and you've got all these pressures on you, and you have no idea what you're really getting into. And so that's what always really kept me away. You can't study that; you can't learn that. That sort of model that my parents had, it doesn't really exist anymore. I don't see it around me at all anymore."

George has similar ideas about marriages that fail. He said, "I had a lot of friends that I thought were better people to get married than I would be and their marriages fell apart. They say a lot of it is around money or sex or things like that, but I don't know. I analyze things a little too much. I thought, 'Well, why would I have any more success than they would?' I thought I was doomed, destined to have a doomed marriage. I could see that if I did get married, I would've been divorced by now."

"Where does that destined-to-fail come from?"

"Five years ago I had this couple as friends. One day, I hear from her that her husband came home from work, after thirty-one years of marriage, and said he met somebody else. They spent the next two years fighting with lawyers and making each other's life miserable. Now, they're back together again."

"What's your biggest fear about being married?"

"I guess it is the fear of failure; I don't like to fail. Sometimes it's beyond your control. Like everything I do is under my control right now. I don't think it (marriage) would be something I'm controlling."

I recognized a lot of my own thinking in what George said. I too have seen others, who I felt were better suited to marriage, fail to keep it together. I think over-analyzing marriage has played a role for a large number of us who have remained unmarried.

Never Been Ready

There are a couple of men who understand the realities of marriage, but rather than feeling overwhelmed by it, their view is that they simply have not been ready for it. They're open to it, just not yet. I suppose what it comes down to is that some people are simply on different schedules. I admire these men. They have thought through the question of marriage, such as the commitment to monogamy, and the answer came back, *not yet*. A man that falls into this category is fifty-four-year-old Martin. He said, "I think I've never been married because I've never been quite ready, and I've known that I've never been quite ready. So, the times that the opportunity came up and I looked at my life and my situation, I just knew it wasn't the time. There were a couple of reasons for that. One reason, I think, was a sexual issue. It was very difficult for me to imagine myself being monogamous with one person for my entire life. I don't really feel that way now, but I felt that way at the time. The other issue was that I was an only child with several elderly relatives that had no one to take care of them, and it was always understood that if they ever needed somebody to take care of them, that I would be the one to do it."

There were four elderly relatives he was responsible for and they are all dead now.

"I was living in a different city, and I knew I was going to have to move back at some time and take care of them. Then that happened when I was forty-two. So, I was always in limbo. [How] could I devote myself to a family when I knew I had these other expectations?"

"What is your biggest fear about getting married now?"

"Right now, my biggest fear is the whole financial issue of taking care of another person or having a family. I don't know that at my age I would ever have a family, but you could marry into a situation where there were kids, or you could marry someone and you're still responsible for that person and their welfare. My own financial situation has deteriorated somewhat since I went ten years when I didn't work a lot and was pretty much involved as a caregiver."

"How would you feel if you got to the end of your life and you had never been married?"

"I think I would feel a bit disappointed, [like] I missed something important."

James also stated that he was heavily influenced by the intimidating limitations of monogamy. "The reason I haven't been married in the past is because I get into a relationship and get scared—the whole stereotypical thing—that the grass is greener. I get into a relationship and two years later I get bored, lose interest and want to get something else. I guess diligence towards keeping the relationship flourishing diminishes. So, eventually it falls apart and it's not always been 100 percent my fault. There were lots of times [when] there was fault with the other party too, but I can say generally speaking, it was my disinterest over time."

"What do you think is the single greatest influence on why you have not been married up to this point?"

"It's going to sound horrible, but my ability to get laid pretty much whenever I wanted to definitely made me think twice [about] settling down."

"I am sure that has affected a lot of guys."

"It's never been an issue. I've never had a problem going out and picking up women, if that's what I chose to do. So, in the past, not so much recently, but definitely earlier than five years ago, why settle with one, when you can just have the best parts of many?"

James's story was the one I had been waiting for. The playboy-bachelor who "loves 'em and leaves 'em." Why settle for one when you can have a variety? James is still relatively young at forty and it's not surprising he thinks that way, and yet I can begin to see chinks in his armor. From my own experience and observations, men in their early forties tend to view themselves as thirty-something, at least as far as sexual prowess is concerned. They are still young, virile and on the prowl. As we get into our late forties, however, not only does our sex drive start to diminish, but we become more reflective, and that drive for the next conquest suffers from diminishing returns. The need for variety, rather than being a strong motivator, seems laborious, and our old way of thinking begins to dissipate. In essence, the chase gets old. It would be interesting to speak with James again in seven or eight years and ask him the same question.

Mitch is another forty-year-old who thinks like James, but it took awhile to get to his real feelings. I began by asking him what he thought was the single greatest influence on why he had never married. "My father," he replied.

"Explain that."

"I see a lot of how I react to women as how my father reacts. I think he had high standards, but he seemed to always lower them on occasion."

"Do you do that?"

"I think you lower them so that you get what you need versus what you want."

"So, in the back of your mind you know what you want and you know this isn't it, but it's going to serve the purpose right now?"

"That's right."

"What makes you see a girl, she's not the right one, but you go for it anyway? What is it that keeps you from thinking to yourself, 'She's not the right one; I am just going to walk away?'"

"Horniness."

"That is honest."

"I love being a virile man and there is something about the chase that is wonderful."

"Do you have any guilt over that?"

"I do."

"Why?"

"Because I intentionally hurt people that I love."

"In what way?"

"By deserting them. By being non-communicative with them and by hiding my motivations or my feelings. The sad thing is, when it comes to women with children, there's kids involved too. You develop a bond."

Not exactly what you would expect to hear from a guy just trying to get some. Think what you will about the forty-year-old skirt chasers, they are not oblivious. They know what they're doing and they understand it has consequences, and at least as far as integrity of the family is concerned, they have chosen appropriately to remain unmarried.

Not a Priority

There are several men for whom marriage has not been on the radar screen of life's priorities. Quite a few cited their careers and the satisfaction they derive from it as reasons why. Their careers make them feel complete and, therefore, feel there is no void in their life not having a spouse. There are even a few for whom the sexual void is no big deal. Nathan is a man who fits this category, as I discovered when he shared why he had never married. "Truthfully, I probably haven't put the time and effort into it. I've put more time and effort into my job."

"Why is that?"

"I like the work I do, and I like helping others. I think that's where I get my satisfaction in life is helping others. Even the little things that you do sometimes, it's incredible. One of the things I do in my guidance job is I go to almost every sporting event these kids do and [I] take pictures and then post them on the website. That alone—it's just incredible the feedback you get from the kids."

"That has got to give you a great sense of joy."

"It really is incredible."

"So, you get the same sense of fulfillment a parent could get on a daily basis."

"Absolutely. Then I come home and I don't have to deal with it."

"It sounds like your job has been a priority over getting married."

"Correct."

"Why is that?"

"For the first sixteen years when I got out of college, it was all about working at this one residential treatment center with disturbed kids, and we worked between fifty and ninety hours a week, so you really didn't have much time. That's where most of my friends come from. So even when we were out of work, we would hang out at the same places, do the same things."

"When you were working these fifty-to-ninety-hour weeks, did you ever think that you were missing out on an opportunity to meet the woman of your dreams?"

"No."

"Because you had a lot of friends and you were having a lot of fun?"

"Yeah."

"And that set a pattern for the rest of your life, didn't it?"

"Absolutely."

"Did you have any fears about getting married?"

"I don't think so. The only fear is that I would lose my solitude at home."

"You definitely would lose that."

"Yeah, and believe me, it's just so nice to come and go as you please, and you don't have to answer to anybody or anything."

"That independent streak, where does it come from?"

"Being able to be in control. That's important for me."

"Do you have control issues?"

"It's funny because I used to very much want to be in control of everything. Now, I don't really care that much, but I also enjoy the freedom of not having to be in charge of everything."

"So, you want control plus freedom? That is your winning combination?"

"Right."

"How would you describe your sex life as a never-married man over these last thirty or forty years?"

"You know what, it's been mostly taking care of it myself. It really hasn't happened that much and you know what, I don't really care at this point."

"Was there ever a time that you did care?"

"Yeah. I had some sexual relationships and things like that, but it's not a big thing for me."

"Has it always not been a big thing for you?"

"No, not at all."

"How would you feel if you got to the end of your life and you had never gotten married?"

"Doesn't matter to me if I don't have dates to go to weddings and funerals with. You have friends to take with you."

"It sounds like that sense of connection a person would get from marriage you have in your friends."

"Yep."

"What is your feeling on being alone or being lonely? I know you have all these friends, but does that play a role?"

"There are times when you would like to have somebody to go out with. Like I went out to breakfast this morning and it would have been nice if I didn't have to go by myself."

"But in terms of maybe having a special someone in your life, as opposed to just friends, do you ever think about that?"

"You think about it, but [do] you want to give up everything else for that? I don't think so."

Nathan is definitely not the man you think about when you think about fifty-two-year-old confirmed bachelors. He is a man whose life is so full of friends and children, he does not even think about marriage or kids or even sex. He has found true contentment in a never-married life. He enjoys his independence and has not been unhappy or wanting along the way, and he is not unhappy or wanting now. How could any other decision but to remain single have been the right one for him?

Paul, who echoed similar sentiments to Nathan, believes he is here for a reason other than to be a husband and father. He said, "You know how some people grow up and all they think about is, 'Oh, I'm going to be married and have kids?' Even as a small child, I never did picture myself in that light. I never pictured myself as married and having children."

"Why do you think that is?"

"I'm just not sure."

That is as close an answer to the question of why *I* have never been married as I heard in all my conversations: I never pictured myself married. It wasn't that I pictured myself as a bachelor forever, or I had some inherent disdain for marriage. I just never pictured it, the same way I never picture myself as a concert cellist or an international soccer star. It simply was not in my conscious mind. The question, of course, is why not?

Paul continued, "I went to a numerologist one time, and I don't want to go way off the deep end on you here, but I can tell you what the numerologist said."

"I am curious to know because it means something to you."

"Basically, what she said was that I didn't have to come back [this lifetime]. I chose to come back and I chose to come back as a master's chart."

"A master's what?"

"A master's chart, which means I didn't come back for me. I came back to help other people through their lives, not really to live my own life, but to help other people through theirs. I think about that, and that was twenty years ago, and it really does seem true. I meet people that are having problems in their lives, either male or female. I'm a good listener and I try to help them understand themselves. Part of the work I do is [to] go out on the reservation at some tribal hospitals. One day I was walking in with a CFO to a hospital out on the Navajo Reservation and there was this very old woman sitting there at the door in a wheelchair. As I'm walking by, she grabs my hand and she goes, 'An old soul.' I just thought, 'Oh my God—you know.'"

"Would it be fair to say that you get more fulfillment out of helping somebody than being a husband?"

"Probably. I feel like that's really why I was placed here."

"The only thing I cannot resolve is the fact that you love helping people and yet you are turned off by dependent women. It seems to me you would want to help dependent women."

"I know. That's a contradiction and I've thought about that."

"How do you explain it?"

"I guess I don't want someone I'm involved with to be needy, if that makes sense. I know it's kind of a contradiction."

"No it's not. It is the primary love in your life. You want her to be independent so that you can go out and help other people. Would that be fair?"

"Yes, that would be fair."

"What is the biggest fear you have about getting married?"

"I don't really have a fear. I guess I just haven't met the person I feel like I could spend the rest of my life with."

"Would you marry her if you met the right one?"

"I don't know."

"Is that because you do not really see any purpose to marriage without children?"

"I think it's possible. As I'm getting older, I really don't want to grow old by myself. It'd be nice to have somebody to grow old with, whether you're married to them or not."

"So, it is not the formal institution you care about, it's being in a relationship?"

"Right."

"How would you feel if you got to the end of your life and you had never been married?"

"I don't think it would bother me."

"Really? Why not?"

"Like I said, it's because I just feel like that was not really my purpose."

Kyle's feelings are similar to Nathan's and Paul's in that marriage has not been a part of his plan.

"Well it's never been a goal of mine," he said.

"Why not?"

"I've just had other things going on. Life is what happens when you're busy making other plans, right?"

"Where does that come from, the concept of not having a plan?"

"Part of it is just my own individuality."

"Has it been more of a concept of wanting to, but there are other things that are more important? Is it lack of desire? Or has it been more of not thinking about it that much?"

"I just don't think about it. It doesn't enter into the equation for me right now. If there's anything of interest to me, how about we begin with a good healthy relationship. How about I just begin having a girlfriend. How about I begin just on the level of meeting somebody, interacting with somebody in which I feel there can at least be the possibility of just having a girlfriend. It's not like I'm looking at life through this looking glass of marriage. If anything, I'm moving through life with this looking glass of just a healthy relationship, and that could begin as fundamentally as just a healthy friendship with somebody."

"I think that aligns well with your merging of the hearts being as important as the piece of paper."

"Yeah, plus sex is the easiest thing to have, but that's not a relationship, nor is it love."

"How would you feel if you got to the end of your life and you had never been legally married?"

"I could die happy."

"There is no pull for marriage for you, is there?"

"Well, I think that's the whole crux of the issue of marriage. I think maybe I'm just [a] result of this kind of new paradigm of people who have seen marriages come and go. Marriage is not as inevitable as birth and death. It's not this big huge monolithic entity that one has to go through. It's not a sign post of a valid life. I'm not even sure that marriage, outside of a religious function, really serves any real purpose. If you look at the history of marriage, outside of the continuance of a community and their reflections of its laws and its religious implications, I don't know if marriage serves any other purpose."

If I could choose a single message for this book to convey, it would be what Kyle had to say about marriage: It is not as inevitable as birth and death, and it is not a sign post of a valid life. I could not have said it better. It's an empowering belief because it grants us the freedom to choose a less-traveled path and not feel as though we are less because of it. Maybe these men are a new paradigm, at least as far as their thinking toward marriage is concerned. I'm glad Kyle articulated that so well.

Manny has also not made marriage a priority, but unlike Nathan, Paul and Kyle, he is living with a woman. A reason why it has not been a priority for him is because it has not been a priority for her, as he explained when I asked him why he had never married: "I'm very happy with my life."

"That woman you are living with now, how long have you lived with her?"

"Officially for a year."

"Do you have any intention of marrying her?"

"She's been married twice and she says she doesn't want to get married. Do I have any intentions? No. Will it happen? Maybe. If we're still together when we're fifty-five or sixty, it comes a time where we'd probably get married. I don't think it's a priority for either one of us."

"Is one of your attractions to her the fact that she has been married twice and she is not putting any pressure on you?"

"You know, that could be. I don't know the answer for sure, but now that you said that, yes."

"Do you see yourself spending the rest of your life with her, or do you see other women in your future?"

"I don't know the answer. We're pretty comfortable with each other. We certainly have found that we have differences. She suffers from depression to some degree and that's not something that I really understand, and maybe over time that might come between us, but we're very happy together."

"For now you have learned to live with the differences?"

"That's exactly right."

Winston had so many explanations as to why he had never been married it was difficult to discern the real reason. There were strong influences from earlier in life, the inability to find the right one and even a woman who was too young. I think the real reason Winston has never married is because it has not been a priority for him. He said, "In my twenties, I had a dream to get married, have a wife—I wanted a large family [because] I came from a large family. I absolutely love kids. I had a fantastic childhood myself. I'd love to pass it on to children of my own. It just hasn't happened for me."

"What happened to that dream?"

"I think it was shattered by the reality of mature relationships. I fell in love, there was nothing in my sights except for marriage, children, the whole bit, and then I think human nature took over. I was cheated on. I could see that when you fall in love, it's lust, and I think the whole concept of American love is wrong. I look at my parents and I think they influenced me a lot. I wouldn't want the marriage they have. They've spent forty-seven years bickering and I can't stand it. I think it might have played a role in why I'm single today."

"Do you think that was the biggest role?"

"No. It played a part, don't get me wrong, but the biggest role was the reality slap of human nature when I reached my late twenties and early thirties."

"Was there one event or person, or was it an accumulation of things?"

"Just an accumulation of things. I looked around, I saw my friends getting married, immediately getting divorced. I looked at marriages that weren't happy, so I chose to establish myself economically before I took on a wife."

"Let's do a real quick synopsis. Why do you think you have never been married?"

"I'm anal retentive."

"How does that relate to not being married?"

"I feel a man's role is to go out and make money, and that's a lot of what I've been focused on. I did it through my twenties and may have been too focused on that. I just never found a girl that I felt I could last fifty, sixty years with. That's really a huge part of it. I always thought, hey, I can retire; I can travel the world and meet women. I think there's a lot of sexual conquering that goes on in men."

"Is that important to you?"

"Yes, it is. But that's not to say that one woman couldn't recognize that and fulfill that role."

"Do you feel like you have done enough sexual conquering, or do you feel like there is still some more that needs to be done?"

"If I found the right woman, there doesn't need to be anymore. But you know, yes, there's a little more that needs to be done."

"What is your biggest fear about being married?"

"In a marriage, if it's going to break up, I feel the woman's got the total upper hand. Half of whatever you've earned is going to go [to her]. You've got no control over that other party. So, I'm thrilled about prenuptial contracts, and at this point I'm not afraid of marriage because I would go into a pre-nup."

"Do you think you have a commitment problem?"

"Yeah, I do. I definitely have a fear of commitment."

"How would you feel if you got to the end of your life and you had never gotten married?"

"I've got no problem with that."

Haven't Found the Right One

Of course, there are those men who feel the reason they have not gotten married is because they haven't met the right one. Randy is amongst the men who fall into this category. "Just haven't found the right one," he stated. "Early on, I think I probably could have settled and stayed with somebody, that woman with the great family. I think we could probably still be married, but as you get older and you meet more different types of women, I certainly am not going to settle for anybody."

"In your mind, what constitutes settling?"

"Just marrying somebody that I didn't think was nearly a perfect fit. Nobody's absolutely perfect, but I think there are enough women out there. Like when you fill out the survey on some of these websites: what's the deal breaker? There's enough (women) with the things you do want, that meet the criteria. I'm not willing to settle for less than that."

"What's your biggest fear about getting married?"

"I never said I was afraid of it; I just happen to not be married."

"So, you have no fears?"

"No."

"As long as you pick the right person."

"Yeah."

"Anything else?"

"My parents had a torn relationship. There's five [siblings] in my family, four boys and one girl, and all [of us] are single. I think, more than anything for us, it was just our upbringing. My father had a nasty, nasty temper and he took it out on the boys. Growing up it was nearly intolerable, and we could never understand why my mother put up with it. I think it was probably the most deep-rooted reason that we're all single."

"How would you feel if you got to the end of your life and you had never gotten married?"

"I'd feel pretty fulfilled; I had a pretty good life. I think it'd be different if [I] never dated, and was just a loner, but I don't feel that way."

Dylan also insists he has not met the right one. At first, it seemed as though he simply has not been ready, preferring to concentrate on career achievement, but as I dug deeper, it was apparent he told a similar story. He said, "I hate to use that as a crutch, but I work a lot and the hotel business is great. I work with great people, I meet great people, but it's been [my] downfall. I've dedicated my life and my work to moving up the corporate ladder and neglected my social life. I've had time for friends and family, but I haven't traveled much and I haven't dated much. Maybe I'm trying to secure my future because I don't want to work until I'm sixty-five or seventy. I look at my dad, he's retired at fifty-one. I don't want to work all my life. I want to work hard now while I'm single. If I found the right one, I'd cut back a little bit, but right now I'm just working and having fun."

"Would if be fair to say you would not get married until you felt great about where you were career-wise?"

"I would do it, I think, if I met the right woman."

"Do you have any fears about getting married?"

"No, there's no fears. On my part, it's just meeting the right one who has a college degree. I'm trying to find the one to put all four, five components together. It seems easy, but it's difficult."

"It is difficult."

"To find a woman who's twenty-eight to forty-five, who can have kids, who is educated, who maybe her parents are still together, that would be nice. Every woman I meet, her parents are divorced. I come from a good, solid family. It would be nice to meet somebody where I could go over and have dinner with Mom and Dad."

"Would that keep you from marrying a woman if you could check all the boxes, but her parents were divorced?"

"That would make a difference. I met a guy at work, and he said he's going to get married, and the parents were divorced, and her three sisters were divorced, and I looked at him and said, 'Good luck, buddy.' There's a pattern, you know."

"Exactly."

"My brother's been married twelve years, and my little brother's been married two years. The men in our family usually get married, and I don't know why I haven't."

"How would you feel if you got to the end of your life and you had never been married?"

"Don't want to think that. I saw a survey that says if you are divorced, you're normal; if you've never been married, you're abnormal."

"We are abnormal. There is no doubt about it."

"Women look at a guy who's (never married) in his forties and their first question is why. It doesn't bother me. I tell women if they want to ask. Once they hear my life story, they realize, 'Oh, okay.' There's nothing to hide. I'm pretty open."

"I think it would be fair to say you really would like to get married to the right woman."

"Yeah. I'm not a millionaire; I don't make $100,000. I'm just a solid, normal, honest guy who comes from this family who's looking for just the same."

Sandy also understands the impact of the shopping list on finding the right one. What is intriguing about Sandy is that he is open to evaluating the shopping list, and maybe even modifying the list as he evolves. He said, "In the beginning, my standards were shallow, definitely with regards to the physicality of the woman, and way too narrowly focused in terms of their intellectual pursuits and demeanor, and I got into   relationships that were not good. I learned and I grew myself, and I became way more flexible with regards to the qualitative things, education, background, IQ, all that. I became more flexible about that which broadened the field, but at the same time, I really started raising my   standards on things such as spiritual maturity and emotional maturity."

"Do you recall what age that kicked in, starting to shift your standards?"

"I'd say seven or eight years ago." (He was thirty-five then.)

"What would you say is the single greatest influence on why you have never gotten married?"

"The single greatest thing is a realization that the dynamics had to be right, and if they weren't right, I was going to be miserable and I don't want to be miserable. So, I'm not going to commit to being married and then expect the relationship to have favorable dynamics."

"Obviously, you have not found the right dynamics yet."

"Not exactly, no."

"What is your biggest fear about being married?"

"I don't have one."

"Do you think you have a commitment problem?"

"No, I don't have a commitment problem."

"How would you feel if you got to the end of your life and you'd never been married?"

"I guess I'd be okay with it. I'm not going to measure my success by getting married. I got an intuitive feeling that it's not going to go that way."

"So, you will get married some day?"

"Yeah."

Wanted To, But It Didn't Work Out

Then there is the collection of men who wanted to be married, really wanted it, but for whatever reason, it has not happened. Perhaps no different than an actor working hard at their craft who has yet to be discovered, you can have good intentions, work hard and desire a specific result. However, luck, timing and even serendipity all play a role in this thing we call life, especially when it comes to affairs of the heart. Sometimes we are in the right place at the wrong time, or we meet the right one at the wrong time, as happened to Perry. He said, "I do realize there's different kinds of love. Like one girl I dated was eleven years older than I was, and I did love her, but as soon as I found out how old she was, when she finally told me, I knew that could never be."

"*Why is that?*"

"She had done everything that I wanted to do. She was done running around, done partying, she already had a child who was in his teens, and she was done. I wanted to go and do, run around all night and dance and party, and she's like, I did all that. She did all that while I was in grade school. On that level we just didn't connect, but she was a good person, and had good heart, and I was really ready to settle down."

"*Why didn't you get married at that time?*"

"[Another] girl I dated, she was looking for a guy to have a kid with, but her plan was like these other two girls she knew. They wanted kids, they didn't want husbands. They just wanted some guy to get them pregnant and then pay them child support [so] they could run around and party on the money. Then another girl that I dated for a long time was completely in love with me, but it was that kind of high school infatuation love that I knew in a few years probably wouldn't be real. I didn't feel the same for her. I loved her, but I didn't love her the way you would if you got married."

"*What is your biggest fear about getting married?*"

"It wasn't a fear of being married, it's knowing whether you really love the person or not. If you know you really love them, then there is nothing holding you back. I did ask one girl to marry me, but she turned me down. Basically, it is a logistics problem. She didn't want to move to St. Louis and I didn't want to move to [her]. She had a career and I had my job, and the long distance relationship fizzled out after two years."

"Would it be fair to say that you wanted to be married and just kept missing opportunities?"

"Yeah, that would be very fair to say. That's exactly what it is."

"How would you feel if you got to the end of your life and you had never gotten married?"

"I'd think, 'How come I'm not married?' I've been in every position there is in the wedding [party] except the groom. I'm actually angry in a way now that I realize what I should have done, and where I should be. I'm not anywhere near there. I should have a rock-solid, steady marriage that has a lot of history behind it. You have that kind of relationship where you don't even think about it, because you're so used to being together and you totally trust them, and I should have that. I should have a lot of history to look back on with somebody right now and I don't."

"A lot of guys are afraid of marriage and you're not. You wanted it. You wanted that picture and it just hasn't worked out yet."

"Yeah, pretty much."

Life's not fair. Perry should not even be in this book. I could hear it in his voice. He wanted to be a husband for a long time and it simply has not worked out that way. The good news is, Perry is only forty-two and there is a lot of game left before the clock runs out.

I was pretty sure I already knew the answer, but I had to ask Samuel, who had only ever had one-month relationships, why he had never been married. He said, "There's a number of reasons. One is it takes two to tango, and if you don't find somebody who's interested, it's tough to get married."

"Have you ever found anybody you were interested in and they didn't return that?"

"I've found several people that I was very interested in and would have liked to have pursued a long-term relationship with. Whether it would have resulted in being married, I don't know, but you can't figure that out in one month."

"What is your feeling on being alone?"

"It's a double-edge sword. On the one hand, it doesn't bother me because I'm very used to it. I'm also involved with a lot of different groups and I know a lot of people. I always have to laugh and say, what would I do if I caught a woman or she caught me? I'm not sure I would know what to do because I'm good at entertaining myself. I'm good at finding ways to fill the time."

"How would you feel if you got to the end of your life and you had never been married?"

"I think in some ways I might view it as a lost opportunity, but in other ways I'd have to say, it was really sad that it never happened. But it takes two to tango, and though it would be sad from my end, I would say it's sad from the other side that nobody took the time and effort to think I was worthy of them."

CHAPTER 7

Lessons Learned

If being never married *is* the final destination for some men, the journey should have taught them something about women, about relationships or about themselves. In particular, I wanted to uncover which lesson, of all the lessons learned from past relationships, did they feel was most important. I wanted to know which nugget of wisdom they believe is most useful to them as they continue on their journey, regardless of their desire to marry or not. I was also hoping they would play amateur psychologists and see if they could discern any patterns or behaviors in their past relationships that repeated themselves. And I wanted to know not only *what* they learned, but how long it took, and if it was something they learned at an early age and carried with them through life or a more recent discovery. For many people, including myself, extracting life lessons from previous relationships is one way of dealing with situations we either did not understand or found untenable. I was counting on at least some of the men to have done this: examining their life and carving out their accumulated relationship wisdom. They did not disappoint me.

There were a handful of lessons learned that were mentioned frequently: the importance of good communication, the impact of sexual behavior and the difficulty in making any relationship successful. Most men I spoke with were introspective, honest and objective, especially as it related to their own complicity in those lessons. What is not clear, however, is if there is any correlation between the lessons learned and an increased chance of them marrying in the future. Only time will tell.

Lessons Learned About Relationships

The men have learned important lessons about how to act in a relationship and, in particular, how to communicate effectively. I was not surprised to hear that. By the time they hit their forties, most men at least recognize the importance of proper communication in a good relationship (even if they have not mastered it). Beyond that though, this group also discovered that *when* you begin to communicate openly and honestly is also extremely important, and I agree with them. In my experience, effective communication is either established early on in a relationship— from date one—and an environment is created in which the two people can discuss anything, or somehow it never seems to take hold at all. When two people are not completely honest right away, they set a precedent for themselves that lingers, making it okay to be less than truthful with each other. There are, however, two ways to be dishonest in a relationship: there are acts of commission (outright lies) and omission (secret thoughts we keep to ourselves). I think men are more often guilty of the latter. Our attitude is, ask us any question and we will tell you the truth. But is that enough? What about the questions that are never asked or are not asked soon enough? What about the information we keep to ourselves, such as I don't want to have children or I don't see this relationship going anywhere? What responsibility do we have to volunteer certain information? But when should the man volunteer information in a relationship? Is date one too soon? Is six months too late? Of course, there is no one right answer, and it depends on the people and the circumstances. Nevertheless, as we hit our forties and beyond, in line with women's inherent desire, we do accelerate the volunteering of critical information in our relationships. After all, women are not the only ones who have a ticking clock. In addition to being the right thing to do, being honest up front just seems to cause less strife in the long run.

Danny, who has had only a few serious love relationships, talked about the importance of communicating when I asked him what he thought was the most important thing he learned from his past relationships. "Keep your heart in control. I bought *Men are from Mars, Women are from Venus* and I bought this other one, *Smart Dating*. I figured I at least want to find out what makes women tick."

"What else have you learned in addition to keeping your heart in control?"

"To listen, because that's women's biggest complaint about men. And not trying to solve their problems or give them a solution, but to just agree with them and validate their feelings and empathize with them. I have to remember that because I'm really solution oriented and women don't want a solution, I guess."

"I struggle with that, too."

With observations similar to Danny's, Gabriel spoke about the importance of communication, and he added his own unique perspective on why it is difficult to do. "Talk about anything, even trivial things, because what usually happens is if you don't talk about the   trivial things, you're more hesitant to talk about the more serious things. Things can become a big issue when they shouldn't have been a big issue in the first place."

"What do you think makes it so difficult to talk to women?"

"I think we're not trained to do so. I think a lot of times, especially in our early twenties, guys tend to hang out more with guys and guys don't usually deal with emotional stuff. My impression from women—including my sisters—is they talk about this stuff all the time, and I think there's a big disconnect between men and women, in that women talk about this among themselves. My dad was in the military and I was raised that part of being a man is that you don't cry. If you're upset, you just deal with it."

"What do you think is the biggest hurdle to communicating in a relationship?"

"The brooding non-communication, and usually women tend to do this more than men. I think something will set them off and they don't want to tell you what it is; they want you to discover what it is. Of course, men being kind of literal in a lot of ways, we don't necessarily get all the subtleties. So, they think, oh, I'm leaving fifteen clues, and the guy thinks why the hell is she being so moody? What the hell is wrong with her? He doesn't have a clue as to why she's pissed off, and women can drag this out for days, sometimes even weeks."

"Have you learned anything else besides proper communication?"

"I was feeling really guilty when I was thinking about breaking up with my last girlfriend. In the last year of the relationship, we started to talk about the possibility of getting married. We were talking about the possibility of having at least one or maybe two kids and, in breaking up with her, I kept thinking, I'm sure she's going to think that I'm her last chance of having kids, because she's thirty-eight. When we were breaking up, originally she didn't believe me and I made a huge mistake: I thought we could be friends. I guess because I was the one breaking up and she's a good friend. I'd like to at least see her again. We can chat and go out to dinner, but I didn't realize from her perspective, she's still in love with me, still wants to be with me and it's just pure torture for her to be around me if I'm thinking we're just friends. It took me a couple of months to realize, 'My God, what am I doing to her?'"

"Can you add anything to that?"

"One of the things she said to me was, 'You were my last chance to have a child, and if you break up with me, that means I will never have a child and it's your fault.' I was feeling so bloody guilty about that at the time, but then I thought afterwards, if she wanted a child—if a child was so important—we would have had it earlier on or else we would have broken up and she would have found the guy that she wanted to have the child with. In thinking back, I think for her it was just a means of trying to keep me in the relationship. That essentially she could guilt me into staying."

In addition to the importance of being a good communicator, Gabriel also learned the realities of trying to remain friends after the relationship ends. It is inevitable that relationships end. But as we get older, it becomes harder to just "throw it away." We want to keep it— or at least a little piece of it—because we still care for the person and because keeping them in our life, even in some small way, makes the relationship seem more purposeful. We get to take something away from it: a friendship. In my observation, when a relationship ends by mutual agreement, where both parties agree that ending the relationship in its current form is for the best, staying friends is possible. Conversely, when one of the two parties "breaks up" with the other, as Gabriel did, the likelihood of remaining friends is severely diminished. That might be the most important lesson Gabriel learned.

Like Gabriel and Danny, Donald also learned the importance of good communication early in a relationship, but he also learned a lesson from his sexual behavior. A noteworthy confession from some of the men is their acknowledging that basing a relationship purely on sex, or having sex too soon in a relationship, ruins its chances for success. Donald eventually got around to admitting this. "I think if you have great communication early on in a relationship, you're going to find out a lot more about the person and it'll lead you in the direction you want to go. A lot of times the excitement of dating someone new and the sex is great, but you haven't really communicated and really don't know the person deep inside. I try now to get to know them early on in the first five or ten dates and figure out if it sounds like we can coexist together."

"How do you do that?"

"I think you've got to experience some things. You can talk about a lot of things, but it's how people react under certain situations."

"How would you describe your life right now relationship-wise?"

"I would say [there is] confusion as far as relationships go; other than that, I'm happy. I've just gotten out of a relationship, so maybe I'm just a little down on that aspect of it. I'm leery of starting to date women just because I know you tend to jump into relationships after you get out of one, and I think I just have to cool it for awhile. But [I am] just a little confused in what I want to do in my next step as far as a woman goes."

"Why do you think you are confused?"

"Because I'm getting tired of the same thing, of dating a woman for two or three months, and it not working out and starting over again. The starting over again takes a lot of work, to figure out if that's the one. It's just an investment of your time and, unfortunately, to find that out, you've got to date a few women, and I'm not really into going out with three or four women a week. I'm just not into that, so I'm just gathering my thoughts and figuring out more of a concrete plan of attack after all these years."

"Looking back on your past relationships, do you see any patterns in either your feelings or the way you behaved?"

"Yeah. I think sexually that it's always great at first for maybe a month or two, and as time goes on, it's not quite as exciting. I'm seeing more and more that if you're basing your relationship on sex, it's never going to work because that's not going to be as exciting as it was initially. I'm in the process of trying to just find something else you like about her more than sex and her looks, that's going to be long lasting."

"Why do you experience a cooling-off period after a month or so?"

"Well, I think it's human nature. I don't [know] too many people who are as sexually happy ten or fifteen years down the road, [as they are] after the first two or three years."

Gerald also learned a lesson about sex when he observed a pattern in his behavior from a previous relationship. "Sex early on in the relationship probably destroyed it," he stated.

"Why do you say that?"

"There's a lot of physical passion at first, and when the steam ran out, there was nothing else there. So, I kept that in mind. Next time around, I would try to take it a lot slower."

"What is the most important thing you learned from your past relationships?"

"Take a cold shower before I get too hot and bothered about anybody. Probably be a little more aware of the warning signs. My last girlfriend, going on a couple of years now, wasn't entirely honest with me about what was going on in her life. She was crying poverty to me for six months and I believed her. So, I was springing for meals and groceries and stuff like that. [Then] she let it slip that she made $90,000 the previous year. I said, 'You're making $90,000 a year and I'm paying for everything—forget it!' I just walked away from it."

Take it slow. Get to know her. Don't rush into sex. These are good lessons to learn at any age. Why does it take some of us into our forties and fifties to learn them? The only thing that comes to mind is the last scene from the *Wizard of Oz* where the Wizard tells Dorothy she had the power to go home the entire time. Why didn't he tell her sooner? Because she wouldn't have listened. She had to experience the drama along the Yellow Brick Road to open her mind and prepare her for the journey home, and so did Gabriel.

The Most Important Relationship Lesson

There is one lesson above all others that these men have learned about relationships: it is difficult to make them work. Martin fits into this category. He said, "Relationships are very difficult, and I'm surprised anybody gets married at all because, in my experience, they've been very difficult, and the people that I've had relationships with have had a lot of issues and baggage that made things very difficult. I had my own issues too, and it just seems like it's an insurmountable thing to overcome all that."

"How would you describe your life right now?"

"I would say, right now, I'm pretty lonely."

"Do you have any plans to do something about that?"

"I'm a little bit relationship-shy right now because I've had a couple of fairly recent relationships with women that have ended pretty badly."

"What caused them to end so badly?"

"I chose poorly or tried to push someone into something they weren't ready for."

"Do you see that as a common theme?"

"The women I got involved with were quite a bit younger than me, and maybe they weren't looking for marriage and they had some issues with trust."

Manny also sees relationships as difficult to pull off. In that regard, he is introspective and open to evaluating his past relationship decisions. For him, the lesson came by watching and observing others, which enabled him to see the patterns in himself. He said, "We're always very happy at the beginning. I guess that's a pattern."

"Then what happens?"

"I get annoyed with the person. Not necessarily bored, but those certain antics that the person has, whatever it is they do. Over time I'll just say, you know, I'm happier alone than I am putting up with this crap."

"These would typically be things you would not care about up front?"

"That's right. You probably like [it] at the beginning. I look at the situation and say I'm happier single, or there's somebody better, and I make the decision to move on, not that I've always been the one to make that decision."

"Have you ever stayed in a relationship too long?"

"Absolutely."

"Why did you do it?"

"Fear of hurting the person. So, even though I know it's imminent, sometimes I'll let it string along."

"What do you think is the most important thing you learned from your past relationships?"

"I'm getting better at putting up with these annoyances. That I'm really becoming more—what's the word?"

"Tolerant?"

"Tolerant—exactly."

"Why do you think that is?"

"I look at it and say, what is wrong with me? Maybe I should be more tolerant because obviously men that get married for thirty years, they're obviously more tolerant. So, why can't I learn from that and make myself more tolerant? And I really am. I'm not just putting up with tolerance more, I really am becoming more tolerant."

"What is causing you to become more tolerant?"

"I think learning from other people. In knowing that other people are more tolerant, I should try to be tolerant. To work at it over time. And I think, by default, if you work at something, it happens."

"So, in your case it is just a matter of working at it?"

"Probably so, yeah. I don't think getting older has anything to do with it because, you know, I'm happy being single."

There is a great deal of insight us never-married men can garner from others. At times we feel overwhelmed at the idea of trying to make a relationship work, because we think they are too difficult. But others make them work, and we can use them as role models from which to learn. If you want to be a concert pianist—which may be more difficult than making a marriage work—you would begin by taking lessons from someone who is already successful at it. Why can't we do that with relationships? Any difficult undertaking seems much less daunting if you are watching someone do it successfully right in front of your eyes.

Jason has experienced relationship difficulties too and he also assumes a good deal of the responsibility for that. He told me of a pattern of behavior he saw running through his past relationships.

"Maybe I fall out of love," he confessed.

As he said that, I could not help but think the reason he gave is the same reason many marriages do not last.

"What causes that?" I followed.

"The person emotionally drains you and emotionally turns you off, [is] upset with you, never happy with you. I did go through some therapy several years ago and it made me realize that I can't be with people who are going to turn my life in a negative way, so [that] I'm going to be unhappy. I want to be happy. I want the person I'm going to be with to be happy."

"You said you have fallen out of love. Has the other person in the relationship ever fallen out of love with you?"

"No. It's always been me."

"Have you ever stayed in a relationship too long?"

"Yes."

"Why?"

"I think when you're in a relationship with somebody you become used to that person no matter how good or difficult the relationship is. It reaches a point of no return where if it's not going any place, I've tended to stay with it because I've always feared the fact, well, geez, I'm out there on my own again and I have to find somebody else and I know the difficulty of finding somebody. So, that's been the issue."

For whom hasn't that been an issue? At its core, it is an economics decision—only with emotion as the currency rather than greenbacks. The cost of staying in an unsatisfying relationship versus the cost of finding someone new. I don't think this conundrum is unique to never-married people. I think this happens to everyone, married and otherwise, only with marriage, the cost of looking for someone new is higher—especially financially. And that may go a long way in explaining why some of us have never married.

Myron also mentioned the challenges of making a relationship work as a lesson he learned and, like Jason, he is accountable for his own contribution to that. He shared patterns in his past behavior with me.

"It's very obvious that when I meet somebody I like, I enjoy getting close to them and sharing feelings, communicating thoughts, feelings, ideas," he explained. "As time goes by, the pattern that repeats is my reluctance or my fear or concern about going to the next level, where I anticipate negative feelings. So, I pull back, and some women don't like that and will leave at that point. You can go on that way indefinitely."

"You talk about anticipating negative feelings. Has your experience been, in longer relationships, where eventually you do get to those negative feelings?"

"In all of them, but if I'm not living with someone, I could always go home to my own apartment and they go away faster. I seem to be able to deal with them better if I have time away. If I was married, it'd probably be good for me to take two days a week and go somewhere else. Have a vacation every fourth day."

"That sounds nice."

"The pattern is that sometimes I will start to pull away a little bit and a lot of women want to move forward, and they want to live together and get married. There have been a number of women I've met that have broken things off because I didn't want to get married. So, that's the pattern that has repeated itself. I'm aware of it and even laugh and say, 'Oh, here we go with the nonsense again.' I see it, actually, while it's happening."

"Have you ever stayed in a relationship too long?"

"Yeah. Probably the current one because we're not really sharing as much as we should be. We don't fight much, but it's a little flat and dull. It might be because I don't want to go forward."

"Why are you staying in the relationship?"

"I think because it's like a comfortable old shoe. You see each other and you trust each other enough to get along. Also, my expectations for romance and excitement have declined as I've gotten older. I care about that less than in my twenties and thirties. Sex was always a great motivation, but as the sex drive declines a little, and the women in my age group are not as attractive as when we were in our twenties and thirties, sexual motivation is somewhat less. That's part of it."

"What is the most important thing you learned from all your past relationships?"

"That other people deal with anger and confrontation better than I do. I don't like conflict. I don't like criticism and that probably plays a big role in why I've avoided [marriage]. But I haven't learned anything practical from it; I'm telling you theoretical things. What I've actually learned is probably nothing, because I haven't changed my behavior that much."

"Has sex played a role in your not marrying?"

"I think that it did play a role in not being married when I was younger, because I felt that if I was married, especially in my twenties, that I would be unable to have different sexual experiences, and I needed that to stroke my ego."

"How about since your twenties?"

"It seems to be less so. I remember one weekend when I was about thirty-four, because it was like an epiphany. That weekend I went out with three women, which I thought was ridiculous, and by the end of the weekend I thought, this isn't even fun. That's when I realized I no longer cared about undressing new women. When I was twenty-five that would have been a very big feather in my cap, but at thirty-four I thought that was silly. The idea of chasing women just for sex lost a lot of its appeal during the preceding few years. Since then, sexual activity has not played a big role in getting married."

Lessons Learned About Ourselves

For some men, their most important lessons learned were about relationships. For others, they used those relationships to open a window into themselves so they could peer in and see themselves better.

In this way, their past relationships were simply a part of the growth process, getting them ready for who they were meant to be. The most encouraging part for me was the acceptance these men displayed. They have learned who they are and, maybe more importantly, they accept themselves for the way they are. One man who increased his understanding of himself through past relationships is Evan. As he shared when we talked about what lessons he had learned, he said, "You have to contrast my younger self with what I am now at forty years old. Things are very different. When I was young, I would get jealous easily and I think that sometimes interfered with my relationships—and maybe even led to the destruction of them. Now I'm more sure of myself and have accepted myself as an introverted person who spends a lot of time alone. The pattern sometimes develops where I don't share enough affection with the person and that causes conflict. If that conflict can be resolved in an appropriate way, then I try to stay in the relationship with them."

"Good for you."

"Yeah, relationships are a lot of work and if I find someone who is not willing to put that work in, then I would just as soon move on and go back to my own life or move onto somebody else."

Another person who learned about himself through relationships is Ryan. Even with his limited experience in relationships, Ryan mentioned that he saw some patterns in his behavior that led him to understanding and self-acceptance. "Well, I'm definitely not the aggressor, and again that's why things [never] really worked out, always being introverted and growing up kind of shy in high school."

"Do you ever wish you weren't shy?"

"Oh yeah. I think it would have been a lot easier in all situations."

"Did you ever try doing anything about it?"

"I realized it was something that was holding me back, especially in college and in my twenties. I was aware that it wasn't helping me, being shy. Specifically, did I do anything about it? I tried going to group counseling or a therapist for a few sessions to talk about it, and the suggestions were valid. Suggestions on what I should work on to improve if I wanted to change the way I was. I made some effort to improve that, but I didn't really see a lot of success. I didn't enjoy it. I didn't enjoy having to make those efforts. Thinking back, if anything, it just made me more embarrassed."

"Do you have any insight as to where that shyness comes from?"

"When I was thirteen, my family moved from the city out to the suburbs at the end of seventh grade. I guess going to this new school, and seemingly everyone who was there had known each other since kindergarten, I was just automatically a loner. Starting out in middle school, those might have been some formative years. So, I think that could be the cause of it."

Dwayne, like Ryan, learned that something from his past was holding him back and keeping him from the relationship he wants, and he, too, sought help to address it. "The heart is a very tender aspect of human nature and may very well be the most important aspect," he stated.

"Can you add anything to that?"

"I guess I really haven't resolved the pain and the grief in some important aspects. I'm very protective of my heart."

"Do you have any desire to work on that pain and grief issue?"

"I have been working on it in various ways. I've done it professionally over the years, and now I'm doing some interceptive work. I'm writing and I'm also looking at the kinds of deep connections I've made, the patterns. I don't know if you're familiar with Carl Jung."

"Sure."

"And trying to understand some of what's going on in terms of his approach to psychology of relationships. I'm also looking at the whole notion of past lives and reincarnation. That some of these profound heartbreaks that I've had, whether in real life or online, could very well have links to past lives."

Whether it is from shyness, as Ryan experienced, or the early pain and grief that Dwayne went through, these men have acknowledged things about themselves they know are holding them back. I admire them for having the courage to see it and to try doing something about it. There is only one question: will anything change going forward or is this how the story ends for them? I'm pulling for them.

Winston actually recognized two patterns in his behavior that contributed to his never marrying. And while he has acknowledged these about himself, it is not clear if he is going to use these understandings to change anything. He said, "I go for trashier women.

I set myself up to fail without a doubt."

"How do you do that?"

"I could go find a girl that's just looking to get married and have kids, but I go for the women that aren't looking to settle down. I go for a wilder woman that I know ain't going to last. I'm going to have some fun with them and I'm going to move on."

"Has that worked for you in the past?"

"I enjoy moving on. I like women for a month, six months, maybe a year, and by going for a woman like that, there's a built-in reason to leave."

"Anything else?"

"I know that I sabotage the relationships by choosing a woman that I can leave and not feel bad about."

"Why do you sabotage it?"

"I don't want to settle down. Believe me, if the woman of my dreams came along, I would go for it. But she hasn't, and I'm not going to settle for less. I'm not going to settle for what's out there, and really what I'm looking for isn't there. The ideal woman that looks good, takes care of herself and doesn't let herself go, just has not come along, or she's out of my grasp. I'm a realist; I'm not going to get Christie Brinkley."

If my theory that you cannot find the right person until you become the right person is correct, maybe Winston has not found the right one because he is not willing to change. I continued by asking him what he thought was the most important thing he learned from past relationships. He responded, "I guess I haven't taken the time to really think about that or to examine it. What comes to mind is I think of women as almost disposable in the relationship. I try not to get involved with their feelings, to be honest."

"How would you describe your sex life as a never-married man?"

"Probably better than most."

"Did you ever leave a relationship too soon because the sex wasn't good?"

"I put a lot of value on a woman's sexuality and I have absolutely dumped women who just were lousy lovers, and never gave them a second chance, never gave them a second thought."

"So, you have this certain level of sexual satisfaction you demand from a relationship and it is not always met. What role has that played in your never being

married?"

"I don't think it's played a big role because I've met women that have satisfied me and I haven't stayed with them either, and I could have."

I do not think Winston is a bad guy, and I admire him for his brutal honesty with me (and himself). He shared ideas with me a lot of married and unmarried men think, but would never admit, at least not out loud. He is clearly not the only man to let sexual desire influence his behavior, and it *did* contribute to him learning about himself. But perhaps with Winston, there is something larger at work here: restlessness, which I am of the opinion that each one of us has a certain amount of. If we have an IQ, then why not an RQ (Restlessness Quotient)? Restlessness tends to manifest itself as continual dissatisfaction, always wanting to try something new. And whether it is their career, physical appearance or relationship, we all know someone who is restless. Some people have only a little restlessness and are generally content, while others, like Winston, have it in abundance. I have met men whose ideal woman is the *next* woman. If restlessness is the explanation for Winston's behavior, I suppose the best thing is at least he did not lie to himself (or a woman) by getting married.

Another man who learned about himself through his sexual experiences is Kyle. One of his lessons learned stemmed from a change in his sexual behavior, as I discovered when he told me about his sex life as a never-married man. "Having not been married, I think my sex life compared to married people is probably damn good."

"Please elaborate."

"The last major relationship, which was probably the most difficult emotionally for me, ended in 1999. I haven't been in a relationship since. I've hung out with women, but in terms of really making myself vulnerable and being open to the intensity and seriousness that my last relationship had, I haven't really been in a relationship. This last relationship affected me on a very subconscious level. I know last year about this time I was dating a person I'd known for twenty years. She's been in and out of my life as a friend. We used to work together and I guess it just finally came our time. It was like, 'Okay, let's give it a go, let's see what happens.' Immediately, I think within a month, I broke up with her because there's just a level of bullshit that I have absolutely no tolerance for whatsoever, and I'm not willing to negotiate. So, in terms of sex, I've had the casual sex thing, but if I'm going to put that much energy relating to somebody, I want there to be a return that is more significant than just physical. I want any sex that I experience now to be an indication of love. I've actually reached a point now where I don't have much of a sex drive anymore, and I don't know if that's because I've been basically living in abstinence for a while or I just haven't focused on that aspect. It's just not been a thing that has been that strong for me in terms of an impulse. Frankly, I've just been working, living my life, spending time with friends and pursuing my own personal interests."

Kyle's words resonated with me. His sentiments are the first sign of resignation from a man over forty: resigned to middle age, resigned to a diminished sex drive and ultimately admitting to himself that he wants more than just sex—that he really is ready for love. I understand exactly what he meant. Hearing him say that made me believe those feelings are not feelings of weakness, but of strength. Strength to be comfortable with who we are and to stop trying to be who we were, holding on to feelings and behaviors that may no longer work for us. His conversation made me even more interested in the changing role of sex as we grow older and what we can learn about ourselves from that change.

Since he was in the longest relationship of any of the men, I asked Dennis, the 64-year-old retired computer programmer from North Carolina, to talk about the changing role of sex as one gets older. He said, "Well, I think sex is important, but priorities change over a period of time. When you're in your teens and in your twenties, most guys walk around with a semi-permanent erection. Through the years, I've got to admit that I've been slowing down. I've come to the point where, now in my sixties, I have found it necessary to try Cialis and Viagra and the like. I don't use it all the time, but I have found that it's a distinct help. I find that my libido has tapered off slowly all through the years. It has nothing to do with my affections for [Tracy] and I wish that I was as horny today as when I was twenty, but I'm not."

We want so badly to find somebody that we are sexually

compatible with, it is difficult to imagine that, from here on out, sex is going to play an ever-diminishing role in our day-to-day happiness. The saddest thing is not that we have a diminishing sex drive, it is what that diminishing sex drive represents. It is evidence that we are getting older and that our turn here is coming to an end, and *that* has nothing to do with being never-married.

Lessons Learned About Women

Some men learn about relationships while others learn about themselves. Then there are those whose greatest lessons are about the opposite sex. For those who fall into this category, it is the lessons they learn *about* women, and for others, like Andrew, it is the lessons they learn *from* women. Andrew shared what he learned from women when I asked him what he thought was the most important thing he learned from his past relationships. He said, "Not necessarily from relationships, but from women in general, is to try to be as honest and open as possible as quick as possible, regardless of how it feels. I've heard that you can get any piece of information out of somebody in the first three minutes you meet them if you ask and say the right things. After that, a wall seems to go up and you're not quite as honest, for some reason [as] the initial few minutes of meeting somebody. So, that's possibly why speed dating works, if you know how to ask the right questions. I've never done the speed dating thing, but now I'm thinking, maybe it's a good idea."

For those whose most important lessons from past relationships were about women, some were so impacted by a single relationship that it left them with a less-than-flattering belief about the opposite sex. Randy relayed such a belief when he told me what he had learned. "The most important thing is not settling. I think I could've ended up in some bad relationships. You know, everybody's on their best behavior when you first meet. You try to be well-mannered, and then after you get comfortable, the evil comes out."

"Do you see patterns like that in your past relationships?"

"Yeah, sometimes more prevalent than others, but I definitely see a pattern. I date a few women and then find that they're just users."

"What do you mean by 'users'?"

"I dated one woman, we got along fine, but it was very much a one-way relationship. She would have to take a trip and would want to be dropped off at the airport, and picked up, and the cat fed, and the plants watered. [I] pay for everything and she doesn't offer. I'm giving and providing and she's taking."

Gordon had two relationships that impacted him as a younger man. One of these was to a separated—not yet divorced—woman. Like Randy, the lesson he took from that relationship impacted how he saw women in general. He said, "Since I left that one [relationship] eighteen years ago, I have seen a terrible pattern where I find unhappily married women. I seem to run into quite a few of them, dated a couple along the way and had affairs with them. I don't have a problem with dating married women because I try to get an understanding of where they're coming from, what's going on in their life, the mistakes they made and the new direction they're looking for."

"You have run into these unhappily married women. Do you see any pattern in their stories, why they are unhappy? What have you found?"

"A lot of it is sex."

"Meaning?"

"They're not getting satisfied at home, which is common, I guess."

"Do you have any insight as to why that is?"

"No, because this one woman I've known for twenty years, is still married. Her husband is her best friend. This woman is absolutely gorgeous and he never sleeps with her, he never touches her, and she's accepted that for twenty-five years of marriage. I said, 'What is wrong with you?,' and she still lives with it so she's an emotional basket case. She said, 'I love him as a friend. He's my best friend in the world. I can't leave my best friend.' I said, 'Well, get divorced and move next door to your best friend, he's tying you down.' She doesn't understand. She has no freedom. She has no life. She has no marriage. She just has a best friend who lives in her house and pays her bills. I can't understand her because I thought she would be out of it after knowing her ten years, but we're going twenty years strong and she's still in the same exact situation."

"Wow."

"She'll call me four or five times a year and tell me how much she misses me because I had an affair with her and it was a sexual, loving affair. She fell extremely in love with me, but it was based on the physical. Of course, she likes me for other reasons too, but she couldn't let go of her husband to get to know me better."

"And you have no idea why she is not having sex with her husband?"

"Other than she tells me he doesn't like it. The guy is a muscular, good-looking guy—he's God's gift to women. It's a difficult case to try and figure out."

The most important thing that Gordon learned from past relationships is that there are many unhappily married women. I wonder what influence that has had on his never getting married?

For some men, like Dale, the lesson they learned about women is that they keep attracting the same kind. "Well, I date really independent women. Strong, feminist types."

"And why is that?"

"I think that's because my mother was very weak and I don't think it served the family well. I think there's that, and I think I can be very domineering, very intense, and I need someone who's strong enough to push back."

"What makes you so intense?"

"It's just genetic."

"It seems like you are picking the right women. You are picking strong, independent women, right?"

"Yeah."

"You know what you need in a woman and you seem to be finding them, so why have you never been married?"

"I don't know."

"I think you do."

"I had a college sweetheart who I dated for seven years and our families knew each other. It was a huge circle of people that knew us in Houston and I just imagined us being married and living in this particular neighborhood and really being part of society there. It was just my dream; I wanted it to happen."

"So, what happened?"

"There was just a certain closeness and intimacy that wasn't possible with this person."

"You like strong, independent women, but you also want that emotional bond and closeness?"

"Right."

I once heard someone say the thing that first attracts you to somebody is the thing that will ultimately drive you away from them. I don't know if that is true in every case, but it was for Dale. Maybe I think this way because I am a man, but to me *strong* means emotionally strong. So, when Dale says he wants a strong but emotional woman, perhaps he is seeking two mutually exclusive traits, a combination of behaviors that just does not occur in nature, at least by his definition. And maybe seeking this unobtainable combination is what has kept him never-married.

Like Dale, Dylan also has a particular type of woman he keeps picking, even though he has recognized the incompatibilities and that this type of woman does not work for him. He said, "I'm all-American, I'm white, and most of the women I've dated have been Spanish or from another country. I'm open to all, but [Spanish women] are not as romantic. I know what women appreciate, and I like to do the things over the course of a relationship, and I just feel like they don't hold their part. An example, I was dating a girl for over a year, and I never got one card from the girl. I found that ironic. I'd give her cards and flowers and little notes and do little things and some women take it for granted. They just expect it, and that's the thing [about] living down here in South Florida. I can read a woman pretty well. After two, three dates you kind of know if these women are playing you or what they're looking for."

Why do they do it; select women they know will not work for them? Are they slow learners, or like Winston, are they consciously (or unconsciously) sabotaging the relationship because they have no inherent desire to take the next step? I'm not sure, but if men like Dale and Dylan do ultimately hope to be in a relationship with a woman that *does* work for them, I hope they find the answer.

CHAPTER 8

If I Had To Do It Over Again, I Would Have...

I concede that it is a little tricky to get an honest answer about someone's regrets in life. It is not that people don't want to tell the truth; it is that they may not want to admit the truth, especially to themselves. Regret is a form of surrender, conceding to a past with mistakes that we are powerless to correct. It is just a lot easier to believe that our lives worked out the way we wanted. In spite of this, over one-third of the men who responded to the survey do regret having never married; a larger number than I would have predicted.

I asked every man I spoke with to complete the inquisitive statement that is the title of this chapter—*If I had to do it over again, I would have. . .* In one respect, it is a solicitation to find out what they learned. But it is more. It is also an exercise in fantasy to see if they would be a different person given a second chance to get it right. The men had regrets that ran the gamut, including those who would not have changed a thing. I also asked them if they had any guilt over their past relationships. Guilt, in this context, is a specific form of regret: It is regret over behavior directed toward somebody else. I was curious to know if they were sensitive enough to recognize the impact their "mistakes" had on the women in their lives. The men were more than forthcoming with their responses and confirmed what I already knew about them: they may struggle with the decision about marriage, but they are honest, sensitive and have learned a great deal along the way.

Dated More Women

Some never learned to play the numbers game well enough, so it is not surprising there are those who wish they had dated more women. With such a large number of men seeking the right one and not finding her, one logical regret is they simply did not look hard enough. There were a few reasons why they did not date more. For some, like Gabriel, it was staying in the "wrong" relationship too long that kept them from dating more. He said, "I never would have dated for seven years. I would have dated a lot more women. I think in my twenties I probably should have done something to get me over my shyness sooner. I think that limited me in a number of ways and I think it would have helped me open up and realize that I had to be happy myself in order to have a relationship that worked."

For others, like Danny, it was the prolonged recovery from a bad break-up that curtailed his dating efforts, as I discovered when he told me what he would do differently. "I don't know how to answer that because I haven't had that many relationships."

"Could one of the things be to maybe have dated more women?" I inquired.

"I guess, yeah. After Paula, I was really heartbroken and there was too much fear of pain."

"How long did it take to get over Paula?"

"She broke up with me when I was about twenty-one or twenty-two and I probably didn't have another relationship until I was twenty-nine or thirty."

With Ryan, it was just his innate shyness that kept him from dating more. I asked Ryan, thinking back to his twenties, where he thought he would be relationship-wise today. He said, "I thought I would be single, I thought I'd be an artist and I pretty much got my wish as far as being single."

"That was actually a wish of yours?"

"I think it was because I was determined to be single."

"Do you have any regrets about that?"

"If I had made the other decision, if I had been that sort of personality where I would have been drawn to having a partner, I probably would have benefited from a relationship. It just seems that there would have been support and that probably would have been healthy."

"Complete this sentence: If I had to do it over again, I would..."

"If I had to do it over again and actually was able to have some kind of foresight of what would really happen, I would pursue trying to get some type of relationship going."

"How would you have done that?"

"Maybe just been more reckless, maybe more open to making mistakes, not as concerned about being so careful, but taking more risks. And when they fail, you just keep taking more risks."

"I like the idea of taking more risks. What would keep you from doing that starting today?"

"I think lack of skill. I really feel like just kind of a bumbling, inexperienced teenager. I just feel uncomfortable and nervous, and really stuck inside my own head."

He avoided a relationship in the hopes of being an artist. Now, in his forties, he tries to reconcile the possibility that he actually would have increased his chances of becoming a successful artist if he had sought out a relationship. Even at the "young" age of forty, he is powerless to overcome his regret because he is still the same person, and because he is still living that regret.

Dated Different Women

Some men would have dated more women and some men would have dated *different* women. They are different paths with the same regret: they never found the right one. One man that would have dated different women is Andrew, although he acknowledges the reality that it is often easier to say than do. He said, "If I had to do it over again, I would have pursued women that I really cared for a lot more and I wouldn't have let them go. The ones I didn't care for, I would have cut ties with earlier, but then again, I wasn't seeing anybody else, so nah, it's always good to have something on the side."

The power of retrospection collides with the realities of human needs. Life is short; time is precious. Make up your mind. Cut ties. On the other hand, what you are feeling is pretty damn good. It can be difficult to reconcile in the moment. I once heard a motivational speaker say the biggest obstacle to living the great life is living the good life. Meaning, the reason we do not achieve the "great" life is because the life we already have is not too bad. We are comfortable with what we have and there is not a great deal of motivation to change, even though we may be able to do better. Perhaps the same principle applies in the quest for the right one. We want to find the right one, but the almost-right-one we already have leaves us in a state of limbo. We are not completely satisfied with what we have, but also have no great motivation to "upgrade." It makes finding the right one that much more difficult because searching for her comes with a cost: giving up something we already have. This leaves us with two choices. We can either continually succumb to the grass-is-greener syndrome searching for that elusive right one, or we can change our perspective and learn to see the imperfect one right in front of us as the right one. It is something we need to consider.

Another person who would have made better dating decisions is Jason. He said, "I probably would not have gone out with some of the people I was involved with."

"Why is that?"

"I found out that I was being attracted to a similar kind of woman and that was someone who was very, very needy and very clingy."

"Where did that come from?"

"It could've been from my family growing up. Who knows? I went through therapy to realize I can no longer be with that kind of person."

Like Andrew and Jason, Trent would have also dated different women, but with him it was less about changing his selections and more about changing himself. He said with regard to having regrets,

"Yeah, I do. I had a very good education. I went to a very good private school, but I had such a sheltered life from those schools and from the way my parents (who were British) were. You know, a child should be seen, but not heard. I had no idea what I was doing when I finally was on my own. The world was my oyster and I didn't know what to do with it. I didn't have a plan and it took years to figure out where to go."

"Complete this sentence: If I had to do it over again, I would have. . ."

"I would have changed it."

"How?"

"I should have realized that I didn't have any real guidance and I spent all those years trying to figure out a path. They were good [relationships], many of them, but they didn't accumulate into something that I was really happy with. So, I wish I knew what I was doing when I was younger."

Approached Relationships Differently

There is a group for whom the regrets are not about the woman in the relationship, but their own behavior in the relationship. They wish they could have been the men they are today back then. A man who thinks that way is Martin. He said, "I think my biggest regret is that I didn't deal with a lot of the sexual issues earlier in life. Looking back, I consider that what I had was a sexual addiction, and it was something that controlled my life to a large extent. I knew at the time that I was being very self-destructive, but I always said I'll deal with this later."

"So, if you had to do it over again, you would. . .?"

"I would focus on what's really important, which is building relationships. I was very selfish and short-term oriented in my relationships with women I was romantically involved with."

"Thinking back to your twenties, where did you think you would be relationship-wise today?"

"I thought I would probably be married and have a couple of kids and live in the suburbs."

"Did you have a plan for that?"

"No, not really. I just never seemed able to really get to the point where I felt like I was ready for marriage. I think I told myself at the time that I just hadn't met the right person, but looking back on it, it wasn't about the right person. I think if I would have married earlier in life, it would have been a disaster."

At least his regret is closely coupled with his honesty. He acknowledges he would have approached relationships differently if he had been the man he is today. I think that bodes well for Martin as he approaches new relationships in the future, even at the age of fifty-four. Justin also regrets not approaching past relationships with what he knows today, and he also feels some guilt over his behavior. He said, "Well, hindsight is twenty-twenty. Of course, if I had to do it all over again, if I knew then what I know now, I'd do things much differently."

"What would you do differently?"

"I'd approach relationships with confidence and proactively, and with respect and circumspection. If I knew everything about relationships and women when I was twenty-five that I know now, I think I probably could have made it work. And I'd know enough to tell Mom to shut her big yap if she didn't like the girl, too."

"Why can't you do that today?"

"Well, I can, but so far I really haven't met anyone that I particularly want to get involved with."

"I know most of your past relationships were pretty short, but do you have any guilt over any of them?"

"Some. I suppose there were instances in which I misled women about my intentions, where I knew in the back of my mind that it really wasn't going anywhere. I feel bad about one instance in particular, where I got to the third or fourth date with a woman that I liked and we had sex, and then for various reasons I never called her again. That one weighs heavy on my conscience. I don't think it was the end of the world for her, but it just doesn't smell good."

"How have you dealt with it?"

"I'm just very, very careful how I get involved, and the extent to which I get involved, and the speed with which I get involved with women at this point. I think these are probably the lessons a lot of folks learned in high school or junior high school if they dated a lot, which I didn't. I had to learn these lessons in my thirties. So I'm really cautious now, and that's probably why I don't date a lot."

"Where did you think you would be relationship-wise today at forty-one?"

"I guess on one level I assumed I'd be a normal, middle-aged adult with a wife and kids. I think on another level I probably knew I'd be just like I was then. I had some traumatic experiences when I was about thirteen or fourteen. I was kind of a big puppy dog and I got cruelly shot down by some girls and I just felt so bitter. Part of me knew at that point that I wanted to be celibate. I wanted to be like Mr. Spock from *Star Trek*, all logic and no emotion. I kind of got over that, but part of me never did."

"It sounds like rejection in the formidable teenage years has played a role in the rest of your adult life."

"It did. There's a lingering effect to this day."

Sandy is also in that group of men who wishes they could have been the man they are today, and he shared a frank confession of his behavior back then. "I would have been more like I am now than then. It's the lessons I've learned. It's not like I had a great relationship and I blew it by cheating on her. The problems were always attitudes. I think I was unselfish in a selfish way."

"What does that mean?"

"I was very giving of what it is that I thought that she wanted, and in determining what it is that she wants, I'm being selfish. I guess if I had to do it over again, I would only get involved with women that are accepting of me the way I am, and accepting of us and the situation that we are in."

"Do you have any guilt over your past relationships?"

"The guilt that I have is that instead of leaving the relationships before they even started, I hung with them and responded in my own emotional, sometimes violent ways, either physically—that was a long time ago—or emotionally, because I was unhappy with the circumstance. What I learned was that nobody that you respect should ever be on the receiving end of emotional abuse."

"Why did you hang out with these women longer than you should have?"

"I'm just not a quitter. I would see [a] little glimpse of hope, I would hang on. In two previous relationships, when I started to see that it just wasn't going to work out, the next thing I had to wrestle with were my feelings of guilt for leaving them. I was like hey, I'm going to leave you because you're not good enough for me."

"That's how you felt?"

"Yeah. I felt as if I was abandoning them, like you might abandon a pet or a child. I didn't want to abandon the women. They needed me and that was a tough one."

"Do you have any of that 'rescuer' in you?"

"I used to."

"You seem like a really bright guy. Do you ever feel like you can outsmart these problems?"

"That is the attitude that kept me in the relationship I shouldn't have stayed in, and that attitude is all but conquered."

"What enlightened you to that?"

"The real eye-opener for me was back in the eighties, the *Shere Hite Report*. I read it through and through, and I was totally amazed at how women develop their own sense of self. I think that very few men have an understanding of women to that psychological degree, and I think that is what made me seem very attractive to some women. I can understand them, and then the rescuer thing would kick in because they're looking for somebody to understand them."

"And so, in attempting to rescue them, you ended up being in a relationship maybe you should not have?"

"Right."

Communicated Better

With their recognition of the importance of good communications, it is not unexpected that some men regret not being better communicators—and not just verbally, but emotionally as well. Evan gave an answer along these lines when he told me what he would do differently if he could do it over again. "Maybe I'd make more of an effort to show more attention."

"What to you mean by that?"

"Just to communicate my wants and needs better, and not go off into my own world as I do frequently. I have a lot of solitary pursuits and they take much of my time, and sometimes you have to negotiate those things and figure out what the other person needs. Try not to be as selfish with my time."

Jason regrets poor communication in one relationship in particular. He said, "There was one gal in my early twenties, I was in college and she lived in New York, but [she] was going to school in Boston. We were both in love with each other, but never communicated that. I think that caused the downfall of the relationship. [She was a] very nice, very sweet lady. That was one regret. That was probably the one relationship where if we had communicated then, who knows what would have happened."

"How often do you think about that?"

"I've thought of it. I know she's married. I had written to her four years after we broke up, when she went back to school. I've thought about it off and on because she's that one gal that really, really strongly connected."

When I first asked Kyle if he had any regrets, I thought he might be one who would not change a thing, but as I dug deeper, I could see that he also wishes he had communicated better.

"Do it the same way," he said with regard to doing it over.

"You would?"

"What is done is done. You can do that kind of mental aerobics to think about the past, but it's just done, it's over. In retrospect, from some of the relationships I've been in the past, there are certainly things I'd do differently now because I feel I've learned things from my past relationships. But in terms of if I could do it all over again, I'd probably end up doing it all the same."

"What kinds of things would you do differently?"

"For one thing, I tend to have an acerbic wit and very sharp tongue, and I think multitudes of times I've said things that are hurtful, unintentionally, and so now I think I'm a bit more conscious of this kind of innate gift I've been blessed with. I think I'm a bit more aware that people are sensitive and I really need to be gentler with them verbally."

That is the difference between lamenting the past and learning from it. I agree with Kyle that worrying about things you cannot change is a waste, but acknowledging the things we have learned along the way is not. We are not dead yet, and we can use these lessons from this point forward. Kyle may not have any regrets, but he admits he would have done things differently.

Used the L Word

Why is it so hard to say, 'I love you?' Perhaps it's because of the consequences, and for those men who do not want to deal with those consequences, it is better to avoid the subject altogether. There is a general understanding among men that if you tell a woman that you love her, but have no intention of marrying her, you have some explaining to do. If you never say it, you cannot be held accountable. One man who did not want to be held accountable is Dennis. Even though he has been in a loving and committed relationship for thirty-eight years and has no relationship regrets, he begrudgingly admitted he wishes he had used "the L word" more often. He said, "I have regrets, but the regrets don't deal with my love life."

"Do you have any guilt then?"

"Guilt is a powerful emotion. I have tried to live my life in a way to avoid guilt. I am an unreligious person, so I don't have guilt coming at me from any kind of religious teaching. I have felt that I must never tell a woman that I love her in order to induce her to have sex with me, and I never have."

"Good for you."

"However, I feel a little bit of guilt because I've bent over backwards the other way. There were times when I was in love with a woman and I didn't tell her. I was inhibited and I couldn't tell her, 'I love you.' I felt that if I uttered those words that she would say, 'Aha, now you have to marry me. If you love me you have to marry me.' So, there were times when I should have said 'I love you' and I didn't."

Then there was Gordon, who never said "I love you" because he never heard it when he was younger.

"I'm not a person that tells a person I love them because I never heard it as a child," he explained. "My parents never told us they loved us, so I know this sets the course [for] when we get older. Some use the word all the time; I've never used it in my life. I think I told that girl once that I loved her, but I didn't come out and say, 'I love you.' I said it in a general statement, but I never told her eye to eye that I loved her."

"Why is it that you never used the word 'love'? Is it because you parents didn't?"

"I've been studying for fifteen, twenty years why I'm so different than my friends when it comes to this word 'love'. Some people use it like it's an everyday word and I just don't ever use it."

"And you haven't figured out why?"

"Other than I didn't hear it at home growing up."

Been More Honest

Much of the regret I heard during my conversations revolved around better communication. Some wanted to be better communicators in general, some should have said "I love you" while others felt regret having not been more honest. For those who regret not being more honest, it was primarily influenced by their predilection to avoid marriage, as it was with Manny. He said, "I'm sorry I hurt some of the people I did. I've moved on from some good girls in my life basically because I was happier being single than putting up with their little crap, which is sad, because there were some good girls I should have been more tolerant of."

"Complete this sentence: If I had to do it over again, I would . . ."

"I'd probably be right where I am."

"Do you harbor guilt over any of your past relationships?"

"Certainly, I don't like hurting people, and that happens invariably."

"Tell me how that usually happens."

"By ending the relationship where [the women] probably had plans for the future. I think sometimes, at this age, if he's never been married, she's wondering if there's something wrong with him. Then, here I am. I'm in a relationship with her and I end it, and she's just going to think that even more."

"Are you typically honest with them up front?"

"I am. I used to not be, but now I'm very honest. When I start a relationship now, I tell them up front, I'm forty years old and never been married. It's probably not going to work out. It's really the truth; they probably already know."

Myron told a similar story about whether he had guilt over his past relationships. "Yes, I do, because there were a couple of loving women that left because I didn't want to get closer. Although they ended the relationship, they viewed it as me leaving."

"Were you honest with them up front?"

"No, not really, not totally. I didn't say to them, 'This is my history, I'm never getting married.' I would say things to them like, 'This is good, being together. It's nice going out together. Let's stay together.' But I never said I'd never get married or that I wanted to get married. I just sort of left it alone. I didn't talk about it. So, I think there were one or two people that I felt bad that I didn't want to move forward. Maybe they were hurt a little bit emotionally. They felt rejected or felt sad. So, I feel a little guilty, that maybe I should have told them sooner about my pattern."

"What would you change if you had to do it over?"

"I think I might have tried harder to convince that woman not to go back to her parents, when we were in our twenties. It probably could have been done with greater effort, if I had perhaps been more radical in my approach, and encouraged her to go away with me to a different state. If I could have gotten her away from her family, she might have stayed with me."

"Do you think about that at all?"

"Yeah. Once in a while. I remember her and think about her, because that was a particularly satisfying relationship."

"Have you seen her since you broke up?"

"I did see her after, but it's been many years now."

"Do you ever have any fantasies about connecting with her again?"

"I used to, but that was a long time ago."

Even regrets fade with time, eroded away by the years, leaving us a little wiser and a little less discontented with our choices.

Been a Better Boyfriend

Some men regret not being a better boyfriend. Perhaps they should have been more patient or understanding; maybe they should have been kinder; or maybe they should have tried harder. For whatever reason, sex seemed to play a big role for those men who wished they were better boyfriends. Regardless of their motivation, it was nice to hear them acknowledge situations in their past where they had fallen short in that regard. Dale wishes he had been more sensitive to a woman's sexual timetable. He said if he had to do it over again, he would "be more patient."

"In what way?" I inquired.

"As far as sex goes."

"Just take your time a little more?"

"Yeah."

"What do you think that would have done for you if you had been more patient?"

"I think it adds stress to the situation. Women are beautiful creatures, and they'll give when they feel comfortable. If they don't feel comfortable, you're not going to make them more comfortable by pressuring them."

"Do you have any guilt over any of your past relationships?"

"Sure. Not a lot that I carry around right now, but I have experienced it."

"Tell me about it."

"If someone falls in love with me and I break up with them, and they're upset, I feel bad."

"Why do you feel bad? Is it your responsibility to make them feel good?"

"I'm not sure. Maybe it's just an emotional response. I don't think it's anything logical because I try not to be responsible."

"Have you ever stayed in a relationship too long to avoid upsetting a woman by breaking up with her?"

"Sure. I'd broken up because we had a terrible sex life."

"Were you honest about that with her?"

"Well, I tried to bring it up, but it was difficult to bring up because she would get anxiety about it and feel like I was pressuring her, and so in a way, it made it worse. It was like, well, if you didn't bring it up, maybe I would do it. It had to do with blow jobs."

"When you didn't bring it up what happened?"

"It was like six months. C'mon, throw me a freakin' bone."

I suspect many men struggle with this, and not just the never-married ones. If a man is not satisfied with his sex life and he brings it up, it can put pressure on the woman and make her feel anxious to the point where it actually decreases the chances of the situation getting better. And yes, we try being patient, and frequently time rolls on and nothing changes. We view it as being stuck in a no-win situation. Suffer in silence with our sexual frustration, or bring it up and make matters worse. What is the answer? I wish somebody would tell us.

James told me he also regrets not being a better boyfriend, and he regrets the consequences of his sexual promiscuity. "I would be more kind, because I was very self-centered, very into what I wanted, very un-empathetic, very hard to put myself in the other person's shoes."

"Do you think you are better at it now?"

"Much."

"Do you have any guilt over that?"

"I have guilt for a couple of them, sure."

"Talk about that."

"In two of the relationships that I've had, and this was years ago, both girls got pregnant. One was the first time we ever had sex and the second one was just a freak accident that happened, and in both cases they had abortions. There's a little guilt there. Not so much that I feel guilty for not having the kid, but how I left that person feeling, and it was their choice to do that at the time."

"Looking back to when you were in your twenties, where did you think you would be relationship-wise at forty?"

"I never really thought, even at that point, that I would be getting married. I thought I would be the same fancy-free, sexually uninhibited guy that I was back then, and for the most part I am. [Although] I've settled down somewhat. I guess I thought that I would remain the same, but I've seen a lot of changes since I was in my early twenties."

Similar to James, Donald discussed with me how he might have been a better boyfriend, and he too shared some guilt he felt over his past sexual behavior. "I have some regrets of not trying harder to make things work. Just bailing out at the first opportunity a lot of times. Yeah, I have regrets about that."

"Any particular woman come to mind?"

"Yeah. There's actually a woman I dated within the last two years, and she was a black woman. I thought she was beautiful, and she had all these great traits, and I have regrets with her. I had a little hurdle to get over with her as far as the black-white thing, which is a little bit of an adjustment, but we didn't get along all that great and [so] I didn't really try, I didn't really give a hundred percent. I think if I would have, we could have been really happy together."

"Why didn't you give a hundred percent?"

"She had a lot of issues from childhood, probably some issues like I did, as far as not being in a successful relationship. Plus, we fought a lot. When we weren't fighting, we were having a great time. I'm pretty laid back and I avoid arguments at all costs, and I just couldn't avoid them. We were fighting on a regular basis and it just wore me out and her too."

"Do you have any guilt over anything in your past?"

"Yeah, about not being loyal, and not being frank and totally honest with people. I don't really like being that way."

Loyalty outside of marriage. It is an interesting concept for men who cannot commit to marriage. They understand that affairs of the heart do not need a marriage license to be real, and betrayal hurts, with or without those vows. That Donald recognizes that and feels some small measure of remorse tells me at the very least he is not operating in a vacuum—he knows what he did. We continued with this topic because I wanted him to tell me more about being disloyal.

He said, "Just like the girl I dated for a period of five years, and towards the end I wasn't loyal to her. I felt that I should have been honest and just told her, 'I'm not attracted to you and I've been going out with other women and cheating on you.'"

"Did you tell her?"

"No."

"Why not?"

"That would certainly end the relationship with any woman. I liked spending time with her. We got along great. We never fought. We liked sports. We just didn't have any sexual activity."

"Was there a reason?"

"I [wasn't] attracted."

"You were with her for five years."

"I was attracted to her for the first three-and-a-half, four years. The sex kind of tapered off, and then towards the end, we'd have sex every two or three months."

"If you could send a message to all of your past girlfriends, what would it be?"

"I would tell them how much fun they were, even if it was for a short period of time. I've never really been in a relationship I didn't like, whether it was sexual or just the person. I've had the fortunate time to date some really great women, and a lot of them, after I dated them, have gotten married and been happily married. I've dated some really great women that would make most men happy, and they could be content with that."

"How do you feel about that? Hanging out with these great women who went on to get married to other guys?"

"If they're happy, I'm happy. And if they're happy, I don't feel as guilty if I know they're happy, even without me."

I have to admit, he spoke for me when he said that. My biggest fear has always been that I wasted a woman's time, be it from having a family or from finding "Mr. Right." It does feel good to know that we were just a love relationship along the way, and that we did not keep them from their final destination. We were just a stop on the journey: a reason to love, a reason to grow and a way to prepare for who they were ultimately meant to be with.

Not Let Her Get Away

There were even some men who regret letting one get away. I am not sure this is an honest regret though. I think this is a regret in hindsight. At the time, it is almost impossible to foresee this regret coming because we are seeing the world through the lens of abundance. There is someone better right around the corner, or so we think. This is about how someone who is not the right one becomes the right one as the years go by and we gain perspective. It is not that she has changed, it is that we have changed, and we view her in the past as the changed person we are today. And the more time that goes by, the better she becomes as we romanticize who she was. Wayne regrets not marrying a young love, but you can see by his words that this is regret in hindsight, as he readily admits why he did not marry her at the time.

"I do have some regrets," he said. "There was this girl I dated when I was twenty-nine who was ten years younger than I was and I should have married. If I had any sense at all, I would have married her."

"What kept you from marrying her?"

"At the time, it was the late seventies and beautiful women were everywhere, available and easy pickings. She'd been telling me she didn't want to get married. Well, then she turns right around after we break up and marries somebody else, which taught me a very important thing. If a woman says she doesn't want to get married, that means she does."

"So, if you had to do it over again, you would. . ."

"I would have married a girl named Cindy."

"Do you ever think about her anymore?"

"Yeah, I think about her once in awhile."

"Do you know what happened to her?"

"I know she got married and that's all I know."

Randy told a similar story to Wayne, acknowledging that he should have tried harder to win a woman over. I asked Randy to think back to his twenties and tell me where he saw himself relationship-wise at forty-eight. "I thought I'd be married and maybe with a child or two."

"Did you have a plan for that?"

"No."

"That seems to be a common theme among us guys that are still single."

"I think the ones with the plan end up settling."

"Do you have any regrets at all thinking about your past relationships?"

"Just that early one. I regret that didn't work out, because it was such a good match, we just got along so well."

"What would you do differently if you had to do it over?"

"I probably would have fought harder for the first one. I probably would have knee-capped the track guy."

"Do you think about her from time to time?"

"I do. I always think what could have been, because I got along [so] great with the whole family."

"Whatever happened to her? Did she go on to get married?"

"She got married, but got divorced, no kids."

"Did you ever stay in touch with her? Have you ever run into her?"

"Nope."

"Do you want to?"

"Nah, it wouldn't do any good. I think about it, but I'm so over it and past that, if she came on her hands and knees begging for another chance, it's way too late. I've lived an entire lifetime since that point."

"Do you have any guilt over anything in your past?"

"Oh no. I always treat the women I date with a great deal of respect, and when it doesn't work out, I try to be as kind as I can. I've never abused anybody."

"Are you honest with them about your feelings toward marriage?"

"Oh yeah. I've never led anybody on."

Nathan also told me he laments not trying harder to win over a woman when he was younger. "The only regret is that the other woman got married. She moved away too, and she was such a good friend and just good fun."

"What would you do differently if you could do it over?"

"The only thing that I would change is I think I would have spent more time trying to convince her that I was a better person."

"You don't think you gave it the old college try?"

"I abided by what she really wanted, I think, and so I didn't put any pressure on her because I just enjoyed her company."

"If you had to do it over again, you might have tried to convince her, right?"

"Right."

"Why do you think, in hindsight that you didn't?"

"She has four kids now and I'm not so sure I would want those four kids."

"But in hindsight, at that moment, why do you think you didn't do it?"

"Because I was just too good of a person to try and take her dreams away. Also, I was probably too busy doing my work."

Even for men like Nathan, who have clearly traveled the best path for them, there is always the lingering ghost of "what if." They rationalize the outcome because they have to. What other choice do they have, to live a life of regret? It is an easy urge to succumb to, whether it is the girl who got away or a poor career choice. We all have the opportunity to wallow in our perceived mistakes. Thankfully, Nathan did not let that happen to him, and neither did most of the men in this book.

Dylan followed suit with his own story of regretting the one that got away. He said, "The last long-term one I dated, I dated her about a year and four months. I met her on a local chat line and we hit it off the first date. She was Columbian, beautiful. She was close to her family and I got invited to Bogotá to meet them. I went over there on holiday a couple of years ago and found out that her visa was getting [ready] to expire and she wanted to stay [in the US]. Then a family member got sick and she went back and never came back to the states. That was the [one] which I thought, you know, given the opportunity, if she had gotten American citizenship and she had come back, that we would have worked things out, but she left and never came back."

"Did you ever make any attempt to contact her?"

"We spoke by phone, but I guess a lot of people, once they leave here, it's tough to get back into the country."

"Could you have helped her with that?"

"I'm sure, but we had differences in work schedules and what we believed in. She wanted kids. We didn't really speak about it in the beginning, but she showed up on a crutch and I found out that she had polio where one leg is smaller than the other. I didn't know if it was a short term [thing], or if it was something she'd have her whole life, and then we got to talking about kids and she wanted a lot of kids. How's a woman going to be a mother and wife when she's on a crutch and has polio with all these little kids running around?"

"Where does the regret come in?"

"The regret is, I wish maybe I had visited her when she was in Bogotá. She left, I got busy with my work. Maybe I should have chased her down if I loved her and wanted her. Maybe she thought I was going to go to Bogotá and marry her there and leave Florida, but I don't speak Spanish, and I just can't up and leave. If I'm going to do that, it's going to be to one of the fifty states. I just can't up and leave and go to Columbia."

"I think that is reasonable."

"Not that she asked me. To me, it's not the nationality of the woman. Does she have a good heart? Is she honest? Is she intelligent? And this woman was."

"That sounds like the one that got away."

"Yeah."

George's story is unique in this group. He too would have married the first one, not because she was the right one, but because it would have kept Pandora's Box closed. I wanted to know if George had any regrets, and judging by his initial response, it seemed as though he didn't. But as I dug a little deeper, the truth emerged. I asked him how he would feel if he got to the end of his life and had never gotten married. He said, "Well, you can't really have any regrets. I've got a wonderful life. I'm single and a married guy may be jealous of me because I'm able to choose who's sleeping in my bed every night."

"What is the best part of the single life you have, because you pointed out that you have a great life?"

"Just the whole package would be the best part of it."

"The power of hindsight being twenty-twenty, complete this sentence regarding your past relationships. If I had to do it over again, I would . . . "

"Have married the first one."

"Really! Why do you say that?"

"I see a lot of people that got married to their first and only, and if you don't taste it, it doesn't attract you. If you had sex with the first girl and it was just perfect, you don't know that there could be more to sex than [what] you just had."

"So, you think the right thing would have been to just marry the first one and keep yourself in the dark sexually?"

"Yeah, you've go to."

Changed Nothing

And then there are those who have no regrets. It could be a rationalization, they deal with regrets by denying them, or maybe they just do not have any. Either way, they lead a life free from worrying about mistakes, and with the understanding that an imperfect life is just part of the deal. Theodore shared his feelings in this regard when I asked him if he would do anything differently given another chance.

"No. I have no regrets about any aspect of my life," he proclaimed. *"Why do you say that? Because I know a lot of people who do."*

"The reason I say that is in some course work I've done we had a thing called 'Victim Land', which is the idea that something or someone does something to us. My decisions were my decisions—they did nothing to me. I made them at the time because I made them at the time. I don't blame the decision that I made for not getting married. I simply acknowledge that these are the belief systems that I developed and I'm okay with it."

"How would you feel if you got to the end of your life and you had never been married?"

"I wouldn't regret it. I just don't have regrets. I really am in the moment. I'm so thankful for my martial arts and for the fact that I had today with my mother, that I could kiss her and tell her I loved her, that I had today with my brother. I'm a very thankful person. Now, that's not saying I don't have problems. I [just] don't call them problems; I call them situations. I've got some situations, okay. I will deal with them, but this is what I believe. I believe that if I was supposed to be married, I would have been married. That's really the only thing I can tell you."

"Is it a fatalistic approach?"

"I don't like [to be] fatalistic. I do believe I make a choice. I do believe that I could have chosen to marry Megan, the woman that had the kids back in my early thirties when she gave me an ultimatum. I could have made that choice; I did not make that choice."

I like what Theodore said. It was reassuring the way he accepted his decisions and the gratefulness he showed for what he *does* have. If there is one way to counteract regret, it is with gratitude, and Theodore has that in abundance. But because he had broken up with a lot of women, I still wanted to know if he had any guilt over any of his past relationships. His response to that question was even more enlightening.

"No. I believe guilt is a fake feeling. This is the way I look at every relationship. What if every connection we ever had in life, whether it's a one-night stand or a 5,000-night stand, is for the purpose of learning the lessons or teaching the lessons that we're supposed to learn or we're supposed to teach, so that we can move to the next level in our lives."

"That sounds pretty profound."

"Well, that's what I believe, my friend."

Either that belief he has is true, or I just want it to be true. Either way, it casts our life's relationships in a wonderful light. Relationships exist for the purpose of learning life's lessons, and when the lesson has been absorbed the relationship is no longer needed. Now, perhaps that way of thinking is also a rationalization because it absolves us of the responsibility of a failed relationship, but it is empowering and it does away with regret, and there is nothing wrong with that.

Winston responded similarly to Theodore, but his reason was much simpler.

"Nope," he said when asked if he had any regrets.

"Why do you say that?"

"I have pretty much always had a steady outlet of sexual partners and I'm content. I think I'm happier being alone than I would be with a partner that I'd have to entertain. I enjoy being single."

"Complete this sentence: If I had to do it over again, I would . . ."

"I'm afraid I'd do it the same way. You just can't go and pick that woman. If the woman doesn't come along, you're not going to do it."

"Do you have any guilt over your past relationships?"

"Yeah, I do."

"Tell me a little bit about it."

"I've tossed away perfectly good women. I know that they were looking for more and I didn't feel I was as honest with them as I could have been, but at the same time I don't think I did it on purpose."

"If you didn't do it on purpose, why did you do it?"

"Well, one girl in particular, she would have made a perfect mate. I absolutely loved everything about her with the exception that she had kids. I just was not going to be able to deal with that. Had I met her before she had kids, I think it would have been a great relationship."

Samuel's reason for why he had no regrets was simplest of all and, in some ways, the most poignant. He said, "The only thing I can think of is you can't regret what you haven't ever had. I see so many people who've gone through bad situations and unhappy deals. I don't need to deal with that. [It's] like a line from Spock on *Star Trek*, he said, 'Sometimes the having is worse than the wanting.' "

That line is profound and I was shocked I had not heard it before. "Sometimes the having is worse than the wanting," which is why I admire the men in this book who proclaim they prefer to remain unmarried, like Winston. They already have what they want, and they know it.

CHAPTER 9

Hope

Since I had requested the men look back on their lives and share their feelings of guilt and regret, I felt is was only fair to end our conversations by having them look forward. I wanted to know where they see themselves relationship-wise when they peer into the future. If you recall, almost two-thirds of the respondents would like to be married someday, even though only about half that many think they actually will be. What would they do if they found the proverbial right one? Do they see themselves married some day? And no matter how they see themselves, is their future a hopeful one?

Of the men responding to the survey, almost seven in ten have some measure of optimism about their future. Given that a majority would like to be married some day, I also wanted to gauge how important it is that they marry. When asked, twice as many men think it is at least somewhat important to marry as compared to those who do not feel it is important at all. They may not have married yet and their internal reality meters tell them they may never marry, but they want to and they think it is important.

For some, however, meeting the right one does not necessarily mean marriage. When asked what they would do if they met the right one, only a little over half said they would marry her, while a quarter would live with her, 14 percent would only date her and the rest would do nothing. Even though they may not be consumed by the desire to marry, it does not mean they want to end up alone either. Almost half fear ending up alone.

In an effort to gauge their future, I asked each of the men I spoke to where he sees himself in five years, relationship-wise. Almost all displayed some measure of hope for the future. There are those who hope to be married, while others hope to just be in a loving relationship. For some, their hope stemmed directly from changes they made in their lives, for others it was more blind faith: they were hopeful, but could not point to a reason why. There was even a small group that *expects* to be married. For those who see marriage in their future, I inquired as to what they thought was going to change to enable that to occur. Some mentioned concrete steps they had already taken, or would be taking, to make that happen, while others are less proactive, preferring to let life play itself out. Either way, most of the men see their future very differently from their past—and that future is full of hope.

Don't Really Know

When asked where they see themselves relationship-wise in five years, the largest group of men I spoke with responded with "I don't know," but that does not mean their future is not a hopeful one. Many hope to be in a satisfying relationship, whether that means marriage or something else. I did find it curious that they want a relationship, but have little idea of how that will actually come about. That uncertainty was best expressed by Theodore. He said, "I don't know. I have a lot of woman friends, but I like the idea of a traveling companion. I think a lot of it is going to depend on what happens in my overall situation. I have a lot of options open to me, but to sit here and tell you that I know what the next five years of my life looks like relationship-wise, I haven't got a clue."

Dwayne shares that same uncertainty, but gave a more specific reason why. "I don't know; other things are taking precedence. Right now what's taking precedence is my health, and with all the pain that I feel and the disability, I don't feel desirable, and so I'm even more cautious."

"Why do you say you are more cautious, because you don't feel desirable?"

"Fear of rejection. We're a very visual society. People look at you and it's a hard one to overcome for me."

Samuel continued the theme of uncertainty, but was honest enough to admit that some of his uncertainty is his own doing. He said when asked about his future, "Honestly, I don't know."

"Do you think anything will change going forward?"

"I would hope that it would progress, but it's not necessarily my decision."

"Would you like something to change going forward?"

"If I found the right person, [but] finding the right person is becoming more and more problematic."

"Why is that?"

"I'm picky and women are very picky."

"That's true."

"One of the things that I'm seeing [is] the Mick Jagger line that goes 'you don't always get what you want, but you just might find that you get what you need.' There are so many cultural expectations that we have—a laundry list of what we want. What you've got to do is figure out what you need and then everything else is a bonus. My suspicion is that if I do get involved with somebody, I will be involved with somebody much younger than me."

"Why do you say that?"

"There's three reasons. One is I don't look that old. I don't think I look old enough for some of the older women. The other problem is that I don't necessarily have that much in common with them because I'm very, very fit. In my age bracket, as you get older, there's fewer of them that are fit. The other thing is, I find that younger woman are just much more approachable. They're much less judgmental, and I think that they tend to treat guys as a human being."

"What age bracket are we talking about?"

"I would say the women over forty are not very nice, and they're very demanding."

"Do you have any insights as to why that is?"

"I don't know, and so I look at it this way, they've had their chance. They've had their chance for a long time and I've always been wanting. It just seems like the ones in my age group have just never been very friendly or nice."

I do not happen to agree with Samuel, but every man's outlook is influenced by what has transpired in his past. Nevertheless, it is one thing to be influenced by the past and quite another to be trapped by it. I know he would like to have a relationship. I hope he frees himself from his past and opens to the possibility of meeting a woman from any age bracket.

Gerald also does not know where he will be in five years, and that is because five years ago he thought he would be some place different than he is today, but he still has hope. He said, "Well, five years ago I would have said I'll have a life that's different in five years, but I don't know. I still seriously think that I will be able to find someone that I'm compatible with and be happy with. I hope that happens in five years, but again I'm kind of just letting it happen, because some of the avenues I've tried haven't panned out. For example, going online to some of the various personal ads. I haven't had much [luck] with those. The relationships in the past [that] came through there weren't very good at all. Five years from now I would hope something happens, but I really don't know to be honest with you."

Dale was a little more rigorous in his analysis of his uncertainty about future relationships. He said, "Well, I'm a statistician. I think there's two different paths: either I'm married and have children and have a wonderful life like that, or I'm doing exactly the same thing I'm doing now."

"Which one do you think is more likely?"

"From a statistical point of view, I'd have to say that the more likely one is the one I'm doing, but that's not the plan I have. I'm actively trying not to go down that path."

"What do you think will change going forward?"

"When you're thirty years old, you're at your peak of options with women, so you're not concerned about locking down something with one person because you just turn over another rock and there's another girl. That's about the maturity level I was at that age. At this point in my life, my career's developed, I'm financially stable and I'm becoming more mature and better able to handle a relationship and enjoy everything about it."

"And you do not want to spend all of your time turning over rocks?"

"I've turned over enough rocks. It has to do with maturity. Financial stability has something to do with it as well because that was always a concern when I was younger. It might have played into some of my decision making as well because there's a financial commitment to it, getting married, having children, and I didn't feel comfortable enough bringing on extra mouths."

Trent has hope, but of all the men I spoke with, he is the most uncertain. He said, "I project myself ten, twenty years into the future and try to figure out where I'm going to be or how I want to be when I get to that point. I'm not really sure what that is, but I'll know it when I see it. It's serenity of some sort. I certainly don't want to be here. I just want it to be really quiet."

"In those images of the future, do you see yourself being alone or do you see yourself being with somebody?"

"In the very, very long term, probably with somebody. Yeah, I think that would be nice. If we both come to the sense of understanding of where we are in life and what we want to do. Yeah, I think that would be nice."

"You have this vision of the future and maybe there is even a woman in there. What do you think is going to change in your life, going forward, that might allow you to do that?"

"There'll be several changes involved to have gotten to that point. So, I'd have to figure out exactly when and where I want to be, and when and where she wants to be. I haven't figured that one out. I don't know."

For Trent, the five-year time frame was not long enough. I get the impression he felt constrained by such a "short" time frame, but at fifty-two, I wonder how much of his uncertainty is simply fear. The same fear that has kept him unmarried until now. I do not know the answer, but like Samuel, I hope he figures it out, and before it is too late. Everybody deserves to be with somebody.

Paul would also like to find somebody, although it does not have to be for marriage. And while he is content in his current situation, he does not relish the prospect of growing old alone. I think he is hopeful, even if he does not readily admit it. He said, "I would like to find someone. It doesn't have to be marriage, we don't even have to live together, but just someone that, later on, as you get older, you could be together and just grow old together. [I'm] very content where I am, but my only thought is the older I get, I really don't like the thought of growing old by myself. I don't have any kids that could take care of me, not that I would ever do that to a child of mine. It's just one of those things that's probably one of my biggest concerns, is growing old and not having anyone to grow old with."

"How often do you think about that?"

"Not that much."

"You do not have that person in your life right now. What do you think will change going forward?"

"I've just always been one of those people that think that if I meet them, I'm going to know, and that may be too idealistic, but that's what I've always felt. I'm going to know when I find that person. Here I am, fifty-three and I haven't yet. So, what does that tell you?"

"Are you doing anything proactive, or are you just waiting for fate?"

"No. I work too much right now. For the last couple of years I have been working nonstop. It would be very hard right now to actually have a relationship where you're dating and that kind of stuff."

"Tell me why you are hopeful going forward."

"I didn't say I was hopeful."

"I know. If you were hopeful, tell me why you would be."

"Just because I think that, hopefully, someone would cross my path, someday."

"Is there a reason why you might not be hopeful?"

"With this thing about what I think my purpose is[2], I'm hoping that the point comes where that responsibility, if it's even valid at all, is over, where maybe I can find someone and get someone in my life."

Don't Expect Much to Change

There is a group of men, which includes Wayne, that has a hopeful outlook, but that hope is tempered by the realities of who they are. They know themselves well enough, and have taken the honest position that they may not change; therefore, their situation may not change. When I asked Wayne where he sees himself relationship-wise in five years, he responded with, "I have no idea."

I followed with, *"What do you want to happen?"*

"I'd be married to a beautiful woman half my age and she'd be pregnant."

"What do you think will change in the future to make that happen?"

"I don't think anything will change."

"Well, why are you hopeful going forward then?"

"I just am. Even though I don't think there's going to be any change, I still try to maintain an optimistic outlook. But unlike some people, I don't feel my life is incomplete because I don't have a woman in it."

They say insanity is doing the same thing over and over and expecting different results. I do not think Wayne is insane, even though he hopes for a different outcome but expects no changes in his behavior. I do question his motivation though. After researching this subject as thoroughly as I have, I have come to the conclusion that with some men, being married is just not that important. They feel they do not need a woman to complete them, and I see that as being a significant influence on Wayne. And that's okay.

Justin is another one that does not expect his behavior to change, but hopes for something different. When asked where he sees himself in five years he said, "Smart money says probably sitting here in front of the computer just like I'm doing today, single and lonely. But I'd like to be different. I'd like to say I could make the change and find one that works, commit to walking down the aisle and be in a blissfully happy relationship. I still haven't given up hope, and I would love to see it happen, but you know…"

"Do you think anything will change going forward?"

"Maybe God will lead me to the right one. Maybe we just step into the elevator together one day and maybe Yahoo! Personals comes through. You just never know."

Not a surprising response from a devout Christian, and maybe his faith in God will pay off for him in the form of a wonderful relationship.

Kyle echoed Justin's words when I asked where he sees himself relationship-wise in five years. "Well, at the rate I'm going, probably the same."

"You don't think anything will change?"

"It could, it couldn't. It really doesn't matter what I think."

"Are you hopeful going forward?"

"Oh, absolutely."

"Why are you hopeful?"

"Because it's the only alternative. Outside of being hopeful, what's left?"

"Despair?"

"It's a dismal existence. Who wants that?"

He's right. With all the choices available, why not choose hope?

Randy does not expect much to change, but he is hopeful because it is a numbers game and, in his mind, his number is ready to come up. He said, "Well, I'm hoping to find somebody more steady than what I've had."

"What do you think will change in the future?"

"I don't know that anything will change. I may end up following the same twenty-plus year pattern of just bouncing around. I don't know what'll make that change. I suppose it's finally meeting the one that you know has all the checkmarks."

"Tell me why you are hopeful of meeting her."

"I'm hopeful because I know it's just a numbers game. Mathematically it's bound to work out."

Done with the Old Life

Some men are hopeful because they do expect things to change, and the thing they expect to change the most is themselves. They are ready to leave who they were behind and become that person who wants a committed relationship, even if it is not marriage. One man who falls into this category is Andrew. He said, "I'm hoping that if

I'm not married, I'm certainly close to it, or in a good long-term relationship with somebody I care for. I'm not getting any younger and I think it's about time I've mellowed. I used to be completely outrageous and maybe I wasn't ready for a really good relationship. Now I think I've gotten a little bit older and I've mellowed out, and as long as I have somebody that is a good listener and doesn't mind talking, anything can be worked out."

That doesn't sound like the Andrew who is driven solely by his sexual desires. Time changes people, and not just Andrew. This idea of maturing into someone who is ready for marriage came up frequently during my conversations. Donald is not quite there today, but in five years he expects to have gotten the wildness out of his system. He said, "Five years from now would put me at fifty-three. I would say involved and potentially headed to get married. I've got a goal of being married by fifty-five or fifty-six, somewhere in there. I'm hoping by then I've got whatever wildness I have out of my system, and I'm ready to settle down and have a wife."

For similar reasons, Chuck expects to be in a good relationship and shared why he feels the time is right. "I'm sitting back and waiting for it to hit me. I think I'm really starting to feel ready."

"You are starting to feel ready?" I asked with a hint of sarcasm.

"Yeah."

"What do you think is different now?"

"I've experienced a lot of things. I've moved around quite a bit and I think I've gotten that all out of my system. I think I'm beginning to settle into my role in life, and I think that set the stage to be more compatible and to maybe fall into a good relationship."

There is a lot to be said for "getting it out of your system." Many of the men I spoke with acknowledged that in the past, they had too much wildness stored up within them to even think about marriage. When young people marry and subsequently divorce a few years later, I think in many cases it is because one or both partners did not get it out of their system. Chuck has gotten it out of his system and so have I. I know exactly what he is feeling. It is a contentment that can only come from satisfying a curiosity of the unknown. We have been single long enough to the point where that lifestyle no longer holds any mystery or fascination for many of us, and we would consider giving it up for a good relationship. And just the fact that we recognize that, that we are willing to let go of the old life in search of something new and better, that *is* the first step on the path to that new life.

We're Ready

Some men have a feeling about their future beyond hope: they have expectations. They expect to be married, or at least in a long-term committed relationship, within the next five years. They expect it because the uncertainties have faded away: uncertainties about women, about themselves and about the relationship they desire. They have a crystal-clear vision of what they want, and that is the key, as Steven Covey eloquently points out in his book, *The Seven Habits of Highly Effective People.* Habit number two is to begin with the end in mind, and that is precisely what Sandy has done, as I found out when I asked him about his relationship future. He said, "I think that probably in five years I'll be in a long-term relationship and possibly married."

"You are hopeful going forward?"

"Oh yeah. I'm more hopeful now than ever before."

"What leads to that hopefulness now?"

"Because I know what I want. I want a fair, balanced relationship that doesn't have a lot of gender bias. I know what sex has got to be like. I know what types of attitudes I want about bigger picture things and child rearing, and I know for sure that the woman that I'm looking for is out there and I have the means to find her."

"Why are you sure she is out there?"

"I can't tell you that. It's just [that] I've met women that come close, closer, and then closer."

James feels strongly enough about the future for his current relationship that he is willing to lay odds on it. He said, "I think I'll 90 percent for sure be married to the same wonderful woman I'm dating now."

"You are changing going forward then?"

"Yeah, I am. For the first time I'm in a relationship that I absolutely want to be in."

"What is there about this relationship that makes it the right one? Is it you, the timing or both?"

"It's definitely the timing. There were so many things in the past that were more important than finding the right woman, like my career, getting my finances straight, moving and I honestly hadn't the time to devote to it. We're best friends and I cannot put it any clearer than that. There's no one I'd rather vent to, there's no one I'd rather hang out with. [If] one of my guy friends wants me to go out, I have no problem bringing her along if I so choose. She does not even come close [to] being a ball and chain, not at all. She's cool. She's the chick I want to take with me when I want to go out."

Hearing that brought a smile to my face. James has found the Holy Grail; he found *his* right one. It is a powerful admission from a guy who is forty. It is not puppy love. It is the result of a two-decade-long quest collecting information about women and about himself. He has analyzed the data and come to the conclusion that he has found what he is looking for. He became the right one and he found the right one.

Gordon is another man who is filled with expectations. When I asked him where he sees himself with regards to a relationship in five years, he replied, "Married."

"You just feel really good about that?"

"Yeah, I do."

"What is going to change from here on out?"

"I'm being more serious about looking. I'm more seriously looking now for that mate when I look on Match.com. I'm reading the [profiles] and I'm looking for total seriousness in a connection, not wasting much more time on that friendship stuff."

"Tell me, why you are hopeful going forward?"

"[I'm at] the age where you think how great it is to have a mate, whatever level it's at, as long as you have someone that you would consider to be with you for the rest of your life. I don't have that fear of being alone, and I'm not afraid of that, but I don't want it. I don't choose it. When you're beyond the forties, the marriage word is a different word. As long as I have a mate and somebody I can travel with, eat with, do things with and sleep with, it feels ok. That equation doesn't equal marriage anymore, but if the woman wants to be married or we both want to be married, I'll get married. But if we're just living together, I have no problem with that either."

I could not agree with Gordon more. After you turn forty, marriage no longer means the same thing. For one, *"till death do you part"* is a lot less intimidating. The sexual voracity that consumed us as younger men starts to wane. We slow down, time speeds up and we see the world (and marriage) differently. And yes, while having someone who you care about and someone to do things with no longer automatically means marriage, for some of us, we no longer have the strength to fight it. We give into the notion that if she wants it, we'll do it for her. For the right one, we will do it: for her and because we see things differently than before.

Keeping with a theme, Martin sees himself married in the next five years because he feels he is close to clearing the last hurdle. He said, "I guess I'm always the optimist. I do see myself being married, whereas before I never thought I could be sexually monogamous. I spent quite a bit of time being celibate, so I feel that's still an issue that I struggle with and deal with, but it's not as severe as it was in the past."

Dylan was the most optimistic about his future, in fact, he would bet his house on it. And he does not just want a wife, he wants a family too. He said, when asked where he sees himself in five years, "Happy, healthy, hopefully at least one kid, if not two. It would have to be somebody younger. I'm normally used to meeting women in their forties, so it has to be a woman in her early to mid thirties."

"Can I assume marriage is part of the plan in the next five years?"

"Of course. I would bet my mortgage."

"What do you think is going to change for you?"

"I'm focused on it. I just said when I reached forty back in May, this is going to be a good year. I'm going to find somebody, and whether it's forty or forty-one, I'm going to find a woman who I'm compatible with and we complement one another. It would be nice if she's single and doesn't have kids, and she can travel and be spontaneous and stay the night or the weekend."

"Tell me why you are hopeful going forward, because it sounds like you are."

"I'm pretty confident, no matter what I do, when I set my mind to something. Living down here I heard a survey that said for every single man, there are six single women, so the odds are in my favor to find somebody down here in Florida."

"Sounds like you found a good place to live."

"I'm on the online dating as a different avenue to meet somebody. There's a lot of single women. I have my picture up there, so I have nothing to hide. [I] try to get out there and meet people."

For The Next Generation

Since these men took such a distinctive path in life and have such unique perspectives of marriage and relationships, I felt it would be a waste not to capture some of that accumulated life experience and perspective. I thought it would be fun to corral this collective knowledge, bundle it up and pass it along to the next generation, for better or worse. With that in mind, I ended each of my conversations with the same question: "If you could speak to a room full of twenty-something young men about relationships, what advice would you give them?" What follows is an unadulterated snapshot of their offering. And it should not be surprising that who they are and what they have experienced showed up again in the advice they offered.

I would just tell them to go with their heart. I think a lot of people get caught up in the idea of the institution of marriage and think they have to do it. You see a lot of people end up in relationships that they are not really happy in. Some of them seem like they are in jail. (*Chuck*)

I would say that they may not think it now, but chemistry, especially if they're looking long-term and thinking about getting married, that chemistry is more important than anything else. You definitely have to be attracted to the woman you're with, but far beyond that, they really have to be someone that you can talk to about anything. When you get older, it's not so much about looks, it's far more about the person you're with. And yeah, the person ideally should be someone who's your best friend, and not get so caught up in just the sex aspect of it. (*Gabriel*)

I would say have more confidence in yourself, whether you're right or not, and be yourself. Don't worry about rejection. If someone rejects you, it's okay. They're not a worthwhile partner. Relationships are a lot of work. If you decide to get into a relationship, be prepared—eventually—[for] a lot of work when the novelty wears off. (*Evan*)

You've got to do what makes your heart feel good. You've got to do what you want. You shouldn't date the woman who is just like your mom, unless you really think that much of your mom. So, I would say even though it may not be in your comfort zone, or your family's comfort zone, if you want to be with somebody that's completely outrageous and wild, as long as they make you happy and they're giving you what you need mentally and physically, by all means do what you've got to do, as opposed to, 'Oh, this is a nice person. I think I'll just spend the rest of my life with this person and grow old and be bored to tears.' (*Andrew*)

Be open-minded, patient, kind and sensitive to a woman. The one thing I learned, a woman will bring you into their life if they feel safe and comfortable. If you want a relationship with a woman, you have to give it time, have the person get to know you. You have to get to know them as a person. So, I think it's patience, I think it's time. I think it's that time they need to be comfortable and safe with you. (*Jason*)

I would say to not base your relationships on physical attraction and sex, but to try and find a woman who you can communicate with and be open with, and not change who you are. I find that so many of my friends get married and have kids, and they're just a shell of the person they were before. They're unhappy and it's because they don't have communication. I think if you can communicate and actually get to know the person, and still hopefully have good sex with them—knowing that sex is probably going to wear thin after a period of time—and love the woman, then you'll have a chance to succeed. (*Donald*)

Treat them with respect. One of my pet peeves is this so-called gang-land culture that's calling them bitches and ho's and that kind of crap. And cool it on the sex thing. Just have some good clean fun. I sound like an old fuddy-duddy saying that, but it's true. (*Gerald*)

I would suggest that they get in touch with all of their belief systems, both subconscious and conscious, that run their lives that they may not be aware of so that they can either choose to change those belief systems or they can accept and love themselves the way they are, whether they are single or married. (*Theodore*)

If you find somebody who's 80 percent, take it. I would also say it's great if you can find somebody,

but don't necessarily sweat it. One of the issues that
we've got right now is that women have been told for
the last twenty years, a man is a nice thing to have,
but it's not the most important thing. Whereas men
have been told, hey, to be validated you have to have
a woman. I think we need to tell guys, you know
something, enjoy your male friends. And if you have
female friends, that's good—enjoy them as well. But
don't forget your guy friends. Don't forget you're still
a guy and you've got guy interests. (*Samuel*)

Learn to open your heart and experience feelings.
Learn to communicate from your heart and not
from your mind. (*Dwayne*)

Don't get married until you've known her for at
least a year. (*Aiden*)

Have a plan. Talk to people. Be aware that you don't
have a plan and ask, 'What do I do?' (*Trent*)

Focus on what's really important, and I think what's
really important for anybody is having a kind of
spiritual connection to the person. Figure out what
your philosophy of life is, where you stand spiritu-
ally about things, and then find somebody that you
have that spiritual connection to. Still focus on the
physical aspect—I don't think there is any way you
can get away from that—but I think it's got to be
balanced out. (*Martin*)

I would tell them that they have to understand themselves best. They can't have a relationship until they
understand what they want. They have to understand
what it is they want from the relationship before they

seek out women for dates. To know themselves well enough to know what kind of woman they should be meeting, and be honest with themselves. (*Myron*)

There's no rulebook or instructions. You've just got to wing it. You've got to start feeling like a woman almost. A man just looks at a problem and tries to find a solution, but what a woman wants is just to be hugged. (*George*)

I would tell them, first of all, be yourself, unless yourself is a jerk. Don't try to be something you're not, and treat women with respect. Develop a good sense of humor—even if you don't have one. For some strange reason, that's important for a woman, to have a good sense of humor. Have integrity and character, be true to your principles and be true to yourself. (*Wayne*)

Don't settle, you virgins, for the first woman. Certainly don't settle for somebody that just says she wants what you want, or what you think you want, because you're still young. Absolutely do not get hooked up with one of the users. If you earn a good living, that's all they're interested in. You'll see right away, they'll bleed you. So, you definitely don't want to do that. (*Randy*)

I'll tell them how happy I am never being married. Don't just necessarily go by what the rules of society are. Go by what you want to do. (*Manny*)

Date a lot of people. Don't get locked into one relationship. I'm not saying you have to fuck a lot of people, just date a lot of people and find out. I

spent seven years in my twenties in one relationship
and that was not good. I should have dated a lot of
people and just enjoyed life and learned about
things. Learn about yourself, learn about what
works, what types of personalities you get along
with and that sort of thing. And one more thing,
learn how to dance. I think the greatest little
moments I've had with women was dancing with
them. (*Dale*)

You have to be nice to the person you're with. You
really have to be nice and honest and open.
(Nathan)

Grow up before you make any major decisions in
your life. And when I say grow up, grow up inside
yourself. Know what's going on inside your mind,
your soul. The more you know about you, the more
your life will be. You'll look at it differently. You'll
avoid a lot of confusion, a lot of difficulty. We all
have trial and error, of course. None of us can
escape trial and error, and that's part of growing up.
Just take your time, don't put pressure on anything.
(*Gordon*)

I'd say never give up hope, but don't settle. Look for
the right person, a person you can live with, but on
the other hand, based on what I've seen my parents
do, you can live with someone who's not absolutely
compatible if you just make a commitment to live
with them. And don't have sex with them and then
stop calling. (*Justin*)

You're going to fuck up and you really have to make
efforts at getting at the core of what you really need,

which is beyond what you think you want. That may just come with maturity, but in any and all things, one needs to strive to be much more aware of their motivations, of what's informing their decisions and how they express those efforts. And it's not just in terms of marriage or relationships, but as you move through your life, it's important for you to really spend some time continuing to unfold who you are as a human being. Forget the idea of what it means to be a man, or anything about what society tells you you are, and respond to the core of who you are as a human being. Be sensitive to that movement, that's really where the reflection of your life comes from. (*Kyle*)

I'd tell them [about] the myth of marriage and that marriage is for women. I'd tell them don't do it—you're going to fall in lust. There's a big difference between lust and love. Love is something that fits together like a puzzle and lust is just smeared jelly. There's nothing clear about it. You're going to chase your heart, but you're going to fall in and out of lust throughout your life. If it's with the same person in the structure of a marriage that's great, but chances are that's not what's going to happen. I would advise to avoid marriage at all costs. Look into a marriage for the sake of structure in your life, not for love. (*Winston*)

Get your education, take your time, find a good woman, establish your goals, work hard, be honest, sincere and be close with your family. You've got to be honest. If you don't like yourself or your life, you're not going to be able to be a good person. You've got to be a strong-willed person. (*Dylan*)

Have a pre-nup. (*Paul*)

Take everything it is they learned about being a
man and toss it right out the fucking window,
because I think the focus needs to be on being a
person, being a human being. (*Sandy*)

I'd say don't settle, and don't fall in love with the
first person who has sex with you. When you're that
young, you're having sex for the first time in your
life, you have a tendency to fall in a little more head
first than you normally would after you've had a
few years to digest some of that stuff. I would say
try not to take life so seriously and just have fun.
(*James*)

Don't fear a relationship, it could really be helpful.
(*Ryan*)

The first and perhaps only thing to talk about is
honesty and direct communications. Tell the other
person what you need, and that is true in the sexual
realm and it's true in every realm. Say straight out
what you think, what you want, what you can give,
what you can't give and what you expect of the
other person. Lay it all out. (*Dennis*)

Coming from my age and the fact that when I go
out and see all these guys with great looking girls,
the kind I would want, and I'm thinking where in
the hell did you meet? Well, a lot of these guys met
them when they were real young. They had kids
with them, and luckily they're still together. I think
I would tell these guys, the twenty-somethings, if
you want a family, find the best looking girl you can
now, and grab her up. Because if you wait, there
ain't going to be any available. Or if there is, you're

going to have to take on a whole bunch of baggage. The way it is with divorce right now, you might as well find a really hot chick when you're young, grab one up and hope for the best. (*Perry*)

Lessons For Women

If you are a woman and you are reading this book, maybe you are never married, or perhaps you are dating a never married man. Either way it is my hope that you gained some insight by reading this. If you are a woman who has never married you know you are not the only one. If you are never married out of choice, you know you are not alone, and if you have not married but wanted to, you too are not alone. Perhaps you think you are too shy, or you were with the "wrong" man for too long or you just decided to make your career a priority. Somewhere out there is your male counterpart. Some of them are lonely, some of them are contented and almost all are still looking for answers...and the right one.

Do not forget that never married is what you are, not who you are. And I accept you for that because I am one of you. You already know that my wish is for society to accept us as is. My greater hope is that all of us never married ones accept ourselves for the choices we have made (and have not made). We have taken a unique journey, and the best part of all is that it is not over yet. We still get to end it any way we want.

If you meet a never married man over forty, chances are he has financial issues. It is likely that he either feels he does not make enough and is therefore unworthy, or he is doing fine and is afraid of the financial impact a bad marriage could have on him. Many have homes and savings (and pensions) and are wary about putting that at risk and you need to be sensitive to that.

If you are a woman dating a never married man, my experience tells me you are probably dating a good guy. He may have taken a less-traveled path, but that does not mean he wants to remain on that path forever. Most would like to marry someday, or at least they say they would. Admittedly, when all the research is done and the conversations

are concluded, it is difficult to know if they really do want to marry—
and make all the changes and sacrifices that entails—or are they just
saying that because it is what they think they want. I am sure there are
those who say they would like to marry, but probably don't. They
simply have not admitted it to themselves yet. So, will he marry? Only
the future knows for sure. What I think can be said with greater
certainty is that most would like to be with the right woman in a good
relationship, no matter what that looks like. Will that be enough?

What should you remember if you are dating a never-married
man? Foremost is that they are all different. You are as likely to
encounter one who has been with a hundred women as you are to find
one who has been with only a few. Nevertheless, if you assume that
they are not a womanizer, you will be right more than you are wrong.
Recall that these men are more likely to be serial monogamists. They
love one woman at a time until hopefully they find the last one.

Most men—not just never-married ones—feel as though they
have some sexual conquering to do in their lives and they all respond
differently to that urge. Some are done with it in their twenties, some
in their forties and some are never finished. As you have read, that
need for sexual variety has played a role in why some of these men
have yet to marry. But it has also played a role in why some men
divorce.   Which path is better? And as the years roll on, and forties
turn into fifties, you can see the desire for sexual variety begin to wane.
There comes a time for most of us when the joy and comfort of a
good relationship outweighs all the other stuff. If you are dating a
never-married man, maybe your timing is perfect.

The truth is that some won't ever marry. For those, marriage is
just not that important, even it they meet the right one (and many are
not even looking). But some men will marry.

As we live longer, first time marriages after the age of forty will
become more common, and people will give up the notion that "if he
hasn't married by now he never will." Some will, because they are ready
to leave their never-married pasts behind. The good news is that if you
do happen to marry one, it is something special. When a man who has
no inherent desire to marry does, you know it's real. And you can feel

extraordinary knowing that there were those who came before you and none could get in until you. I do not know the exact statistics for men marrying for the first time after the age of forty, but it would not surprise me to learn that the retention rate for those marriages is very high.

When it comes to taking the plunge, these men can be frustratingly pragmatic, and with an acute hypersensitivity to the institution's downside. And almost without exception, they would all be okay if they never married. They self-actualize in other ways and are far more afraid of divorce than of never marrying. None of these men "need" a woman. If you needed to be needed, that may be a challenge. They may love you completely without ever needing you completely. You have to be okay with that.

Yes, these men have tended to stay in relationships too long. Since, in general, they do not crave marriage they were not ruining their chances of getting married by staying in a relationship longer than perhaps was warranted. Today, these men know themselves very well and none of them has lied to himself as to why he has yet to marry. Consequently, like most people over forty, they have little patience for going down the wrong path. If you are not the right one, you should both discover that sooner rather than later. And if they do decide to get married, I suspect they will not feel any great sense of urgency. The status quo is fine with them. If getting married is important to you, and you happen to be the right one, more than likely you will still have to be patient in that regard. Forewarned is forearmed.

What I Learned

I began this project be seeking answers to two questions. The first was, "What is wrong with me?" Of course, the answer to that rhetorical question is *nothing*. I already knew that, but now I also know that I am not alone. I am in a fraternity of brothers who see the world with the same exceptional view I do. And we are not alone; there are over six million of us, and there are over twelve million if you count women. That would make for a pretty nice party.

The other question naturally was, "So, why have I never been married?" I suppose if I were cornered, my answer would be a combination of two answers I heard during my conversations: I was never really ready and it just was not that important to me. But I learned much more than the answers to those two questions. I have been exposed to many new ideas. Consequently, I have increased my awareness about marriage and what I hope for my future.

One of the most important things I learned is that marriage is for some people and not for others. My only hope is that we get to a point in society where we see marriage as an option, not an inevitability. And either choice is equally acceptable.

I believe the men in this book fall into two general categories with regard to their overall feelings toward marriage. There is the small minority of men who have no desire to ever marry. Some knew it at a young age, others only realized it over time. For those men, the only thing they owe is honesty to themselves and the women they are with. I am sure there are plenty of women out there with no desire to marry (or marry again), and these two groups should do their best to find each other.

Then there is the other group: the vast majority who would like to get married—or at least they think they would. If I were forced to select the one predominant trait that separates these men from men that have already married, it would be their lack of fear of being single. Everybody who intends to marry wants to marry the right one, but what do you do if you don't find the right one? You can compromise or you can continue to look. These men have placed a premium on finding the right one over being married. The who is more important than the what. Couple that belief with their fearlessness about remaining single and you get never-married men over forty.

I do think it is important to find the right one, and I count myself among the men who will marry the right one or remain single. I will not compromise. And I have reaffirmed my belief that part of finding the right one is becoming the right one. That means opening our minds to meeting someone we might not ordinarily be open to meeting. Everyone is looking for the perfect person, the perfect "gift."

But what if that perfect gift arrives and is wrapped differently than you had expected, would you recognize them? Would you be smart enough to get to know them and love them for who they are? We must take responsibility to open our eyes to see things we were unwilling to see before. We have to open our hearts so that we can overcome fear. There will be risks, and if we wait until everything is certain and there are no risks, we will remain members of this fraternity forever. And for some men, that's okay too.

The rules of marriage may not change much in the future, but the expectations of it surely will. For one thing, I believe we will cease to judge the quality of a marriage by whether it lasts forever. We are just living too long, and I believe the single lifelong marriage will become the aberration, and the norm will be several loves in one's lifetime, with or without a marriage certificate. For some, that piece of paper will still be important. Many people will continue to validate all of the loves of their life with a marriage contract, some will only require it the first time, while others may never need it. I do not think it changes the quality of the love.

I will continue to be a big advocate of the renewable marriage. Should that ever become widely adopted, it will be evidence to the fact that we have finally come to terms with multiple loves in a lifetime as being an acceptable option. I also believe the renewable marriage contract, if it has any effect at all, actually strengthens the relationship. The only people who would be against it are those unwilling to continue to "earn" their relationship, and you have to question the long-term viability of that relationship anyway.

As I finish writing this, I have a new lady in my life who is a wonderful person. It is too soon to know for sure where the relationship is headed, but I do feel pretty good about it. She just might be *my* right one, or maybe this spry "young" forty-eight-year-old has simply become the right one. God knows it's time.

APPENDIX A

The Survey

The following survey of never-married men over forty was conducted online in late summer 2006. There were 1533 respondents. Due to rounding errors, totals for each question may not add up to 100 percent.

Personal information

1. Do you own or rent your primary residence?

Own	59.0%
Rent	41.0%

2. Your current age is

40 – 45	62.2%
46 – 50	21.9%
51 – 55	10.0%
56 – 60	4.0%
Over 60	2.0%

3. Your race is
Caucasian (White)   84.6%
African American (Black)   3.1%
Hispanic   3.7%
Asian   3.3%
Mixed Race   3.0%
Other   2.3%

4. Your highest level of education is
Did not graduate high school   2.0%
High school graduate   9.1%
Some college experience but did not graduate   30.5%
College graduate   37.3%
Advanced college degree (Masters, PhD, MD, etc.)   21.1%

5. Your current annual salary is
Less than or equal to $25,000   11.1%
Greater than $25,000 but less than or equal to $50,000   31.1%
Greater than $50,000 but less than or equal to $100,000   36.5%
Greater than $100,000   21.3%
None of the above   11.9%

Information about family and friends
6. Do you have one or more siblings?
Yes   90.5%
No   9.5%

7. If yes, which sibling are you?
Youngest   33.2%
Oldest   31.8%
Neither youngest nor oldest   35.0%

8. If you have at least one sibling, have any ever been married?
Yes   90.4%
No   9.6%

9. If you have at least one sibling, have any ever been divorced?

Yes	56%
No	44%

10. How many parents were actively involved in raising you?

None, I was raised by someone other than my parents	2.4%
Just my mother	15.8%
Just my father	2.3%
Both my mother and father	79.5%

11. If your parents were married, have they ever been divorced?

Yes	33.6%
No	66.4%

12. If your parents were divorced, how old were you when they divorced?

Under 5 years old	22.5%
Between 5 and 10 years old	23.2%
Between 10 and 15 years old	23.6%
Between 15 and 20 years old	14.3%
Over 20 years old	16.5%

13. If your parents were married, how would you describe their marriage?

Very happy	12.0%
Somewhat happy	28.2%
Neither happy nor unhappy	14.2%
Somewhat unhappy	14.5%
Very unhappy	23.2%
Cannot recall	7.8%

14. What influence did your parents' relationship have on your never being married?

A great deal of influence	12.5%
Some influence	22.9%
A little influence	12.5%
No influence	52.1%

15. Do you have any children?
Yes   14.5%
No   85.5%

16. If yes, are you actively involved in their life?
Yes, at least some   80.8%
No, not at all   19.2%

17. How would you describe your closest friend?
Never married   26.7%
Currently married   50.3%
Currently separated   3.2%
Divorced   19.8%

18. What influence does your closest friend's situation have on your never being married?
A great deal of influence   2.6%
Some influence   9.0%
A little influence   13.9%
No influence   74.5%

Information about past relationships
19. At what age did you first become sexually active?
Under 15 years old   18.4%
Between 15 and 18 years old   28.7%
Between 18 and 21 years old   38.6%
Over 21 years old   14.3%

20. How many sexual partners have you had?
Less than or equal to 10   24.4%
More than 10 but less than or equal to 25   23.2%
More than 25 but less than or equal to 50   19.6%
More than 50 but less than or equal to 100   14.7%
More than 100   18.1%

21. How many different women have you lived with (as more than just roommates)?
None, I've never lived with a woman   31.5%

One	20.7%
Two	20.3%
Three	12.1%
More than three	15.4%

22. If you lived with at least one woman, what is the longest time you lived with a woman?

Less than one year	14.7%
Between one and two years	22.1%
Between two and three years	17.0%
Between three and five years	18.7%
Longer than five years	27.0%

23. How many serious love relationships have you had?

None	8.5%
One	11.7%
Two	22.9%
Three	25.9%
Four	11.8%
More than four	19.2%

24. To the best of your knowledge, have you ever unintentionally gotten a woman pregnant?

Yes	29%
No	71%

25. How many times have you been engaged?

None, I've never been engaged	69.2%
One	20.9%
Two	7.1%
Three	1.6%
More than three	1.1%

26. What influence have your past relationships had on your never being married?

A great deal of influence	19.2%
Some influence	33.2%
A little influence	17.1%
No influence	30.4%

Information about current situation

27. Are you in a love relationship right now?

Yes	23.8%
No	77.2%

28. Do you fear "ending up alone"?

Yes	44.0%
No	56.0%

29. Do you think you are afraid of marriage?

Yes	27.6%
No	72.4%

30. Do you think you are afraid of divorce?

Yes	45.4%
No	54.6%

31. Your view of marriage is mostly?

Positive	40.4%
Negative	17.1%
Neutral	42.4%

32. Which of the following statements best describes your feelings about soul mates?

I do not believe in soul mates	32.7%
I believe in soul mates but I am not waiting to meet mine	32.6%
I believe in soul mates and I am waiting to meet mine	34.7%

33. Which of the following situations scares you most?

Marrying the wrong person	47.7%
Never getting married	4.9%
Both scare me equally	17.5%
Neither scares me	29.9%

34. Which of the following is most important to you in a long-term relationship?

Physical attractiveness	11.9%
Sexual compatibility	14.7%

Intelligence	13.2%
Personality/sense of humor	49.2%
Financial stability	4.7%
Spiritual/religious compatibility	6.3%

35. Which of the following best describes your feelings about being over forty and never married?

Happy/glad	8.4%
Unhappy/sad	6.3%
Angry/mad	0.8%
Indifferent/neutral	26.2%
Confused/lost	4.2%
Uncertain/undecided	15.8%
Lonely	15.1%
Content	17.2%
None of the above	5.9%

36. Which of the following best describes why you never married?

Haven't found the right person	47.5%
No desire to ever get married	8.1%
Haven't been ready	8.7%
Not important/not a priority	13.0%
No time/too busy doing other things	4.2%
Enjoy being single	6.7%
None of the above	11.9%

Outlook for the future

37. Would you like to be married someday?

Yes	61.7%
No	7.6%
Undecided	30.7%

38. Do you think you will be married someday?

Yes	33.9%
No	17.7%
Unsure	48.4%

39. Would you like to have (more) children someday?
Yes   29.9%
No   42.2%
Undecided   28.0%

40. How important is it for you to be married someday?
Very important   13.9%
Somewhat important   29.7%
Neither important nor unimportant   35.2%
Not important   21.3%

41. If you found the right partner which would you most likely do?
Marry them   55.6%
Live with them but not marry them   25.2%
Date them but live separately   14.4%
None of the above   5.5%

42. Do you think you can be satisfied with just one sexual partner
for the rest of your life?
Yes   59.6%
No   15.5%
Unsure   24.9%

43. Looking to the future, what is your outlook on life in general?
Very optimistic   35.3%
Somewhat optimistic   34.5%
Neither optimistic nor pessimistic   17.3%
Somewhat pessimistic   10.2%
Very pessimistic   2.7%

44. Do you have any regrets having never been married?
Yes   37.2%
No   62.8%

♂

APPENDIX B

The Men

This appendix contains a brief description of each man with whom the author had a conversation, along with the pages in the book where you can find their dialogue.

Aiden is a fifty-year-old mortgage and real estate broker from Southern California. He is originally a lawyer from Texas, is financially well-off and wary of women who are not. *(Pages 24, 82, 149, 234)*

Andrew is a forty-six-year-old professional DJ from Florida who was dramatically impacted by his parents' break up at an early age. He speaks with great frankness and honesty about sex, which is a constant theme running through our conversation. *(Pages 66, 101, 129, 142, 191, 197, 226, 232)*

Chuck is a forty-one-year-old soft-spoken engineer from Colorado who had just broken up with a woman when we spoke. He is comfortable operating on instinct and feels as though he is going through some form of mid-life crisis. *(Pages 21, 66, 227, 231)*

Dale is a forty-five-year-old mortgage analyst from Seattle with a Ph.D. in finance. Originally from Texas, he is intense when in a relationship and prefers strong, independent women. *(Pages 36, 71, 116, 193, 207, 222, 235)*

Danny is a forty-eight-year-old nurse from Washington state who grew up in a broken home with no father around. He is captivated by a woman who has come in and out of his life for the past thirty-four years. *(Pages 61, 127, 177, 196)*

Dennis is a sixty-four-year-old retired computer programmer from New York who now lives in North Carolina. He has been in a loving, monogamous relationship with the same woman for thirty-eight years. *(Pages 130, 144, 190, 204, 238)*

Donald is a forty-eight-year-old owner of an electronics retail business in Arizona and the father of a grown daughter. He was heavily influenced by his parents' unhappy marriage. *(Pages 38, 63, 93, 143, 179, 208, 227, 233)*

Dwayne is a sixty-three-year-old retiree from Oregon who grew up in a conservative, religious home. Influenced by his parents' divorce at an early age, he has never really bought into the concept of marriage. *(Pages 27, 55, 74, 96, 187, 220, 234)*

Dylan is a forty-year-old working in hotel management in South Florida. Originally from New Jersey, he is the oldest of four children from a happy, healthy Irish Catholic family. *(Pages 67, 84, 119, 169, 194, 213, 230, 237)*

Evan is a forty-year-old mathematician from Virginia. A self-described introvert, his beliefs run the gamut from liberal to conservative. *(Pages 33, 71, 97, 118, 141, 186, 202, 232)*

Gabriel is a forty-seven-year-old media developer from Canada who was heavily influenced by his Catholic upbringing and rigid, military father. Although he no longer considers himself a Catholic, he is of high moral and ethical fiber, but with a streak of pragmatism. *(Pages 59, 110, 122, 177, 196, 232)*

George is a fifty-two-year-old bookbinder from Canada who has antiquated views of man-woman roles in relationships. Getting close to retirement and with his financial worries behind him, he is generally happy with his life as he continues to build his dream house by hand. *(Pages 45, 90, 104, 157, 214, 235)*

Gerald is a fifty-two-year-old bus driver from Seattle who had an emotionally cold father and an indifferent mother. His parents' divorce when he was fourteen impacted his self-confidence, and he feels as though he has nothing to offer women in the way of financial security as a result of some questionable career choices. *(Pages 74, 152, 180, 222, 233)*

Gordon is a fifty-year-old real estate investor from Atlanta who comes from a large family with nine siblings, which forced him to become self-sufficient as a young child. His entrepreneurial struggles early in life have had an effect on his never marrying. *(Pages 43, 57, 86, 119, 150, 192, 204, 229, 236)*

James is a forty-year-old software technician from the South who was a stereotypical male in his younger years with his share of casual sexual experiences. He bores easily and is self-centered by his own admission. *(Pages 24, 79, 137, 147, 158, 208, 228, 238)*

Jason is a fifty-six-year-old accounting manager originally from the East Coast, but has lived in Los Angeles for the past fifteen years. He prides himself on his East Coast values and believes he probably would have been married already if he still lived there. *(Pages 41, 54, 112, 183, 198, 203, 232)*

Justin is a forty-one-year-old attorney from Washington, DC and an only child from a conservative Christian family. He is a momma's boy by his own admission and started late in life sexually, but managed to sow some wild oats in his late thirties. *(Pages 70, 91, 133, 145, 200, 225, 236)*

Kyle is a forty-eight-year-old massage therapist from Texas and an adopted child of parents who are still together. He is cognizant of his own personal development and has no strong desire to get married. *(Pages 28, 54, 69, 166, 189, 203, 226, 236)*

Manny is a forty-three-year-old software developer from Raleigh, NC who mentors children. He has a strong need for independence even though he was living with a woman at the time of our conversation. *(Pages 64, 80, 104, 121, 166, 181, 205, 235)*

Martin is a fifty-four-year old writer and actor from Missouri and a Christian who claims he relates better to women than to men. His recent role as a senior caregiver has greatly impacted him to where he now considers himself a little selfish and emotionally closed off. *(Pages 20, 79, 83, 148, 157, 181, 199, 230, 234)*

Mitch is a forty-year-old self-employed single father, from an unplanned pregnancy, living in Oregon. His single life was heavily influenced by his parents' early breakup and he is honest in his assessment of his own questionable behavior in the past. *(Pages 42, 117, 159)*

Myron is a fifty-seven-year-old librarian from New York who hung out with hippies and spent time on a commune in the sixties. He believes his freedom is more important than all the compromises he would have to make to be in a committed relationship. *(Pages 45, 55, 76, 94, 123, 151, 184, 206, 234)*

Nathan is a fifty-two-year-old student counselor from New Hampshire who was affected by repressive parents. He loves children, enjoys his solitude and has many plutonic female friends, but has not had a proper sexual relationship in years. *(Pages 30, 72, 89, 125, 161, 212, 236)*

Paul is a fifty-three-year-old CPA from Texas who is financially cautious and into numerology. He bores quickly, seeks variety in his relationships and sees himself as a rescuer who was put here to help others. *(Pages 23, 62, 78, 106, 120, 163, 224, 238)*

Perry is a forty-two-year-old sheet metal worker from Missouri and a single father raising his daughter on his own. He believes in the traditional family and has very much wanted to be married. *(Pages 107, 136, 172, 239)*

Randy is a forty-eight-year-old engineer from Southern California who is the product of an abusive father. Originally from Virginia, he has four siblings who were all unmarried at the time of our conversation. *(Pages 73, 88, 122, 168, 191, 211, 226, 235)*

Ryan is a forty-two-year-old sculpture designer from Wisconsin who wanted to be an artist from a young age. He is shy, introverted and a loner, which has left him with very limited relationship experience. *(Pages 77, 154, 186, 196, 238)*

Samuel is a forty-seven-year-old teacher from Colorado who is jaded over women and dating as a result of many brief, unfulfilling relationships. Because of his background coaching and teaching children, he relates well to younger women. *(Pages 30, 53, 68, 92, 132, 173, 221, 233)*

Sandy is a fiercely independent forty-two-year-old hypnotherapist from Cleveland. He is a spiritual person with multiple master's degrees, and while he did well financially at one time, he was struggling somewhat at the time of our conversation. *(Pages 58, 77, 98, 135, 170, 201, 228, 238)*

Theodore is a fifty-year-old telecom worker living in Florida who had recently been laid off at the time we spoke. He was affected by his father's death to cancer and his mother's bouts with depression, and as a consequence has done a lot of personal growth work. *(Pages 114, 147, 215, 220, 233)*

Trent is a fifty-two-year-old retiree from Vancouver who moved frequently as a child which caused him to become introverted. He described himself as "not very macho" and his overriding theme during our conversation was fear. *(Pages 26, 134, 155, 198, 223, 234)*

Wayne is a fifty-eight-year-old draftsman from Houston with a Southern Baptist upbringing. He has only had a few meaningful relationships, but still has a practical view of the way things are today. *(Pages 48, 60, 66, 104, 126, 210, 225, 235)*

Winston is a forty-five-year-old corrections officer from Boston who is well-off financially as a result of real estate investments made as a young man. He is an admitted chauvinist, cynical over relationships in general, and leans more toward the European culture when it comes to his ideas of marriage. *(Pages 34, 99, 167, 189, 216, 237)*

---

[1] She already had two children of her own.

[2] If you recall from Chapter 6, Paul believes he came back as a Master's Chart and is here to teach others.